Contents

Series Editor's Preface

Our society appears to be increasingly preoccupied with crime and with criminal justice. Despite increasing general affluence in the post-war period, crime has continued to rise – often at an alarming rate. Moreover, the pace of general social change at the end of the twentieth century is extraordinary, leaving many feeling insecure. High rates of crime, high levels of fear of crime, and no simple solutions in sight, have helped to keep criminal justice high on the political agenda.

Partly reflecting this state of affairs, the study of crime and criminal justice is burgeoning. There are now a large number of well-established postgraduate courses, new ones starting all the time, and undergraduate criminology and criminal justice degrees are also now appearing regularly. Though increasing numbers of individual textbooks are being written and published, the breadth of criminology makes the subject difficult to encompass in a satisfactory manner within a single text.

The aim of this series is, as a whole, to provide a broad and thorough introduction to criminology. Each book covers a particular area of the subject, takes the reader through the key debates, considers both policy and politics and, where appropriate, also looks to likely future developments in the area. The aim is that each text should be theoretically-informed, accessibly written, attractively produced, competitively priced, with a full guide to further reading for students wishing to pursue the subject further. Whilst each book in the series is designed to be read as an introduction to one particular area, the Longman Criminology Series has also been designed with overall coherence in mind.

Ian Brownlee's book is the first in the series to be published. It covers a most important, and yet sometimes neglected area: non-custodial or 'community' penalties. He examines the philosophies underpinning community penalties, traces the history of the probation service, and explores the use of different penalties in practice. As he says in his introduction this is an area of penal policy that has been particularly susceptible to short-termism and 'populist punitiveness'. Too often it has been characterised by 'policy-making by postbag'; the tendency of politicians to pay more attention to the contents of outraged letters from constituents (and to editorials in the tabloids) than to the experience of professionals working in the field or to the results of research. He argues that if penal policy is to move forward in a 'sensible and consistent' manner then policymakers must be prepared to make difficult decisions in the face of what will sometimes be hostile public opinion.

The key tasks Ian Brownlee sets himself in this book are, first, to explain how it is that we find ourselves where we do now (with a prison population which has risen by half in five years) and, secondly, by examining both the philosophy and practice of punishment, to show what a 'sensible and consistent' approach to community penalties might look like. There are some radical changes required, Brownlee suggests, if we are to move to a position in which *reducing* rather than simply *managing* the offender population is the priority. Though for some this may seem now rather a forlorn hope, one only needs to be reminded of what made the 1991 Criminal Justice Act possible to see that it is not that far-fetched. This book will be of great interest to students of criminology and related subjects, to practitioners working with offenders, and to all those with an interest in the future direction of criminal justice policy.

Tim Newburn
London, January 1998

List of Figures

Acknowledgements

As avid readers of acknowledgement pages will appreciate, few books are ever brought to publication without considerable help and encouragement from friends, professional colleagues, family, the landlord of the local pub or whoever else it was who made the awful job of authoring a little more bearable. This text is no exception, and I should like to acknowledge my debt to a number of 'significant others' – some more significant in the genesis of this volume than they probably realised at the time. In order to avoid any potential embarrassment I shall list them only in alphabetical order but each by their own particular contribution helped – enabled – me to do something that I really wanted to, which was to write this book. Thanks, then, to Andrew Ashworth, Terka Bagley, Paul Cavadino, Adam Crawford, John Gallacher, Geoff Kenure, the Library Staff at the Law Library, Leeds University and the Crookesmoor Library, Sheffield, Tim Newburn, Mary Seneviratne, Clive Walker, Frank Walton, Sally Wheeler, Brian Willan and to all my former colleagues in the Department of Law at Leeds who allowed me to have a study leave to begin the task of writing. Biggest thanks of all to Mary and Christopher, Anna and Sarah who just got on with their lives and encouraged me to think of doing the same.

Ian Brownlee
Sheffield
October 1997

The publishers are indebted to the Controller of Her Majesty's Stationery Office for permission to reproduce extracts from CMND 1650. Crown Copyright, and to Blackstone Press Ltd. for permission to adapt Figure 1.1 from a figure on p. 19 of M. Wasik and R. Taylor, *Blackstone's Guide to the Criminal Justice Acts 1991–93* (Blackstone Press, 1995).

To my mother and father, May and John Brownlee

Introduction

The book you are about to read provides an introduction to the history and politics of non-custodial sentencing and to the range of theories, both penological and sociological, which help to make sense of the way that non-custodial punishments are currently used. The analysis involves (in the main) an examination of how such sanctions have developed in England and Wales over the last thirty years or so, and particularly in the period since 1985. It also looks forward and suggests how the use of non-custodial sentences will develop in the next five to ten years, and how it *should*.

On the night that the first draft of this book was finished I relaxed by going to see a performance of Jim Cartwright's excellent play *Road* at the Crucible Studio Theatre in Sheffield. Those of you who know the play will remember that it is a moving and disturbing portrayal of a working-class community deprived of work by the collapse of the industries that once sustained it and, hence, stripped of the motivations that had previously helped to give meaning to the lives of its inhabitants. This particular performance was by an amateur group called *Blank Slate* which is made up of students from one of Sheffield's largest comprehensives, King Edward VII School. The production and the individual performances were outstanding and should have provided sufficient food for thought for the night; but my head was still full of my own writing and I was constantly drawn into making analogies between the play and the way in which, as a society, we organise our penal system, particularly that part of it which takes place outside custodial institutions.

No doubt, many of these analogies were contrived and banal (particularly after the interval in the bar!) but two are, I hope, worth recording here. The first is to remark that none of the characters in the play is naïve enough to believe that unemployment and the associated loss of dignity and purpose *just happened*: each in his or her own way displays a refreshing (or alarming, depending on your point of view) lack of false consciousness. Unemployment and all the degrading, dehumanising consequences that flow from it are portrayed throughout as the utterly predictable and, hence, entirely avoidable consequences of deliberate government policies. The same is true of penal policy, the state of our prisons and the way we choose to employ or ignore meaningful alternatives to incarceration. As the book unfolds, I hope to demonstrate as a central theme that none of this happens by accident. Political decisions are taken, policies implemented or reversed and from these human activities great patterns of opportunity or denial emerge. The lesson is that events, circumstance, outcomes even *could be different*, given the political will.

The second analogy I draw from the play, and a second major theme of the book, is the relationship between knowledge, outraged public opinion and the direction of policy. *Road* is a play about real lives and, therefore, contains a realistic amount of swearing and attempts at sexual coupling. The fact that it was to be performed by an acting company from a secondary school drew some adverse commentary in the local press. Two 'outraged' local residents rang King Edward's and the local radio station to complain about the unsuitability of the play. In response, the teachers who produced the play included the following commentary of their own in the programme:

> At the time of writing these notes the 'barrage' of controversy that has surrounded the production has amounted to *two* telephone calls . . . from indignant citizens variously repelled, disgusted and outraged by the very fact of ROAD, and by the fact of a school production of the piece. In both cases the callers were quite clear that they did not know the play, did not intend to find out about it and were certainly not going to see it. They also had no connection with the school. The unhappy callers had, in fairness, reacted to press coverage which was rather lurid, sensational and to some degree more creative fiction than reportage. The journalist did not know the piece either. It strikes us as very ironic that this reflex action, to dismiss without understanding or even attempting to understand, is the response that society at its most cosy generally hands out to people, relationships and environments like those actually depicted in the play that we are performing tonight.

Precisely so. And without depriving 'outraged of Ecclesfield' (or wherever) of their right to criticise, the producers refused to be swayed by opinions that were clearly ill-informed and based solely on misrepresentations in the press. Unfortunately, as the subsequent chapters of the book reveal, penal policy, and particularly any part of it which smacks remotely of humanity towards those who have broken the law, tends to be more susceptible to being blown off-course by criticisms that are often just as ill-informed and media-led and just as determined not to understand what it is they are criticising. It is probably harder to be Home Secretary than to teach drama in a large inner-city comprehensive secondary school (I can't say for sure, not having done either) but *mutatis mutandis* the demands for integrity and the courage to face down hostile, but misled, opinion are about the same. So the second lesson to be drawn from this analogy is that if penal policy is to advance in a sensible and consistent fashion those charged with its formation must be prepared, at times, to take on the task of leading and educating public opinion or, if that seems too ambitious, then at least to face it down when it is clearly wrong and based only on prejudice and fear of the unknown.

Enough of plays and players. The book begins with two general chapters which set the context for the more specific discussion that follows. Chapter 1 traces the emergence of the current sentencing framework in England and Wales and identifies the major shifts in criminal justice policy which have given that framework its particular structure. Here we are introduced to the notion that punishments which are 'tough on crime' can be at one and the same time both politically necessary and penologically limited in terms of their capacity for crime control (Garland, 1990: 80). In Chapter 2 we examine the main philosophical theories that have been used to justify the imposition of state punishment in order to gain a better understanding of the importance currently attached to the concept of 'just deserts' and of some of the challenges to that particular justification. This is followed in Chapters 3 and 4 by an outline history of the probation service since it had its origins in the temperance mission to police courts towards the end of the Victorian era. Chapter 3 covers the first seventy years or so and charts the influence of the sense of 'mission' which inspired the first probation officers and became part of the ethic of the service when it was first established on a statutory basis in 1907. This chapter also analyses the reception into probation practice of the 'scientific' methods of social casework, questioning the values that lay behind that movement, and uncovering its implications for the structures of the service and the value system that underpinned it. Chapter 4 then examines more recent transformations of the service under the globalised pressures of 'managerialism' and the search for greater efficiency and accountability that have been accompanied by a resurgence in punitiveness in penal policy. The detailed analysis of the changing role of the probation service is intended to illustrate its relationship to the sorts of community punishments for which, chiefly, it is responsible, and to help to explain the particular form that those punishments now take.

This leads on to an overview in Chapter 5 of the community-based punishments that are currently available, including probation orders, community service and curfew orders, together with an outline of the procedural requirements associated with their use by the courts. Chapter 6 deals in the same way with fines, other financial penalties and miscellaneous non-custodial orders such as bans and bind-overs. One of the central issues in the book is the question of fairness in sentencing, given that we live in a society that is fragmented on lines of age, gender, race and wealth, and so Chapter 7 analyses some of the particular problems involved in trying to measure how community penalties are being used and how effective that use has been. Finally, Chapter 8 pulls together the themes which have permeated the discussion in order to point up the principal lessons that can be learnt from experience of existing sentences and to suggest ways to avoid repeating previous mistakes.

While this book was being written the General Election of May 1997 produced a change of governing party in Britain for the first time in eighteen years. This circumstance added an extra element of uncertainty to the analysis contained within it because, not unnaturally, the new Home Office team preferred to produce policy statements to their own timetable rather than mine. I have attempted to 'read the runes' as best I can and to proffer some suggestions as to the areas of continuity and those of change that are likely to emerge in the new government's policy towards punishment in the community. If subsequent events prove me wrong, then I hope it is because I have been too pessimistic, too conservative (with the obligatory small 'c') in my assessment of what can be done to improve the situation as I describe it first in July 1997.

Chapter 1

Evolving Punishment in the Community

Sentencing under the 1991 framework

This chapter will relate how the present system of non-custodial sentences in England and Wales emerged from changes in penal policy over the last thirty years or so. In addition, it will seek to identify the central themes in this history of emergence, spelling out their implications for the future use of non-custodial and community-based sanctions. The terms 'non-custodial sentence' and 'community-based punishment' will be used, often interchangeably, to describe a range of criminal sanctions short of immediate incarceration in a penal institution. It might be noted that the two terms are not actually coterminous since the second is wide enough to embrace not only the first but also an extensive range of other sanctions, some of which need not involve the activities of judicial sentencers at all. So, under the heading of community punishment one could discuss, for instance, informal responses to rule-breaking among neighbours and acquaintances such as the ostracising of trade-union members who fail to support the industrial action of their colleagues, or the shunning and humiliation (or worse) of those who are seen to be too cooperative with an unpopular political power, as in some communities in Northern Ireland. As we will see, there is currently a revival of interest in the idea that local communities, rather than the agencies of the state, should take responsibility for 'resolving disputes' between neighbours of the kind which lead to antisocial behaviour. Mediation may often involve the negotiation of some form of reparative or compensatory activity by one of the parties towards the other or towards the community as a whole. Although not so clearly 'punishments' in the traditionally understood sense (indeed, many of the advocates of this approach deprecate the use of that term), such activities usually carry with them a sense of compulsion since reintegration of the 'transgressor' into the community will normally depend upon their compliance with the terms of the negotiated 'settlement'. Chapter 2 examines the rationale and justification for this latter sort of 'informalism' and further discussion of the supposed advantages of reparation/mediation schemes over formal court-centred sanctions as ways of dealing with infractions of social rules (Christie, 1977) is contained in Chapter 6, below.

In the main, however, this book addresses itself to the range of sentencing options after conviction by a criminal court and focuses on those sentences or orders which impose on offenders penalties other than immediate confinement in a custodial institution. It is necessary to phrase it in this convoluted way because, of course, not all custodial institutions are prisons, even in England and Wales. Young offenders (those who are aged 15, 16 or 17) and 'young adult offenders' (18-, 19- and 20-year-olds) who receive custodial sentences are normally held in 'young offender institutions' which are segregated from adult prisons even where they have contiguous locations. In addition, the Criminal Justice and Public Order Act 1994 has provided a new form of custodial sentence for certain 'persistent' offenders aged 12, 13 or 14 in the form of a secure training order to be served in specially constructed secure training centres. At the time of writing (1997) no such centres had yet been constructed and there is speculation that the newly-elected government will repeal the statutory basis for them.

The Criminal Justice Act 1991 ('the 1991 Act') continues to provide the basic legislative framework for sentencing in England and Wales, notwithstanding a number of important changes which have been introduced in subsequent statutes (most notably the Criminal Justice Act 1993 and the Criminal Justice and Public Order Act 1994). In general conformity to the 'just deserts' rationale underpinning the 1991 arrangements (see further Chapter 2), sentences are graded into four categories according to their intended use to punish offences of differing levels of perceived seriousness.

As Figure 1.1 illustrates, the bottom tier of the hierarchy consists of discharges, either absolute or conditional, designed to deal with the most trivial offences. At the next level of seriousness come fines and other financial penalties, then community sentences properly so called. This latter category comprises probation orders, community service orders, combination orders (combining elements of the previous two), and curfew orders, all of which are available for adult offenders, and two other orders, the attendance centre order and the supervision order, which are restricted to offenders aged under 21 and 18 respectively. At the top of the hierarchy are custodial sentences to be imposed when a court feels that no lesser sentence could be justified in the light of the offence or offences which are to be punished. In the case of imprisonment for a person over 21 the sentence may be suspended (a complication which is discussed further in Chapter 5). 'Seriousness thresholds' operate between fines and community penalties and between community penalties and custody so that sentencers are not supposed to move to the next, more onerous, level of punishment unless the criteria of seriousness of offence

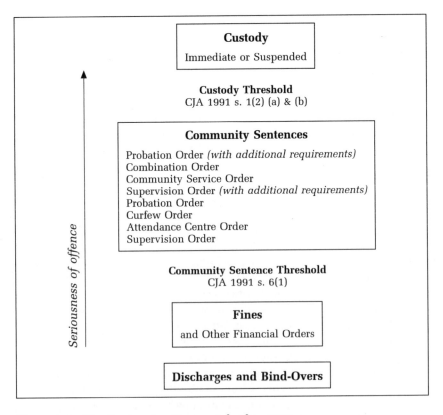

Figure 1.1   The Sentencing Framework after 1991
Source: adapted from Wasik and Taylor, 1994.

for that level are satisfied. Having outlined the current framework, we can now turn to consider how these present arrangements emerged.

Pragmatism and proliferation: the management of crisis 1945–1985

An impressive number of readable and authoritative reviews of penal policy in some or all of the period since the Second World War already exist and it is not intended to repeat here everything that might usefully be gained from reading those other sources (see e.g. Bottoms, 1987; Downes and Morgan, 1994; Hudson, 1993; Newburn, 1995). One of the most important points which emerges from the policy histories of the post-war period is that in Britain as in many other jurisdictions the search for community-based alternatives to imprisonment was not predicated upon any clear or coherent philosophical or other theoretical basis (Bottoms, 1980: 4; Hood, 1974: 377). Rather, it was to a large extent characterised by 'peneological pragmatism' (Cavadino and Dignan, 1997) and motivated chiefly by a desire to reduce or at least contain within affordable limits the escalating numbers within the prison estate (Brake and Hale, 1992: 151–7). This was mainly, but not entirely, a matter of cost. Sharp increases in the number of people in prison not only add to the costs of government, they also have the potential to provoke a number of interrelated crises for penal policy makers and administrators especially when, as is usually the case, such increases precede any planned expansion of the prison estate. High and rising prison populations are associated with overcrowding and poor conditions and with unrest among prisoners and the staff who must guard them. Unless checked, such pressures lead periodically to industrial disputes on the one hand and to riots and lesser disturbances on the other. Such highly publicised and threatening emanations from the seemingly chronic penal crisis place intense pressure on governments to restore the legitimacy of the system and the authority of those who run it either by finding extra resources or in other ways. So, growing prison populations have been seen, at least until recently, as a sign of possible trouble for government and have been, and continue to be, portrayed by more radical critics as evidence of a wider crisis of political legitimacy outside the prison walls (Carlen, 1990; Fitzgerald and Sim, 1982: 23–4). In short, the 'crisis' in prisons is really two crises: a fiscal and a social control crisis (Bottoms, 1980; Cavadino, 1994: 42; Vass, 1990: 33).

Between the two world wars the number of prisoners in England and Wales remained constantly below 13,000 despite a considerable increase in recorded crime, especially in the 1930s (Bottoms, 1987: 178). By the mid-1960s, however, the prison population had reached a total three times its pre-war level, even though the courts were making less use, proportionately, of imprisonment for indictable (i.e. more serious) offences. Assuming that crime would continue to rise, policy makers faced a choice: either they would have to find the costs of housing a continually escalating prison population or they would have to develop new policy initiatives to reduce the use of custody even further. The second option was chosen largely on pragmatic grounds, although the direction of choice was also undoubtedly influenced by a gradual loss of faith in the efficacy of the prison for rehabilitating its inmates or otherwise reducing the impact of reoffending (Clarkson and Morgan, 1995: 107; Vass, 1990: 9).

Attempts at reducing the use of imprisonment

Two main strands were woven into the reductive policy that began to emerge from the mid-1960s onwards (for comparative material drawn from international sources, see Hudson, 1993: ch. 1). The first strand involved the introduction of parole in 1967, its extension in 1975, and the development from 1980 onwards of a growing body of 'guideline' judgments in the Criminal Division of the Court of Appeal. These separate initiatives were intended to lead to (certain) prisoners serving shorter sentences as one way of reducing the average prison population on any given day, although in his authoritative review of these measures Bottoms concludes that any modest success that may have been achieved was at the cost of introducing widespread anomalies and less theoretical coherence in sentencing policy (Bottoms, 1987: 196).

A second strand in this reductive strategy, and the one which more directly concerns the subject of this book, was the creation of new 'alternatives to custody' designed to encourage sentencers not to send people to prison at all. One problem with this kind of 'diversion' strategy is that, in the English context at least, it cannot be achieved directly through government fiat. The concept of judicial independence in English public law has been taken to mean that the choice of sentence in individual cases is the prerogative of the judiciary and that, while parliament is competent to set out the range of sanctions that are available, and to prescribe maximum (and now, presumably, minimum) levels for each of them, the specifics of the actual sentencing decision are within the discretion of each magistrate and judge.

Ashworth questions whether the reluctance of the executive, at least until 1991, to pass detailed legislation on sentencing matters amounts to a constitutional principle as such (Ashworth, 1995: 44). His own view is that it has been more a matter of policy preference which need not necessarily bind existing and future governments, as recent evidence seems to verify. Whether a product of principle or of policy, this reticence has hitherto ruled out the possibility of issuing mandatory legislative guidance on appropriate types of sentence in *specific* instances (Home Office, 1990a: para. 2.16). Instead, those who wished to encourage a diversionary strategy have tended to adopt an approach which involves presenting non-custodial measures in a light which will make them attractive to sentencers at times when other factors in the sentencing process are pointing towards imprisonment as the likely outcome. In line with this 'beauty-contest' approach, three important new disposals were added to the sentencing repertoire in England and Wales between 1967 and 1972, all of which were intended by their framers to operate as 'alternatives to custody'.

The suspended sentence

The first of these new measures was the power included in the Criminal Justice Act 1967 (and subsequently re-enacted in the Powers of Criminal Courts Act 1973) to suspend in full a sentence of up to two years' imprisonment for a period of not less than one, and not more than two, years. (A power to suspend part only of a sentence of imprisonment was introduced in 1977 but repealed by the 1991 Act.) The normal effect of imposing a suspended sentence was that the offender left the court free to resume their normal life subject only to the threat that if they were convicted of a subsequent offence committed during the operational period of suspension, the original prison sentence would then be implemented, usually in full, and normally in addition to any punishment for the later offence. Although there was a power to attach a supervision order to a suspended sentence of more than six months, this was very rarely done in practice.

In recommending the new sentence to parliament the Home Secretary had made it clear that he envisaged the suspended sentence being used only in place of imprisonment and not instead of pre-existing non-custodial measures such as probation or fines (Bottoms, 1987: 183). However, it was not until 1972 that statutory effect was given to this intention by the addition of a stipulation that a suspended sentence could not be passed 'unless the case appears to the court to be one in which a sentence of imprisonment would have been appropriate'. It is clear that in the interim as many as half of those who received suspended sentences would, but for the new provision, have received other non-custodial sentences and were, as a result, being drawn further up the 'tariff' of punishments than would have formerly been the case (Oatham and Simon, 1972, cited in Bottoms, 1987).

The situation ameliorated somewhat after 1972, but most observers concluded that suspended sentences continued to be applied in cases other than those where the offences concerned were serious enough to warrant imprisonment. As a result, rather than effecting a reduction in the overall prison population, the introduction of the suspended sentence may have actually *added* to it indirectly, because some people who would not otherwise have been imprisoned received suspended sentences which were later activated by reason of subsequent offending. The outcome in such cases was almost inevitably a longer period of imprisonment than would have been merited by the second conviction alone and, thus, an overall increase in the prison population. There was also the suspicion that sentencers, especially magistrates, tended to increase the period of imprisonment awarded when suspending it, and so any subsequent activation resulted, once more, in longer sentences being served than might have been justified by the seriousness of the original offence. All in all, the suspended sentence appeared to have done little or nothing in its first twenty years to reduce the prison population (Bottomley and Pease, 1986: 91; Bottoms, 1987: 191).

The community service order

The second innovation of this period was the community service order (CSO), which was introduced on an experimental basis in six pilot areas in 1972 and extended three years later to the whole country despite some equivocal evaluation results. Procedural requirements of CSOs are discussed in Chapter 5, below. The rationale behind the introduction of the CSO has been criticised as lacking in coherence and for trying to embrace too wide a range of objectives (Hood, 1974; Willis, 1977). It is clear, however, that, whatever other penal purposes it was supposed to serve, the CSO was introduced 'with the primary purpose of providing a constructive alternative for those offenders who would otherwise have received a short custodial sentence' (Home Office, 1978: 21). Surprisingly, perhaps, this intention was not given express statutory force, and as a result practice varied from court to court, with some courts attempting to keep community service strictly as an alternative to custody and others using it as a separate disposal in its own right (Young, 1979).

As a result the precise position of this measure in the tariff of sentences was hard to discern with any degree of accuracy, whether one was a sentencer or a probation officer writing a pre-sentence report. Given this imprecision, the evidence from a succession of evaluative studies that about half of those sentenced to community service would, save for the availability of that disposal, have received *non-custodial* sentences is hardly surprising (Pease *et al.*, 1977; Young, 1979, and see Bottoms, 1987: 193 for discussion of some of the pressures that could lead to CSOs being passed in lieu of other non-custodial measures). This still represents a significant diversionary effect in the short term, in the sense that up to about 50 per cent of those who received CSOs might otherwise have been imprisoned, but the extent to which this lowered the overall prison population was undoubtedly reduced by an increase in the length of sentence imposed when offenders were reconvicted after having received a CSO. If the second court were to assume that the CSO had been imposed as an alternative to custody, this might incline them to imprison for the subsequent offence when, in other circumstances, they might not have done so. From the offender's point of view this was unfortunate enough when the court's assumption was true; when it was false, this process merely served to accelerate the progress of that person deeper into the penal system faster than their offending justified, and as such it provides a classic example of the so-called 'up-tariffing' effect thought to afflict the indiscriminate use of 'alternatives' to custody. A requirement from 1986 onwards that courts state in writing when a CSO was *not* being imposed as an alternative to custody ameliorated but did not always prevent the up-tariffing effect. There is considerable room for doubt, therefore, as to the extent to which the CSO actually did replace custodial sentencing overall, and nothing in the sentencing statistics suggests that the introduction of this particular measure had any impact on the proportion of sentenced adult offenders receiving immediate custodial sentences: in 1975 this figure stood at 16 per cent, while by 1985 it had *increased* to 21 per cent (Bottoms, 1987: 192).

Probation with special conditions

The final innovation was the introduction in the Criminal Justice Act 1972 of a special condition which could be attached to a probation order to require an unemployed offender to attend a Day Training Centre (DTC) during working hours for up to 60 days. In 1982, the strategy was extended by legislating for the growing (but technically unlawful) practice in many probation services of requiring offenders to attend other sorts of centres (called '4B' orders after the section of the 1973 Powers of Criminal Courts Act in which they are found) or to take part in other specified activities (4A orders).

This initiative had both rehabilitative and retributive purposes, being intended to offer some social training to recidivist offenders while increasing the 'punitive bite' of the probation order by increasing the restriction of liberty involved in it. This circumstance, in particular, was intended to commend itself to sentencers who were motivated by other than rehabilitative purposes, and so increase the take-up of probation as an alternative to making a custodial order. However, the courts seemed reluctant to take up these new options and comparatively few 4A or 4B orders were made. Nor was there any overall increase in the use made of probation generally. Only 7 per cent of known adult male offenders in 1985 were made the subject of a probation order, exactly the same proportion as in 1971 before the possibility of special requirements was introduced. There was a small increase in the use of probation for adult female offenders in the same period but this amounted to a rise of only three per cent from 15 to 18 per cent (Bottoms, 1987: 184–5). Once more, the introduction of this 'alternative' appeared by the mid-1980s to have had little effect in reducing the growth of the adult prison population.

Increasing leniency and severity: laying down the 'twin track'

This move towards a greater use of non-custodial penalties was never intended to be applied universally to all convicted offenders. While it may be acceptable (in a political sense) to pursue a policy of 'decarceration' with many run-of-the-mill or 'ordinary' offenders, it was felt that public sensibilities would be alarmed by the failure to lock away those whose crimes marked them out as especially dangerous and as posing an enduring threat to public safety, whatever the objective validity of such alarms might be. Even in the days when 'law and order' was not such a dominant electoral issue, politicians of all shades were still wary of being seen as 'soft' on crime as this could be interpreted by their opponents as a failure to offer the public the sort of protection they expected from the risks of criminal victimisation (Downes and Morgan, 1994: 186–99; Willis, 1986: 24). So, for instance, successive changes to the parole rules implemented by the Labour government in 1975 and the Conservative government in 1983 which were designed specifically to reduce the numbers in prisons drew a sharp distinction between prisoners thought unlikely to commit serious offences in the future and those whose early release might constitute a future threat to public safety.

The emergence of an increasing number of non-custodial sentencing options was, therefore, accompanied by a tendency to reserve their use to less serious offenders. For those who were categorised as 'dangerous', imprisonment retained its predominant position in both official and popular expectations. Indeed, for the latter category of dangerous prisoner, there was a marked tendency in many jurisdictions to *increase* the length of sentence as the clamour for 'law and order' grew, on the grounds that it was necessary to protect the public from such 'exceptional' criminals by imposing greater restrictions on their liberty than their current offending actually merited (de Haan, 1990; Home Office, 1990a: para. 3.5).

This 'bifurcation' strategy, as it has come to be known, depends upon notions of predictability of recidivism which have come in for serious criticism (von Hirsch and Ashworth, 1992a: ch. 3). Nonetheless, the strategy commanded considerable support among politicians anxious to be seen to be taking crime 'seriously' while still attempting to contain some, at least, of the escalating costs of imprisonment, and its influence helps to explain the increasing use made in England and Wales of longer than average prison sentences between 1948 and 1974 in a period when there was generally a *decrease* in the severity of other sentences (Bottoms, 1977: 88). However, as a means of reducing numbers in prison, a bifurcated sentencing policy may actually prove counter-productive, since the size of prison populations can increase either because more people are sent to prison or, less obviously perhaps, because those who are imprisoned each spend longer inside and so have a greater chance of being included in censuses of prison numbers (Bottomley and Pease, 1986: ch. 4). Depending on the 'precise mathematics' of who gets caught and for what, the 'escalating' tendency of one side of a bifurcation strategy might actually *increase* the overall number of prisoners (Harris, 1992: 158).

The continuing relevance of the bifurcation or 'twin-track' strategy will be discussed below in the context of the Criminal Justice Act 1991. For the present it is sufficient to note that the possibility of differentiating penal responses between dangerous and less dangerous offenders allowed the development, even the proliferation, of non-custodial sentences without really calling into question the centrality of imprisonment in the penal system. Because of an enduring tendency to conflate within the bifurcation approach two distinct policy objectives, namely reducing the prison population and decarcerating non-violent offenders, without distinguishing sufficiently between them (Harris, 1992: 158), non-custodial sanctions emerged as 'alternatives' to custody rather than as complete, rational and viable responses to rule-breaking *in their own right*, a characterisation which might have emerged under different, more radical philosophical transformations.

The pressure for a new coherence in sentencing

To summarise the argument so far, penal policy in the period between 1965 and 1985 was marked by a range of pragmatic responses to a deepening series of crises in the prisons involving rising numbers and falling levels of legitimacy and control. These crises were fuelled by escalating crime rates and exacerbated by the collapse of welfarist economic principles and their replacement, under globalised imperatives, of a monetarist fiscal policy predicated on 'sound money' and the reduction of public expenditure, factors which David Garland has termed 'the broader dynamics of social policy, class relations and cultural development' (Garland, 1996: 445). Despite all the innovations outlined in the preceding sections, the prison population in England and Wales in 1985 stood at a record high level, and the proportionate use of immediate custody had increased slowly but steadily over the previous ten years, reversing trends in earlier decades and outstripping imprisonment rates in many other European countries on commonly accepted measures (Brake and Hale, 1992: 143, but for a sceptical view on the utility of international comparisons see Nuttall and Pease, 1994). As a result, overcrowding in prisons increased, conditions for prisoners and for staff continued to deteriorate and serious riots and other lesser forms of disorder and indiscipline spasmodically rocked the system.

By the early 1980s the failure of the proliferation of 'alternatives' to address the continuing penal crisis was seen by many inside government as a symptom of the lack of coherency and of consistent rationale in sentencing policy more generally (a failing which had also allowed wide disparities in the level of sentences imposed for similar offences to persist throughout the country). It is important not to overlook the influence which significantly placed individuals can have on policy formation. While individual actors do not operate in political or cultural vacuums, much of the detail of the policies which did emerge in Britain and in other countries after the Second World War resulted from the influence of particular individuals in positions of authority operating within the precise circumstances of the moment (Bottoms, 1995a: 17–18; Downes and Morgan, 1994: 212; Downes, 1997). For many of these prominent figures in the penal policy 'network' the sense of lack of coherence in sentencing policy increased the desire for greater rationalisation and formality in what had hitherto be seen as more of an 'art' than a 'science' (Wasik, 1992a: 119, 127). Moreover, this desire was in keeping with wider policy developments, including the drive towards greater systemisation in the criminal justice system as a whole (Home Office, 1986: ch. XII; Raine and Willson, 1993). Once more reform came in an incremental way, building on existing practices but achieving quite radical outcomes, nonetheless.

The move towards 'punishment in the community'

The first stage of this renewed process of reform of adult sentencing involved drawing comparisons with the dramatic reduction in the use of custody that *had* been effected for juvenile offenders since 1981 (Allen, 1991). In the area of juvenile justice, a coordinated, multi-faceted strategy bringing together the activities of a range of agencies in pursuit of a common objective, bolstered by legislative restrictions on the use of custody and supported by additional government funding (through the DHSS Intermediate Treatment initiative) for a range of innovative alternatives to custody, had succeeded in bringing the number of custodial disposals for male juveniles in 1988 down to less than half of what it had been in 1981. This fall was greater than might have been predicted merely on demographic changes and, moreover, it had been achieved without producing any appreciable increase in the number of offences committed by juveniles (Home Office, 1990a: para. 3.6). The lessons were there to be learnt, and they were not lost on those civil servants and penal administrators who were helping to construct government policy at the time (Downes and Morgan, 1994: 212–13).

In 1988 a discussion document entitled *Punishment, Custody and the Community* was published which proposed extending the policy of reducing the use of custody for juvenile offenders upwards into the next age group, the 'young adult offenders' aged 17–20 (Home Office, 1988a). This paper laid great emphasis upon the central role that community-based penalties could play provided that they were perceived by sentencers and accepted by the public as 'tough' rather than 'soft' options. The underlying presumption here, that the courts and the public would only have confidence in community punishments which were tough, demanding and disciplinarian, is a manifestation of what Bottoms (1995a: 18) has called 'populist punitiveness', a political stance in which politicians adopt 'hard' law-and-order postures which they believe will be popular with the public. Its implications for sentencing policy are discussed more fully in Chapter 2, but it should be immediately obvious that the adoption of such a stance would influence the nature and, indeed, the philosophy of the community-based penalties that would be provided thereafter. The previous failure of existing non-custodial disposals to commend themselves sufficiently to sentencers was put down to their being seen too often as 'let-offs' rather than 'punishments' and, therefore, suitable only for relatively minor offences. This perception was, in turn, officially interpreted not as an expression of punitive excess on the part of magistrates and judges but as a failing on the part of the probation service to operate community sentences in a uniformly rigorous way, and as evidence of the need to 'strengthen' community punishments by building into them extra punitiveness in the form of increasing restrictions on the liberty of the offender.

This policy initiative was continued and reinforced in a circular to Chief Probation Officers later in the same year, *Tackling Offending: An Action Plan* (Home Office, 1988b), which put flesh on the conceptual bones of the Green Paper. *Tackling Offending* called on probation services to draw up detailed proposals to provide a range of tough new community-based disposals which courts could realistically be expected to use to punish young adult offenders (i.e. those aged 17–20) who were seriously in risk of custody. Curfews, attendance requirements and 'tracking' (i.e. intensive, close, one-to-one supervision) were all suggested as possible adjuncts to probation orders which would 'strengthen' them sufficiently to make them suitable for 'heavy-end' offenders and so provide a genuine alternative to custody for this age group.

These action plans laid the basis for programmes of 'intensive probation' for young adult offenders in seven areas of England and Wales which are discussed further in Chapter 4. At about the same time the government also introduced National Standards for community service orders emphasising the need to make such orders consistently tough and demanding so as to commend themselves to sentencers and command the support of the public. Significantly too, probation action plans were to include elements of 'partnership' working with charity and other non-statutory organisations which might provide some of the diversion schemes under the general direction of the local probation committee. Partnership working had at least two advantages from the government's point of view. Partnerships were seen as providing more cost-effective ways of working because they brought elements of competitive tendering into the provision of probation services, and they also avoided, at least to some extent, the industrial relation difficulties that might have been anticipated had all the control functions implicit in the new style of orders been imposed on probation officers, more used to a rehabilitative, welfarist relationship with their clients (Brake and Hale, 1992: 152–3; Home Office, 1988a: 17 and see Chapter 3, below).

Towards a new framework for sentencing

Alongside and integral to the process of transformation that was gradually turning 'alternatives to custody' into 'community punishments' a more general shift in sentencing policy was taking place. In 1974, when, somewhat unusually, the Court of Appeal had turned its mind to determining what might be the principles underlying judicial sentencing, it had managed to enunciate four – retribution, deterrence, prevention and rehabilitation – without giving any indication of how the four might be related or ranked in order of preference. Over the next ten years, however, there emerged among judges and policy makers a marked preference for making retribution or 'just deserts' the principal aim of sentencing. The precise meaning of these terms is discussed in Chapter 2 but, simply put, retribution involves making the punishment 'fit the crime' in the sense that the type and intensity of sentence awarded is determined primarily by the seriousness of the offence for which it is imposed, rather than by reference to any personal characteristic of the offender or in pursuit of a wider social purpose, such as deterrence. The origins of this shift lie in a general disenchantment with the rehabilitative 'ideal' and, to a lesser extent, with deterrent sentencing, due to the apparent lack of impact of either on the growing crime rate. This was coupled with a growing acceptance of the argument by American liberals and others that the disparities produced by indeterminacy in sentencing arising from the attempt to 'match' sentences to offenders rather than their offences worked to produce great injustice in the judicial process (von Hirsch, 1976). A third element, the need to limit the discretion of sentencers in order to control the costs of an untrammelled expansion of the use of custody, undoubtedly also infected the minds of the policy makers for the reasons discussed above, but was less often enunciated, at least until the direction of reform process was firmly established.

The coming together of these elements by 1986 produced a climate in which the primacy of retribution – 'the justice model' or 'just deserts' as it was being called in the United States – could be declared as the official government policy on sentencing (Home Office, 1986: 21). However, declarations of this kind, while not out of line with the broad thrust of judicial thinking, were not binding on judges and magistrates and, as we have seen, previous initiatives to persuade sentencers to make more use of non-custodial sentences usually floundered on the rock of 'judicial independence'. This time the government was determined to make the new policy direction stick even though it was clear that this would require legislation to fetter the discretion of sentencers (Wasik, 1992a: 127; Windlesham, 1993: ch. 5). The basis for such legislation was set out in the White Paper *Crime, Justice and Protecting the Public* published in February 1990, which promised 'a new and more coherent statutory framework for sentencing' in order to promote 'a more consistent approach to sentencing, so that convicted criminals get their "just desserts" [*sic*]' (Home Office, 1990a: paras. 1.5–1.6).

One further theme underlying the steady development of penal policy which had led up to the 1991 Act was the increasing centrality afforded to 'loss of liberty' as 'the connecting thread' of a range of community penalties as well as custody. The government of the day took the view that a greater consistency of approach to sentencing could be achieved if courts ceased to think of non-custodial sentences as 'alternatives' and focused instead on the concept of 'graduated restrictions on liberty' which related to the seriousness of the offence (Home Office, 1990a: paras. 4.5–4.7). This idea derived originally from the proselytising of a right-wing American criminologist, James Q. Wilson (1975), and while it undoubtedly provided a convenient unifying principle to underpin the systemising tendencies of policy makers and administrators at the time, it also served to blur the boundaries between incarceration and non-custody in ways that threatened a wholesale extension of social control (of which, more later) (Hudson, 1993: 32–8, following Cohen, 1979, 1985 and Foucault, 1977).

Without doubt, the 1990 White Paper is still a fundamentally important document, the publication of which marks an important watershed in penal policy and, in some senses, a new beginning for sentencing theory in England and Wales. In it the government of the day proposed to go further than any of its predecessors in challenging traditionally held notions on the meaning of judicial independence by establishing more precisely than ever before a legislative framework for sentencing which set out the principles and priorities that were meant to guide the discretion of judges and magistrates in individual sentencing decisions (Gibson *et al.*, 1994: 33). But the White Paper also represents a continuation of the evolutionary process described in the paragraphs above. As such, it brought together the themes and philosophies that had been emerging in government thinking through the 1980s, among them the primacy of retribution as a justification for punishment, 'loss of liberty' as a unifying principle in sentencing, increasing 'bifurcation' between violent and other types of offenders and the encouragement of greater resort to non-custodial sentences by introducing statutory restrictions on custody while making available 'tougher' community-based sanctions. It also restated the need for the various parts of the criminal justice 'system' to work together efficiently and cost-effectively, and it continued the government's flirtation with the vagaries of 'community' as an all-encompassing arena in which effective crime control could take on a democratic gloss. The proposals in the White Paper were implemented in the main in the Criminal Justice Act 1991 which came into force in October 1992. As we have seen, the 1991 Act, together with some significant subsequent amendments, provides the current framework for the use of custodial, community and financial penalties.

Non-custodial penalties in the Criminal Justice Act 1991

Given this genesis, it is hardly surprising that at the heart of the White Paper and of the 1991 Act is the idea of 'desert' – that the severity of the sentence of the court should be directly related to the seriousness of the offence. This principle can also be expressed in terms of the need to ensure 'proportionality' between offence and punishment (see further Chapter 2 for a detailed discussion of the philosophical and practical difficulties implicit in this task). It is predicated on the idea that the level of seriousness of each offence and the severity of a particular type of sentence can be gauged accurately enough to allow some sort of scale or 'hierarchy' of punishments to be established, so that punishments can be 'traded', as it were, against offences of equivalent seriousness (see Figure 1.1 again).

Neither the idea of 'just deserts' nor the imposition of seriousness criteria is novel as far as custodial sentences are concerned. Proportionality constraints on the use of custody can be identified in decisions going back to 1962 (Thomas, 1992: 232) and restrictions on the use of custody for offenders under 21 (in terms broadly similar to those in the 1991 Act) had been included in the Criminal Justice Act 1982. What is new is the extension of proportionality constraints to community sentences. Section 6(1) of the 1991 Act provides that a community sentence (meaning a probation order, a community service order, a combination order, a curfew order or, for younger offenders, a supervision order or an attendance centre order) can be imposed only where a court 'is of the opinion that the offence or offences with which it is dealing are *serious enough* to warrant such a disposal' (emphasis supplied).

The introduction of proportionality constraints of this kind, which make the use of a community-based punishment primarily dependent on an assessment of offence seriousness, has had important consequences for the way in which non-custodial sentences can be used or, indeed, described and recommended to courts. Gone is the idea of 'alternatives' to custody. As the 1990 White Paper makes clear (Home Office, 1990a: para. 4.1): 'No other penalty can place the same restrictions on liberty as a custodial sentence; if it did, it would be another form of custody: so there can in reality be no "alternative" to it, only other ways of punishing.' Therefore, non-custodial punishments must now be recommended to the courts as 'punishments in their own right', having rehabilitative possibilities, perhaps, but justifiable *primarily* on retributive criteria. In order to promote the use of non-custodial sentences for 'appropriate' offenders, the 1990 White Paper challenged the assumption that custody is the only 'real' punishment. However, far from offering any radical deconstruction of traditionalist notions of punishment and of societal responses to anti-social behaviour, the White Paper chose instead to recast community-based sanctions in terms of their punitive possibilities. It acknowledged that a new approach was needed if the use of custody was to be reduced, but the 'new approach' was launched on a wave of punitiveness, consistent with the prevailing tide of law-and-order rhetoric evident in much of what the governing party of the time had been saying. Punishment remained at the core of the response to offending but offenders could now be 'punished' in the community in the same way, if not to the same degree, as in prison.

To the extent that the characteristics of the offender can enter into consideration, it was the government's intention that they would affect only the choice as between different community penalties, not between a community-based sentence and a custodial one (Home Office, 1990a: para. 4.8). In keeping with the policy of bifurcation, community penalties as a whole were to be used principally to punish offenders convicted of property crimes and less serious offences of violence, when financial penalties were deemed insufficiently retributive, while more violent or sexual offenders were to be punished with custody (*ibid.*, paras. 3.12, 4.3). This neat symmetry was soon distorted, however, by two decisions of the Court of Appeal. In *R.* v. *Cunningham* ((1993) 14 Cr. App. R. 444) the Court ruled that, contrary to the spirit of the 1991 Act, sentence severity could be increased in appropriate circumstances for the purposes of general deterrence rather than as a reflection of the intrinsic harm and culpability of the instant offence. A further 'refinement' of the desert principle was effected by a later decision in the same volume of the reports, *R.* v. *Cox* ((1993) 14 Cr. App. R. (S) 479), in which the Court of Appeal held to the effect that mitigating circumstances personal to the offender (rather than the offence) *are* relevant at the stage when the court decides the *type* of sentence to be imposed as well as the *length* of that sentence (in the case of custody). The fact that an offence is so serious that only a custodial sentence can be justified for the purposes of the Act does not mean that the court *must* pass a custodial sentence: the court is still under a duty (as it was pre-1991) to consider whether such a sentence is appropriate having regard to any mitigating circumstances relevant to the offender (rather than relevant to the offence) (see Thomas, 1993). In *Cox* itself the Court of Appeal accepted that the offence with which Cox had been convicted was 'so serious that only [a custodial sentence] could be justified' (the custody threshold in the 1991 Act) yet substituted a probation order for the four months' custody originally imposed on the basis of the appellant's young age and relative lack of previous convictions. This case seems to be so at odds with the rationale underlying the sentencing provisions of the 1991 Act that it must call into question the extent to which, in the deliberate absence of more rigid and specific statutory guidelines, the Court of Appeal can be relied upon to implement in a 'coherent' way the legislative framework in quite the way that the White Paper anticipated (Ashworth, 1995: 237; Home Office, 1990a: paras. 2.16–2.17).

Changing the role of the probation service

Neither the apparently recidivist tendency of some judges to persist in old habits nor the fact that it required greater uniformity and more administrative accountability in the provision and implementation of community sentences stopped the then government pursuing its new, more punitive approach to non-custodial sentences. In those parts of the criminal justice system, notably the probation service, where government can command rather than 'persuade', rules and guidelines have continued their pre-1991 tendency towards prescription and formalism. Of particular importance is the expanded version of the National Standards for the Supervision of Offenders in the Community (first published in 1992 and revised in 1995). These emphasise the role of community sentences in restricting the liberty of offenders and making very real mental and physical demands upon them. Further, the National Standards require that in preparing pre-sentence reports for the courts probation officers first evaluate the seriousness of the offence or offences involved and tailor the content of reports accordingly, addressing the possible reductive effects of a community sentence only where such a disposal is not rendered unlikely by retributive considerations.

This is not to suggest that the sentencing framework imposed by the 1991 Act was entirely punitive or retributivist. The 1990 White Paper contemplates the use of probation, for instance, to help offenders not to reoffend by making treatment for alcohol or drugs dependency a condition of the making of the order or through the work that probation (day) centres were already doing with anger management or other rehabilitative programmes. As a result, 'securing the rehabilitation of the offender' remains one of the three statutory purposes of a probation order. The crucial point, however, is that rehabilitative and other reductivist objectives were subordinated under the 1991 Act to the principles of retribution and the requirements of commensurability or proportionality between the seriousness of offences and the severity of *punishments*, and, for the first time, community-based penalties were unmistakably included within that punitive phrase.

Response to the 1991 Act

Therefore, it seemed to many within the probation service and elsewhere, including some for whom the reduction of imprisonment was a moral as well as a practical imperative (Rutherford, 1993), that compromises would have to be made with the new language and, indeed, with the new approach, if non-custodial sentencing was to have any viability in the foreseeable future (Mathieson, 1992). For some senior managers, the sort of thinking that had permeated the 'pre-emptive' 1988 discussion document *More Demanding than Prison* published by the Association of Chief Officers of Probation (ACOP, 1988) seemed to represent the only rational response to the changed and changing circumstances. As a result, non-custodial options were increasingly 'sold' to courts (and more generally to the public) in language that emphasised the efficiency, effectiveness and economy of community-based sentences, their status as 'punishments' and (where this can be demonstrated) their superiority over imprisonment in terms of protection of the public over the longer term (May, 1994: 875; Oldfield, 1996: 51).

All of these terms resonate with key concepts in the wider political economy of current criminal justice policy. For some, this willingness to embrace language and practices that would once have been considered regressive (perhaps 'oppressive') is simply a new strategy in the continuing struggle towards a real reduction in the use of imprisonment, a strategy born out of necessity and nurtured by the new tide of 'realism' on the centre-left of politics (Matthews, 1989). It has also been portrayed, however, as at best a diversion, at worse a betrayal, of the struggle for a truly humane system of justice based upon a radical change in the structures of power in Western societies and more immediately upon nontraditionalist ways of thinking about crime and crime control (Drakeford and Vanstone, 1996a; de Haan, 1991: 213). The debate to which these two opposing conceptualisations has given rise is reviewed in more detail in Chapter 4 in the context of the attempt to create a set of values for the probation service in the 1990s and beyond.

Other constraints on the local autonomy of individual probation services and officers both before and since the 1991 Act include the increasingly interventionist roles of the Audit Commission, the National Audit Office and the probation inspectorate, the introduction of management information systems and the cash-limiting of probation budgets by central government (see further Chapter 4 below). Such managerialist initiatives are by no means unique to the probation service. Under the impetus of the Financial Management Initiative (launched in May 1982) and the government's drive for 'economy, efficiency and effectiveness' in the delivery of public services, similar features have become a commonplace in all the criminal justice agencies and in other areas of the public service as well (Hood, 1991; Windlesham, 1993: 210). But May is undoubtedly correct when he asserts that the effect of these 'new public management' practices on the provision of community sentences by the probation service has been to undermine further the 'professional/therapeutic' ethic which traditionally sustained such practices, opening up the possibility of a transition into a 'punishment/administrative phase' in which the community itself, rather than just the prison, has become a place for punishment (May, 1994: 870).

This process of transformation has not been accomplished smoothly or without encountering resistances along the way. Even before the implementation of the 1991 Act the National Association of Probation Officers (NAPO) had adopted a highly critical stance, actively campaigning against what it saw as the increasingly punitive direction of government policy (Windlesham, 1993: 225–31). Local resistance had also been encountered, as, for instance, in the initial reluctance of main-grade probation officers to become involved in the 'tracking' scheme in Leeds, held out in the 1990 White Paper as a model for the new style of intensive probation (Brownlee and Joanes, 1993). But increasingly the discourse around non-custodial sentences has been changed. Faced with clear financial imperatives, those responsible for securing the continuing funding of the service have been prepared to accept the increasingly punitive – and managerialist – language in which central government has cast the debate (Kemsley, 1992; Oldfield, 1994).

What seems undeniable is that the 1991 Act presented a fundamental challenge to 'a long history of theory and practice' in this field (May, 1994: 874). This shift now seems irreversible, at least in the short term, especially in the light of other significant lurches in policy which were to follow and which added to, rather than reduced, the punitive aspects of sentencing policy. The longer-term consequences of the shift are considered at the end of this chapter. Before moving on to that, however, it is instructive to examine how far the 1991 Act was successful in achieving its own, short-term objectives of introducing greater coherence into the distribution of punishment and, as a result, reducing the reliance of judges and magistrates on custodial sentences.

The impact of the 1991 Act on sentencing patterns

1991–1992

Few legislative measures are universally welcomed. The 1991 Act had its critics but, by and large, it won cautious approval from penologists, criminologists and many criminal justice organisations. Writing in the *Criminal Law Review*, for instance, Andrew Ashworth suggested that the Act provided a much clearer structure for non-custodial sentencing than had ever been provided before, in this country or in most others. If he had misgivings, they concerned the lack of precision in the legislation about the ranking of severity of the various community orders, and he doubted the willingness of the Court of Appeal to supply the necessary details in the way that the government envisaged (Ashworth, 1992: 250). NACRO also gave the Act a guarded welcome. Paul Cavadino, its senior information officer, agreed that the Act had 'the potential to bring about a more rational and coherent sentencing framework which uses custody more sparingly and community sentences more appropriately' (Cavadino, 1992) and similarly optimistic comments were attributed to the organisation's director, Vivien Stern. Both regarded the ability of the various criminal justice agencies to work together in securing the Act's 'positive intentions' to be the crucial determinant of whether the proportionate use of non-custodial sentences would increase as a result of the Act.

At first the combination of legislative restrictions on the use of custody and the positive encouragement of the use of community penalties in 'appropriate' cases, together with the 1991 Act's other major reform, a new and streamlined early release scheme (Maguire, 1992; Wasik, 1992b), seemed to have had the desired effect on the prison population. A special Home Office data collection exercise covering a sample of courts revealed that up to February 1993 the implementation of the Act had been associated in the majority of them with a fairly substantial rise in the proportionate use of community sentences and a fall in the proportionate use of immediate custody (Home Office, 1993). The juxtaposition of the two observations was particularly pleasing to those with reductionist concerns, given the tendency of earlier initiatives to increase the use of new non-custodial penalties at the expense of other *non-custodial* options. The same monitoring exercise also reported an increase in the proportionate use of the fine in magistrates' courts in line with another objective underlying the introduction of unit fines by the Act (see Chapter 6, below). Taken together, these statistical indicators provide good grounds for supposing that in the earliest days after implementation the Criminal Justice Act was achieving its objectives in relation to sentencing and was beginning to have some effect in arresting the rise in the prison population.

1993 onwards

This positive trend was short-lived, however. Having fallen at first in both the Crown Court and the magistrates' courts, the proportionate use of custody began to rise from early 1993. By the fourth quarter of that year the proportionate use of immediate custody in Crown Court centres across England and Wales was 12 percentage points higher than at the same time in 1992; in magistrates' courts, which make less use of custody in any event, the rise was shallower at 4 per cent (Home Office, 1994a). During the same period the use of community sentences including the new combination order also expanded from 21 to 27 per cent but without having any apparent effect on the imprisonment rate. It appears that most of this increase in the use of immediate custody came at the expense of the suspended sentence, which declined in use in the Crown Court from 18 per cent before the 1991 Act to just 2 per cent after the 1993 Act. Sentencers seem to have taken to heart the restriction in section 5 of the 1991 Act that henceforth a suspended sentence should be imposed only in 'exceptional circumstances'.

From a point in early 1993, then, the prison population, having dipped temporarily to about 40,000 in the immediate aftermath of the implementation of the 1991 Act, began to climb again on a steep ascent which has been unrelenting ever since and which the concurrent rise in the use of community sentences has been unable to ameliorate. The temporary reduction in prison numbers had done much to ease the chronic overcrowding at least in parts of the system and all but put to an end the (very expensive and otherwise unsatisfactory) practice of using police cells as emergency prison accommodation. By March 1994, however, local prisons (where the pressure on places had always been more acute) were *on average* 20 per cent overcrowded; three prisons actually recorded *70* per cent overcrowding and throughout the system 8,500 prisoners were sleeping two to a cell designed (largely in Victorian times) for one (Sparks, 1996: 209). A year later the prison population exceeded 51,000 for only the second time in history and over 300 prisoners were back in cells in police stations.

By the time the prison population reached a record 58,000 in November 1995, with 10,000 prisoners sharing a single-occupancy cell, the Home Office were planning for the building of 12 new prisons in addition to the 22 built since 1979 and the extensive refurbishing of existing facilities

(Home Office, 1996a: para. 13.8). The suddenness and scale of this surge in the prison population can be indicated by the fact that *actual* population in 1996 had already overtaken government projections for the numbers likely to be in prison in the year 2003 (Home Office, 1996c). That this further massive expansion in the prison estate could even be contemplated is due to the then government's confidence in the ability of its Private Finance Initiative to provide the necessary capital investment from the private sector rather than the public purse and to an entirely unsupported assumption that the deterrent effect of introducing mandatory penalties would reduce the requirement for prison places by 20 per cent (*ibid.*, paras. 13.4, 13.9). The viability of expansion on this basis seems highly questionable, but on the government's own estimates at the time the full costs of the expansion policy would not reach their peak until 2009–10.

The reshaping of the 1991 framework: full steam backwards

So why had the Criminal Justice Act 1991 not maintained its initial promise? One answer lies with the judges and their apparent reluctance, as Ashworth demonstrates in a meticulous examination of early decisions, to take the custody threshold seriously. The effect of judicial inconsistency on the level of seriousness necessary to justify custody has often amounted, Ashworth argues, to 'emptying the custody threshold of all meaning, and undermining any policy of restraint' (Ashworth, 1995: 238, and see further Ashworth and von Hirsch, 1997). The principal answer, however, is that the 1991 Act was not given the chance to work as it had originally been intended to. A combination of poor drafting at key points, media distortion of some of its unintended consequences, and sheer political opportunism resulted in the dismantling of significant parts of the compromise between restraint and severity in sentencing that had been at its heart. Within six months of implementation the government announced major concessions to hostility among judges and magistrates against the restriction on sentencing for multiple offences and on the basis of previous bad record.

The 1991 Act as originally enacted required that the choice of sentence in any individual case should be based on at most two offences – the most serious of which the offender had been convicted and one other 'associated' with it. This provision, together with the prohibition in the original section 29 against treating the instant offence as more serious simply because the convicted person had previous convictions, was intended to safeguard against 'up-tariffing' and incremental or predictive escalations in severity of sentence. As such they might rightly be regarded as essential components of the deserts-based theory that underpinned the whole sentencing framework established by the Act. Despite the fact that these provisions seemed to be working entirely as the drafters of the 1991 Act had intended (Ashworth and Gibson, 1994; Brownlee, 1994a: 298), the multiple offences prohibition and the restrictive version of section 29 were scrapped in the Criminal Justice Act 1993 (along with the unit fines scheme, which many magistrates had resisted), thereby sabotaging the reductive intentions towards less serious (but persistent) offenders that had been woven into the 1991 framework by the policy of bifurcation.

It cannot be coincidental that the announcement of this first reverse in policy came shortly after a humiliating by-election defeat and within days of the publication of a national opinion poll in which, for the first time ever, the main opposition party had taken a lead over the Conservative government on the issue of law and order (*The Guardian*, 3 March 1993). Clearly, the government was now vulnerable on this key area and it appears that a decision was taken to re-establish its credentials as the party that was 'tough' on criminals. A landmark speech by the newly appointed right-wing Home Secretary to his party conference on 6 October 1993 made this intention unmistakably clear. Announcing a 27-point plan of 'emergency action to tackle the crime wave', Michael Howard spelt out the punitive intent behind the new thinking:

> Prison works. It ensures that we are protected from murderers, muggers and rapists – and it makes many who are tempted to commit crime think twice . . . this will mean that many more people will go to prison. I do not flinch from that. We shall no longer judge the success of our system of justice by a fall in our prison population.
>
> (Reported in *The Guardian*, 13 October 1993)

Such a bleak philosophy was not entirely at odds with the rationale on which the 1991 Act had been built. The 1990 White Paper had been quite frank in conceding that prison could not be regarded as an effective means of reform for most prisoners and it was also largely pessimistic about any general deterrent effect in sentencing (Home Office, 1990a: paras. 2.7–2.8). It did, however, leave open the possibility that imprisonment could be justified in terms of public protection, denunciation and retribution, and it was precisely these objectives which the post-1993 policy sought to promote. But this element of continuity was at best superficial and at worst mere sophistry. If some of the details were still intact, the spirit of the earlier policy had clearly been abandoned, and the tone of pronouncements on sentencing which followed was to resurrect the law-and-order rhetoric and all the narrow moral conservatism on which the Tories had first been elected under Margaret Thatcher in 1979 (Brake and Hale, 1992: ch. 2). The result, as Ashworth and Gibson note (1994: 101), was that 'policies based on mature reflection, consultation and research findings were abandoned in an instant in one of the most remarkable volte-faces in the history of penal policy in England and Wales'. Although never explicitly stated, it was abundantly clear that, in the minds of those who were now driving sentencing policy in the Home Office, custody was once more 'the real punishment'. Other sanctions would now have to measure up, more than ever, to that ultimate yardstick and to do so primarily in terms of their punitive 'bite'. Further tightening of the custodial screw came in the Criminal Justice and Public Order Act 1994 in the form of a new sort of custody for 12–14-year-olds (the 'secure training' order) and a watering down of the requirements in the 1991 Act that courts obtained and considered probation officers' pre-sentence reports before imposing custody or certain kinds of community sentence (Wasik and Taylor, 1995: 18).

The direct practical consequences of this renewed punitiveness in political rhetoric were marked by an immediate increase both in the number of people being sentenced to custody sentences and in the proportionate use of custodial sentences. By 1995, the use of immediate custody for indictable offences at all courts was 20 per cent, the highest recorded figure over at least the last 20 years. The number of people sentenced to immediate custody in that year was 79,100, an increase of 14 per cent compared to 1994 and the highest figure since 1985. It is right to mention that recorded crime figures fell 10 per cent overall in the period between 1993 and 1996, but this statistic must be qualified by estimates of the extent of all crime (recorded and unrecorded) based on the Home Office's British Crime Survey which continued to show an increase of more than 20 per cent between 1991 and 1995. And even on the evidence of recorded crime, crimes of violence (i.e. those for which the use of custody could most easily be justified) increased by 11 per cent between 1995 and 1996 (Home Office, 1997f). In addition, an international victimisation survey in 1996 showed that people in England and Wales were more likely to have been the victim of a crime and more fearful of becoming a victim than in almost any other industrialised country, including the United States (*The Guardian*, 26 May 1997). So it appears that the populist punitiveness of the period following 1993 produced the worst possible outcome, namely a vastly expanded custodial population up to the limits of the capacity of penal institutions to accommodate it, accompanied by persistently high levels of criminal victimisation and fear of crime.

In March 1995 the Home Office published a further consultation Green Paper entitled *Strengthening Punishment in the Community* (Home Office, 1995a). The significance of the title is made clear in Chapter 4 of the document where the government's view that 'the role of community sentences is poorly understood . . . [p]robation supervision is still widely regarded as a soft option', is articulated. Inconsistencies in the implementation of orders across the country, and particularly variations in the level of enthusiasm with which different probation services brought offenders back to court in the event of orders being breached, had meant that community sentences were not routinely punitive enough to secure public confidence, in the government's view. The repudiation in the consultation document of the social work ethic which lay at the heart of the probation service's traditional mission to 'advise, assist and befriend' offenders was reiterated in an address by the Home Secretary to the National Probation Conference later in the same month. He rejected, he said, 'an approach which equated punishment in the community with social work with offenders' (*The Guardian,* 17 March 1995) and for this reason the government had determined to remove, and did in fact remove later that year, the legal requirement that probation officers hold a diploma in social work on entry to the service.

The government's suggested solution to the problems which it perceived community punishments to have was to propose the introduction of a single integrated sentence to replace and incorporate all the current orders available in adult courts. It is abundantly clear that a principal aim of the proposed changes was to secure a further shift in responsibility for the implementation of community sentences towards the courts and away from the (sometimes too) 'caring professionals' in the expectation that this would increase the punitiveness of such disposals (Home Office, 1995a: para. 11.1; Ashworth *et al.,* 1995). But consultations on the proposals failed to produce unequivocal support among sentencers for the single integrated order, and as a result the government decided to pursue the principles outlined in the Green Paper 'within the current law' (Home Office, 1996a: paras. 7.18–7.23).

'Protecting the Public': the election looms

Notwithstanding this minor reverse, Home Office ministers continued their war of attrition against the perceived leniency of community sentences. As the prospect of a general election grew nearer, the 1996 White Paper *Protecting the Public* (Home Office, 1996a) proclaimed again that 'the government firmly believes that prison works'. It reiterated that community sentences are often portrayed as a 'soft option' (*ibid.,* para. 7.15) without revealing how much of that portrayal stemmed from the populist punitiveness of government ministers. The rehabilitative potential of supervision in the community was not dismissed entirely, but in keeping with the post-1993 ideology this aspect of non-custodial sentencing was regulated to secondary importance. The first requirement of a community-based sentence was to ensure that 'offenders have to undergo physically, mentally or emotionally challenging programmes and are required to conform to a structured regime' (*ibid.,* para. 7.1), in other words to perform as 'punishments' not 'treatment' in the community. In conformity with the dominant neo-classical representation of offenders as free-willing and rationally calculating individuals and the denial of any social responsibility for the persistence of crime, the part of the 1996 White Paper which deals with community sentencing placed great emphasis on the need for supervision in the community to 'instil a greater sense of personal responsibility and discipline' as an aid to 're-integration as a law abiding member of society'. At least its punitive credentials were clear and the course that it charted for the future direction of non-custodial sentencing unmistakable. As one vehement (conservative) critic of the White

Paper put it, the government was proposing to 'overturn . . . the proposals, principles and philosophies which were put forward as recently as 1990 and embodied in the Criminal Justice Act 1991' (Carr, 1996).

If the government's law-and-order policies up to this point had provoked criticism, the publication of *Protecting the Public* exceeded all that had gone before it in the level of animosity and condemnation that it aroused from sources not normally thought of as hostile to the Conservative Party. Those who spoke out against its sentencing provisions included the Lord Chief Justice and his immediate predecessor, other senior representatives of the judiciary, the Archbishop of Canterbury and other church leaders, several former Home Secretaries and Home Office ministers (all of them Tories), former senior policy advisers who had been associated with the 1990 reforms, at least one Chief Constable and almost every legal academic of note (see e.g. the Hansard report of the debate on sentencing policy in House of Lords on 23 May 1996; *The Guardian* news reports for 10 and 24 May and 5 November 1996; and, for more scholarly but no less telling criticisms, Ashworth, 1996 and Hood and Shute, 1996).

This seemed to offer the possibility of a common front being opened up against the increasing illiberality of criminal justice policy, but crucially the main political opposition party declined to ally itself openly with opponents of hard law-and-order measures or even with those senior judges who were openly critical of some aspects of government sentencing policy. Instead, the Labour Party kept up its pressure to wrest the traditionalist law-and-order vote away from the Conservatives, and in the relentless exchange of rhetoric on the issue the shadow Home Secretary seemed careful to confine himself to the punitive language in which the debate had originally been cast by his opponents. Although Labour's slogan was 'tough on crime and tough on the causes of crime', the language it employed in public seemed too often to emphasise only the first, less radical element of policy. The failure to promote any more radical alternatives ensured that the political argument was conducted almost in the form of an auction in which each side attempted to outbid the other in the punitiveness of its responses towards what was increasingly portrayed as a hard core of committed and persistent criminals maliciously holding the rest of society as hostages and needing to be stamped down on hard. This was an arid, negative debate, informed by what Garland has characterised as 'the criminology of the other' which 'effectively demonizes the criminal, excites popular fears and hostilities and promotes support for state punishment' (Garland, 1996).

Summary

Penal policy in Britain since the war can be said to have been shaped by the influence of certain identifiable intellectual movements. These are

- **Penological Pragmatism**
  (in response to)
- **Crises in Prisons**
  (leading to)
- **Bifurcation**
  (and)
- **Proliferation of Alternatives**
  (followed by)
- **The Introduction of 'Desert' Constraints**
  (accompanied/subverted by)
- **Increasing Punitiveness**
  (in the context of)
- **The Rise of 'Managerialism' in the Criminal Justice System**
  (and)
- **The Rediscovery of 'The Community'**

Figure 1.2   Characteristics of Modern Penal Policy in England and Wales

listed in more or less chronological order of appearance in Figure 1.2. The phrases in italics suggest certain links or relationships between the characteristics but it would be wrong to overstate the strength of these links so as to imply some sort of invariable causal relationship in every case. The impact of what Garland (1996: 445) has termed 'the broader dynamics of social policy, class relations and cultural developments' means that penal policies are not necessarily consciously or instrumentally framed in the unerring interests of crime control (Garland, 1996: 445).

Much of the penal policy that has emerged in England and Wales since the early 1960s has been characterised by a certain 'penological pragmatism' as successive governments struggled to contain the escalating crisis in prisons without thereby undermining their own credentials as guardians of public safety. Earlier experiments with an expanding range of 'alternatives' to custody for those offenders officially classified as less dangerous failed to ease the tension between these two conflicting imperatives. From the mid-1980s onwards, therefore, a wholehearted attempt was made to change the basis of sentencing with the gradual adoption of a retributivist model based on the primacy of 'just deserts' over other aims of sentencing which culminated in the passing of the Criminal Justice Act 1991 (Windlesham, 1993: ch. 5). This change involved casting non-custodial penalties as sentences in their own right to be distributed according to the principles of proportionality, with the seriousness of the offence, not the prospect of future improvement, being the key determinant. It can hardly be doubted that the 1991 Act signalled a shift in both the rationale and the implementation of community sentences away from the rehabilitative/welfare ideal and towards a more punitive/administrative regime (May, 1994). The reversals and changes which have followed and the incremental dismantling of much of the 1991 framework have magnified, rather than diminished, the punitive aspects of that policy as first the governing party and then their main political opponents sought to satisfy the punitive expectations which their own populist rhetoric created.

Taken together, these reforms and counter-reforms have altered (perhaps for ever?) the way in which non-custodial disposals are integrated into the wider sentencing framework in England and Wales. Under foreseeable political conditions, and despite strong support from the Audit Commission for community sentences on cost-efficiency grounds (Audit Commission, 1996), it is hard to imagine any government moving far from the current agenda in which 'the first objective for all sentences is denunciation of and retribution for the crime' (Home Office, 1990a: para. 2.9) and the protection of the public. The Home Office may be under new leadership, but neither it nor the new Home Secretary has been slow in restating that the priorities for the probation service remain the provision of tough demanding punishments which reduce crime and protect the public (*The Times*, 2 July 1997), and the language in which the discourse is pitched remains much the same (see Chapter 8 for a fuller discussion). As long as this remains the prevailing philosophy, community-based sanctions are going to provide 'alternatives' to imprisonment for those genuinely in risk of custody only in so far as they present themselves and are perceived by sentencers to be tough and demanding and to impose punitive restrictions on the liberty of offenders. The policy of bifurcation and the supremacy of proportionality over other aims of sentencing will continue to mean that for a range of offenders a non-custodial sentence just cannot be considered, no matter how compelling the therapeutic arguments may be in any particular case.

In terms of service delivery, 'partnership' working arrangements will continue to develop, opening the way even further to the involvement of non-statutory or private organisations in the provision of community-based disposals; and, alongside this development, 'value-for-money' will continue to be an important performance indicator for any non-custodial measure, whether in the statutory or non-statutory sector. Indeed, one of the first acts of the new government was to announce a review of the operation of the criminal justice system in which one of the options to be explored was the possible merger of the prison and probation services to create a so-called 'Department of Corrections' along the lines of similar organisations in Canada and Sweden (*The Guardian*, 17 July 1997). It is clear that the review is Treasury-led and that a key concern is to secure greater economies and efficiency.

Partly as an adjunct to the quasimarket model inherent in this approach and partly in the interests of greater 'accountability', an increasing emphasis is likely to be placed on the role of external regulation, through increasing of reporting to agency superiors and to the courts, and through the measurement and auditing of 'key performance indicators' of performance and other managerialist tools (Home Office, 1996b: para. 8.13). In this way pressure will continue to be brought to reduce the discretion afforded those (including probation officers) who provide and implement community-based programmes and to challenge the autonomy once thought to be an essential characteristic of the social work

professional (Finkelstein, 1996). These will be among the more important enduring themes which emerged from the 'long march' of policy
formulation that produced the 1991 sentencing framework and which
have survived the subsequent 'purge' of some of the more obviously liberal aspects of that particular piece of legislation. They are likely to influence penal policy in England and Wales for a considerable time to come.

Postscript: but are alternatives to custody always beneficial?

The discussion in this chapter has proceeded on the unarticulated premise
that the promotion of non-custodial sentencing and an increase in the
use of community-based disposals are self-evidently 'good' objectives which
have some sort of invariable relation to the increase in the levels of social
justice. While the case for such a belief can be argued most strongly, it
is not universally accepted, at least not unquestioningly. The tendency
of earlier initiatives involving community-based sanctions to operate as
'alternatives to alternatives' led to allegations that the spread of community sentences, whatever their philanthropic pretensions, actually amounted
to a 'dispersal' of punishment and a widening of the reach of social control mechanisms. Far from producing a less punitive society, diversion
strategies, including diversion from custody initiatives, provided for
'wider . . . denser [and] different nets' (Cohen, 1985: 44). Other critical
voices have drawn attention to evidence of racial or sexual discrimination or discrimination on grounds of age in the use of non-custodial
sentences and the impact that this can have on the 'remnant' prison
population who are not thought suitable for punishment in the community (Hudson, 1993: 137–8; Vass, 1990: 159–61). Hudson has gone as
far as to suggest, with Matthews, that community-based sentencing is bringing about not so much a reduction but a restructuring of the penal population with the creation of a 'a young, white, hopeful penal population in
the community, and a black, mentally disordered, homeless and hope-
less population in the prisons' (Hudson, 1993: 138).

These are clearly important issues for those who advocate the use
of non-custodial sentences on humanitarian, rather than cost-cutting,
grounds and the substance of such claims will be examined further in
Chapter 7. It is right to raise them at this point, however, to remind the
unwary reader of the fact that social policies can have latent as well as
declared functions and that a society as fragmented on lines of age,
gender and race as our own is likely to reproduce inequalities of power
and disadvantage in even its best-intended institutions unless positive steps
are taken to combat this tendency.

Chapter 2

Justifying Community Punishments

The discussion in this chapter concerns the principal philosophical justifications that may be offered for the imposition of state punishment. Do any of them favour community-oriented penalties or, conversely, do any of them rule out the use of non-custodial sentences on any moral or philosophical ground? It should be conceded at the outset that the analysis which follows is predicated on the commonly held assumption that lawbreaking behaviours invite or invoke punishment rather than some other response and that this provides sufficient grounds for maintaining a system of legal punishment. While it is acknowledged that this premise is not one that we can simply take for granted and that there are voices that argue that state punishment is neither necessary or justified (Duff, 1996: 67), its wide acceptance seems to suggest that it is a sensible, if not conclusive, position from which to commence an exploration of this kind (von Hirsch, 1990a: 259). For similar matter-of-fact reasons, the discussion will focus in particular on retributivist or 'desert' theories of punishment, not in order to grant any greater legitimacy to that specific approach, but simply in recognition of its predominant (if not entirely unchallenged) position in the penal policies of many Western democracies at the present time. Retributivism is, so to speak, the 'market leader' in this field and so it is appropriate that the claims it makes for itself and the criticisms that are made of it should receive particular scrutiny.

One other premise should be articulated at the outset. It will become obvious as the chapter develops that I take the view that leniency in sentencing is a desirable objective to be preferred to its opposite, namely an increase in severity. While this is a not uncommon 'credo' among academics, and some criminal justice practitioners (Rutherford, 1993: 18), it is by no means axiomatic that lenient sentencing is a good for all society. At times it is exceedingly unfashionable among what the late Lord Chief Justice, Lord Taylor of Gosforth (Taylor, 1993), was pleased to call 'right thinking members of society' (from which august company he excluded (hopefully only for the purposes of that particular speech) penologists and criminologists 'however forward thinking').

Nonetheless, I believe that this position can be justified on the basis that part (at least) of the function of the criminal law and the sanctions which bolster it is to promote, as far as is possible, a decrease in the level of antisocial behaviour including violent or degrading behaviour and contempt for the integrity of other persons. It seems illogical to me to argue that we can secure those aims by inflicting exactly those social wrongs on those whom we are trying to bring within the compass of society's mores. I might be persuaded to compromise on this principled stand for some sort of utilitarian reason if there were some convincing evidence that by increasing the severity with which we dealt with those who broke society's rules we could reduce the numbers who would so transgress in the future. So far, however, as we shall see in Chapter 7, the evidence in favour of the efficacy of deterrence is pretty unconvincing, at least to unjaundiced observers. I would not go to the other extreme and argue for a system of only token punishments, for I am equally unconvinced that such a tokenistic response adequately addresses the rights of victims of crime to a strong and *meaningful* social response to the fact that they have been wronged by another person's act (Brownlee, 1994a: 88). But, subject to that minimum requirement, I would argue that it is a characteristic of any civilised society that it treats those over whom it claims the right of lawful punishment with humanity and restraint. Some readers may find the logic of this position unconvincing or too idealistic for their tastes, but at least they should not now be surprised when they encounter its implications in the analysis that follows.

The need for justifications

When a court imposes a sentence upon a convicted person it asserts, in a way that is both tangible and charged with wider symbolism, the claim of sovereignty of the political power to which it owes its judicial authority. Given this close proximity between the power to punish and the wider power to *rule*, it has become an axiom of political theory that the act of judicial sentencing requires to be justified by reference to some greater moral or ethical principle than merely the will of either the sentencer or the *de facto* law-giver. Punishment, even where it does not inflict actual physical pain, inevitably impinges in some way upon an individual's personal integrity. Because of this, most theories of law insist that without justification the punishment of an individual by the state is inherently wrong.

Within the somewhat practically-minded jurisprudence of the common law, appeals to higher moral justifications for punishment have commonly been expressed in terms of a range of *objectives* which might legitimately guide a sentencer's choice of penalty. Eliding the philosophical gap between practical objectives and the sort of moral or ethical principles which might, or might not, grant them validity by association, most practitioners and many academics have been content to install the pursuit of legitimate objectives as the distinguishing feature between proper judicial punishment and mere retaliation. Whether expressed as a principle or an objective, however, any supposed justification for punishment is making a *value-claim*, a normative statement about what makes that punishment not simply acceptable, but *right*. The ultimate benefit of such statements is not that they guide the sentencer unerringly to a single, totally defensible outcome in every case (an unlikely circumstance given the diverse range of penal philosophies and the almost infinite variety of human circumstances) but rather that they instil a sense of 'immanent critique' into the sentencing exercise by putting down markers against which the actual impact of a particular sentence can be measured. Clearly, a sentencer who never had to justify a particular choice of sentence by reference to anything more objective than his or her personal whim could never be said to have chosen wrongly.

General justifications for punishment

Consequentialist justifications

General theories providing justifications for punishment may usefully be divided into two broad categories: 'consequentialist' and 'non-consequentialist' (Duff and Garland, 1994; Duff, 1996). Consequentialist theories are forward-looking in the sense that they seek to justify the imposition of punishment (which usually involves some sort of present 'pain'), by pointing to some future 'good' which will follow as a *consequence* of the act of punishment, the value of which will outweigh the pain of the punishment itself. Given the focus on 'ends', consequentialist theories are also often referred to as 'instrumentalist' or 'utilitarian'. A recent critical review of penal policy and its relationship with social justice provides an unequivocal endorsement of the consequentialist principle in the following terms:

> The only possible justification for any state infliction of pain or restriction
> of liberty is that it is necessary for the promotion of some social good or
> the prevention of some greater social harm: the modern state can have no
> justification for inflicting pain for its own sake. Punishment, pain, then can
> never be 'deserved', it can only be socially necessary.
>
> (Hudson, 1993: 159)

Most commonly the goal or end that is pursued by sentencers with a consequentialist philosophy is a reduction in the level of future offending, so that the terms 'consequentialist' and 'reductivist' are often used interchangeably in sentencing literature. For a reductivist the punishment of wrongdoers is justifiable because a greater number of people in a given community derive a generalised benefit from the punishment of those few who break its rules when this leads to a reduction in the level of law-breaking which that community endures in the future. Whether this future increase in law-abiding behaviour is seen as a good-in-itself or as a necessary part of the wider conditions of a good society (see e.g. Lacey, 1988: ch. 5; Braithwaite and Pettit, 1990: ch. 5), the ultimate validity of the court's sentence is seen to be *contingent* upon the extent to which, overall, it promotes this desirable end.

Within this general consequentialist framework sentencers may employ a range of specific sentencing strategies in order to try to achieve their reductivist aim, of which 'deterrence' is probably the most common. Advocates of this approach often hope to achieve a deterrent effect at the level of the individual who is the subject of that sentence (*individual deterrence*) and among the wider public who come to hear of the sentence (*general deterrence*), although hard evidence of such effects being obtained seems remarkably elusive (von Hirsch and Ashworth, 1992a: ch. 2; Walker and Padfield, 1996: ch. 8). Reductivists might also attempt to secure their ends through the *rehabilitation* or *reform* of those who are subjected to punishments with some sort of therapeutic or 'interventionist' element such as drugs or anger-management counselling attached to them. As we shall see below and in more detail in Chapter 7, the empirical evidence suggests that it is difficult to demonstrate the *general* success of a particular type of sentence when measured against a rehabilitative yardstick. More optimism is, however, currently expressed about the possibility that some very closely specified and rigorously implemented rehabilitative programmes might be successful in curbing the recidivism of *some* offenders if carefully targeted at those most likely to benefit from them (Penal Affairs Consortium, 1997). In other words, the former attitude towards rehabilitation of 'nothing works' has been superseded by the conviction (at least in some circles) that *some* things work, with *some* people, *some* times.

More of that, later. The final reductivist strategy is the rather limited objective of *incapacitation*, a policy which emphasises the need to control and contain those who, usually on the basis of prediction derived from their past conduct, are thought likely to offend in the future if they are at liberty so to do. Although a custodial sentence probably affords the greatest level of incapacitation (at least as far as potential victims outside the institution are concerned), non-custodial sanctions, such as a probation order with strict reporting conditions or a curfew order, perhaps enforced by an electronic monitoring requirement, can also point to some level of incapacitation as part of their supposed justification. Incapacitation has recently enjoyed a revival in popularity among populist politicians eager, as we have seen, to manufacture extra votes out of public fears of being the victims of crime. By focusing on the prison's incapacitative effects, right-wing criminologists and 'law-and-order' politicians have been able to claim that 'prison works' (Home Office, 1996a: para. 1.12), thereby overturning the liberal orthodoxy which had long been convinced by the evidence that on almost every other measure prison palpably 'fails' (McGuire and Priestley, 1995: 10–14).

On a very limited interpretation of incapacitation, one which excludes offences committed against other prisoners and against prison discipline and which excludes also any consideration of post-release activity, prison does 'work' in the way that is claimed, at least while offenders are incarcerated. But one might also argue that a custodial sentence is only manifestly superior in terms of public protection if it significantly reduces the total criminal career of its recipient (Jones, 1990: 123). If it merely postpones reoffending, then, viewed in the longer term, the reductive effect of incarceration is diminished. The public might be granted a 'holiday' from a particular individual's offending (see e.g. *R.* v. *Gilbertson* (1980) Cr. App. R. (S) 312 for the appellate court's justification of a lengthy prison sentence on a petty but recidivist shoplifter), but if he or she goes on offending after release, then the holiday is a relatively short and very expensive one. The ultimate logic of the incapacitation argument, that those who are 'incorrigible' should never be released, has been seized on by opponents of the approach, and indeed of reductivism in general, as evidence of the threat which consequentialist sentencing principles are said to pose to individual human rights.

Non-consequentialist justifications

Avoid

Non-consequentialist theories, by contrast, eschew any consideration of possible future benefits and instead look backward towards the alleged wrongdoing, finding sufficient justification for punishing the wrongdoer in the inherent nature of the act that has been committed. Such justifications are commonly called 'retributivist'. What matters here is that a wrong has been committed. This fact alone demands that a reciprocal penalty be imposed, whatever the eventual consequences of this reciprocity of action might be. If punishing a guilty person also achieves some utilitarian consequence, so much the better. But that is not the aim or the justification. For a thoroughgoing retributivist, the guilty should be punished even if no 'collateral' benefit arises from the act of punishment, because punishment is a positive duty not merely a means towards an end.

Just why this duty arises is a matter of debate even among those who hold to such principles (Cottingham, 1979; Duff, 1996: Section III). In order to demonstrate the necessary link between past crimes and present punishments, other than instrumentally, some penal philosophers have used the analogy of a pair of scales. The act of wrongdoing weighs down the tray on one side: equilibrium can only be restored by placing an act of punishment on the other. This restoration of the *status quo* may or may not be linked to the avoidance of supernatural displeasure, depending on which version of the theory is considered. Others assert, less metaphorically, that those who break laws obtain an unfair advantage over those who do not and that punishment is necessary to take away this advantage (Honderich, 1984; von Hirsch, 1976, but see von Hirsch, 1986; 1990a: 264). More prosaically still, it has been argued that the essence of retribution is nothing more than obedience to a rule or a set of rules (usually, but not necessarily, set out in the criminal law) which say that doing this or that must be penalised (Walker, 1991; Walker and Padfield, 1996: 114).

Recently it has become common to ground the retributivist notion of an absolute duty to punish in the concept of 'desert'. Merely to assert, however, that punishment is 'just' because wrongdoers *deserve* to be punished does not take the debate very far unless some convincing explanation is offered of what 'deserve' means in this context. It may be correct to observe that 'most people' feel that a penalty is the appropriate or 'natural' response to wrongdoing (Walker and Padfield, 1996: 112), but to deduce from this that there is an 'intuitive' connection between desert and punishment (von Hirsch, 1986: 52) and then to use that sense of intuition at least in part as the justification for an essentially coercive and potentially repressive system of state punishment is a process of logic that some find unconvincing (Hudson, 1987; Lacey, 1988: 21–6; Ashworth, 1995: 71).

In a recent restatement of his own version of deserts theory, Andrew von Hirsch (1993: ch. 2) gives an essentially functionalist account of the link between wrongdoing and punishment based on the concept of 'censure'. On the assumption that human beings are, and must be treated as, rational, responsible moral beings, he argues that punishment is *the* appropriate response to wrongdoing precisely because punishment conveys 'censure' – blame or reprobation – to the perpetrator of the act through onerous consequences in such a way as to communicate the wrongfulness of the act and society's disapproval of it. 'Such communication of judgement and feeling', von Hirsch asserts, 'is the essence of moral discourse among rational agents.' Additionally, censure addresses the victim of the culpable act and, by directing disapprobation at the person responsible, acknowledges that the victim's hurt occurred through another's fault. Coincidentally, the onerous consequences – hard treatment – of censure also address third parties and announce in advance that specified categories of conduct are punishable. This provides people other than the transgressor with 'prudential' reasons for avoiding wrongdoing in their own conduct, and assists them in overcoming the 'temptation' to do that which (because of the censure) they know is wrong. However, von Hirsch insists that the preventive element in punishment is a secondary, 'supplementary' consideration which cannot be allowed to operate independently of, or to overwhelm, the moral, blaming function of censure (1993: 43). To argue otherwise would be to lapse into a reductivist, consequentialist justification of punishment which would undermine the proportionality requirement in his essentially retributivist position (cf. Narayan, 1993).

Whatever the precise basis that is offered for retributivist sentencing, non-consequentialist theories all emphasise the *non-contingent* nature of the perceived imperative to punish offending. If justice is to be served, then, for the strict retributivist, wrongdoers must be punished for their past misdeeds even where there is no prospect of producing any future benefit by so doing. This strict position is sometimes described as 'positive retribution' to distinguish it from a more limited version of non-consequentialism usually termed 'negative retribution' or 'retribution in distribution' (Hart, 1968). Negative retribution holds that only those actually found guilty of offences should be punished and then only to the extent that their present offending merits. The question of how the extent of harm caused by a particular offence can be measured and how this measurement can be related directly to a certain level of punishment raises some very tricky questions which will be discussed below. For the present it is sufficient to appreciate that the negative retribution principle is thought to rule out the punishment of 'potential' offenders on the basis of their wicked or dangerous thoughts (which certain consequentialist approaches might tolerate) and the punishment of 'whipping boys' or scapegoats, acts which a positive retributivist might deem necessary.

Hybrid or mixed theories, including communicative denunciation

Between these two polar positions of consequentialism and non-consequentialism, one may identify a range of 'mixed' or 'hybrid' theories which attempt to marry aspects of both in varying degrees (Robinson, 1987; Duff, 1996: 8–9). For instance, while some essentially consequentialist theorists argue that state intervention to secure the reform or rehabilitation of offenders is not merely an option but a positive *duty* of sentencers (Carlen, 1989; Rotman, 1990), others would accept that such interventions must not exceed 'upper bounds' set by considerations of negative retribution, especially proportionality to the offence or offences which brought the convicted person within the ambit of the correctional agencies in the first place. Thus, retributive constraints can be used to put a 'ceiling' on the amount of punishment that may be imposed for rehabilitative or other reductivist purposes if this would otherwise allow sentences out of all proportion to any objective assessment of the actual harm caused by the instant offence. Below that ceiling, however (or within upper and lower limits, if considerations of proportionality are also thought to exclude punishments which are too *lenient*), sentencing decisions can be made on grounds other than proportionality (Morris, 1974; Morris and Tonry, 1990, Hudson, 1993: 160–9).

For some mixed theorists, too, sentences which are essentially retributivist can also fulfil educative or reformative functions when they communicate to the sentenced person reasons which induce them as rational, moral agents to choose the path of self-reform (Duff, 1986: chs. 3–4;

1996: 31–41). The idea here is that by denouncing certain behaviours as 'unacceptable' or 'antisocial' and by backing this condemnation up with an undesirable penalty, the criminal law reinforces the moral boundaries of society and enables those who would be law-abiding to appreciate what is expected of them. We have seen something like this in the exposition of von Hirsch's concept of censure above, although von Hirsch distinguishes his own position from a *purely* communicative theory by insisting that there is an absolute moral duty to communicate blame even when it is obvious that the recipient of the communication is either too defiant to heed or too repentant to need it (von Hirsch, 1993: 10). Thus, although the similarities between this communicative justification and more overtly reductivist principles such as deterrence are obvious, retributivist theorists also claim denunciation (or 'censure') as part of their philosophy, arguing, like von Hirsch, that because society has an obligation to express its abhorrence of wrongdoing, denunciation is necessary even if no good consequences will result from it.

Problems of commensurability in sentencing

We have seen in Chapter 1 that current sentencing practice embodies 'just deserts' as its primary objective. The cornerstone of a 'desert' model of punishment is that the severity of punishment should be commensurate with the seriousness of the wrong caused by the offence that has been committed (von Hirsch, 1976: 66). Commensurability, being a term of art, however, is capable of bearing different meanings and confusion can arise if these are not sufficiently clearly defined. In common speech the idea of one thing being 'commensurate' with another implies exact equivalence and complete interchangeability. The *Concise Oxford English Dictionary*, for instance, suggests 'coextensive' as one of the prime meanings of the word. So, if legal concepts were blocks of wood, perfect commensurabilty would require that one could remove the block which represented crime 'type A' from the framework of social arrangements and replace it unerringly with the block representing punishment 'type A', and that the latter would neatly fill the gap left by the former.

A moment's reflection will suggest that such neat equivalence is unlikely to exist anywhere in the world outside philosophy seminar rooms. So how, in the real world, does one go about gauging the harm which a particular crime has inflicted and measuring the severity of a choice of sanctions? How precise can such calculations be, and how much imprecision is tolerable before the claim of proportionality becomes wholly fictitious (as some have claimed it is: see Christie, 1995)? How is the psychological as opposed to the physical impact to be assessed? How much weight is to be given to the views of victims of crimes (Ashworth, 1993) or to wider sections of the public? On the other side of the commensurability equation, one might ask to what extent does one have to take into account the varying tolerances and sensitivities of those who are punished in determining how much a particular sanction 'hurts'? Is the 'collateral' suffering caused to the relatives and dependants by, say, a period of imprisonment to be taken into account in determining the overall impact of that sentence (Ashworth, 1995: ch. 7)?

Even after these issues have been addressed and supposing (and it is a large supposition) that reasonably accurate measures could be produced to indicate offence seriousness and sentence severity, could a precise and neatly tailored relationship be assumed to exist between the two so that 'absolute proportionality' on some sort of mathematical matrix could be assured in every case (Walker, 1992: 534)? Or is it more likely, as some have argued, that the most that can be hoped for is some sort of 'loose' equivalence based on some absolutist notions of restraint in punishment which would help one to recognise 'utter disproportionality' where it occurred, but which made no attempt to impose a 'natural' equivalence between crime and punishment (Morris and Tonry, 1990: 89)? If this more limited role is all that could be claimed for proportionality, would this not merely serve to legitimise a sentencing regime that was so flexible that it could accommodate all but the most draconian sentences within the realm of 'desert'? Clearly, such complex issues are unlikely to succumb to easy answers, but the need to go some way, at least, toward providing reliable guidance for sentencers on practical matters of equivalence is vital if any progress is to be made on encouraging a greater use of non-custodial options in a climate dominated by exhortations to punitiveness.

Gauging the harm caused

Generally, the seriousness to be attributed to any particular crime is taken to be determined by a calculation of both the *harm* caused by the offence and the extent of the offender's *culpability* in relation to it. Hence, both objective and subjective elements play a part in producing a calculation of 'seriousness' against which the extent of deserved punishment can be measured. Gauging harm may be thought to involve essentially objective elements, particularly in relation to offences of theft and other predatory crimes. Even here, however, an element of subjectivity would be included if one were prepared to admit that different victims can have varying susceptibilities to harm, depending on their individual circumstances. Various countries, including Britain, have gone some way towards recognising the need to afford greater rights and protections to victims in the prosecution process, but most have fought shy of allowing individual victims too much direct influence in the choice of sentence, for fear of institutionalising the sorts of disparities that might arise from the different levels of forgiveness or vindictiveness likely to found in such a randomly selected sample of the population (Hough and Moxon, 1985; Ashworth, 1993).

Public attitude surveys, using larger samples of the population and involving stricter methodological controls (Walker, 1978), are thought by some to provide more reliable pointers to offence-seriousness and several such surveys have been conducted in various countries over the last thirty years (e.g. Walker and Hough, 1988). The results of such surveys vary, as one might expect in such a disparate exercise, but many researchers report broad areas of agreement between the views of the public and the relative seriousness accorded to different offences in various criminal codes, at least when opinions on specific detailed examples are examined, rather than attitudes to rather vague concepts like crime and punishment. Given the volatility of public opinion, however, such surveys are inherently susceptible to distortions produced, for instance, by the over-reporting of sensational but untypical crimes in the media and by other more insidious methods of disseminating and entrenching the interpretations of the powerful in everyday discourses (Hall et al., 1978; Box, 1987: ch. 5; Schlesinger and Tumber, 1994).

Moreover, the relationship between public opinion, pronouncements by politicians and changes in criminal justice policy is an extremely complex one (Bottoms, 1995a: 40). The extent to which even sophisticated surveys of public attitudes provide a truly objective basis on which to assess the seriousness of offences may, therefore, be doubted (Ashworth and Hough, 1996). Further, those who wish to promote parsimony in sentencing may actually wish to discourage reliance on surveys of this kind since (as the theatrical analogy in my introduction suggested) they rarely show the public to be particularly well informed about the realities of punishment or (perhaps as a result of this ignorance) any less punitively minded than the penal policy makers and sentencers, whether in England (Walker and Marsh, 1984; Hough, 1996; Walker and Padfield, 1996: 78) or elsewhere (Walker and Hough, 1988; Mayhew, 1994). As we noted in Chapter 1, the population of England and Wales reports itself to be the most anxious about the possibility of criminal victimisation among industrialised nations surveyed in 1996. Since fear of crime undoubtedly reduces the attractiveness of liberal penal policies founded on rehabilitation and decarceration, this opens up the possibility of greater punitiveness and the increased use of custody (Box et al., 1988: 340). Rather than being a resource, therefore, for those who would argue for less severe punishments, generalised public opinion seems more likely at present to provide fertile ground for the 'populist punitiveness' of 'law-and-order' politicians seeking to increase electoral popularity by promising ever tougher measures against 'villains' (Bottoms, 1995a; Christie, 1995: 26).

A more philosophical approach to the problem of gauging relative offence seriousness can be found in the work of Andrew von Hirsch and Nils Jareborg. Together (1991) they have begun to develop what they term a 'living standards' analysis in which, having stipulated a matrix of generic human interests which are potentially violated by criminal victimisation, they suggest a four-point scale on which to measure the extent to which *typical* instances of various crimes would affect the living standards of a hypothetical victim. This *standardised* measure of typical harm could then be supplemented by assessments of culpability and remoteness from the consequences of the criminal act, to arrive at some objective measure of seriousness. This approach or some sort of similar personal-interest analysis might also be usefully employed in assessing sentence severity (Wasik and von Hirsch, 1988; von Hirsch, 1993: 34).

However, the von Hirsch–Jareborg model is not yet fully developed and, moreover, much of its central core seems to depend on 'common-sense' and intuitive 'judgements' by members of sentencing commissions and similar official bodies of the importance that a 'typical' person 'ordin-arily' attaches to various life-chances under specific cultural conditions. Decisions like that are, as the authors concede, likely to be matters of rather inexact judgement (von Hirsch, 1993: 18, 33) and therefore, once again, its claims to objectivity have yet fully to be demonstrated. Further work remains to be done before it can be shown to provide generalisable standards beyond the range of typical-case offences with individual vic-tims on which it is presently predicated (see Ashworth, 1995: 93–100 for some suggested modifications to the basic thesis and Ashworth and von Hirsch, 1997 for further discussion).

Measuring 'blameworthiness'

The second element of offence seriousness is 'culpability', which brings with it notions of 'blameworthiness' and is thus a wider concept than 'intention', at least in the sense in which that latter term is used by crim-inal lawyers in most common law jurisdictions. In relation to this element, desert theorists have been much criticised for founding their argu-ments on the notion of 'standard case', or objective culpability, rather than any more subjective or individually assessed quantum. Echoing earlier strains of classical and neo-classical penal philosophy, desert theory holds offenders personally and individually responsible for their own actions and little account is taken of the social and economic circumstances in an offender's background which might, under more positivistic theories, be taken to provide some explanation of the offending behaviour (for a critical appraisal of this assumption see Lacey, 1988: ch. 3).

In fact, desert theory owes much of its success to the part it played in the attack on apparent disparities in punishments arising from the pass-ing of 'therapeutic' or indeterminate sentences individually tailored to address individual offenders' perceived rehabilitative 'needs' (von Hirsch, 1976; Frost, 1992). Allowing to sentencers, penal administrators and pa-role board members an unfettered discretion to vary the type and inten-sity of punishment primarily on an assessment of the characteristics of the offender was said to lead to unacceptably wide variations in sentenc-ing which could not be justified by appeals either to utility ('nothing works') or to justice (Frankel, 1972). To avoid the negative consequences of such informalism, desert theorists argued that the personal characteristics of individual offenders should play no part in the choice of sentence, once legal responsibility and mental capacity were established. Thus, the notion of objectively determinable culpability lies at the heart of modern retributive or blaming theories and excludes, for instance, sentencing on the basis of any prediction of future behaviour (von Hirsch, 1986) or directly on past record (von Hirsch, 1981, 1991).

Critics of strict proportionality in the distribution of punishment have countered by challenging the existence of 'like-situated' offenders, describing this as an 'illusion' because 'neither offenders nor punishments come in standard cases' (Tonry, 1994a: 69). On a purely anthropological level the first part of that proposition is correct. The issue for sentencers (and for those who seek to influence their decisions through, for example, the writing of pre-sentence reports) is to determine which of the myriad symbols of human diversity should properly influence the sentencing decision, and to what extent. Although there is ample evidence to show that racial or gender difference and social class are influential in the formation of prison populations in most countries of the world (Box, 1987: ch. 4; Hudson, 1987: ch. 4; 1993: ch. 2 and see Chapter 7, below), such factors, presumptively, cannot constitute valid grounds for *worse* treatment in the criminal justice system. But is the converse necessarily true, *a priori*? Do factors of social disadvantage provide any basis on which offenders should receive *better* or preferential treatment? To express the same question less abstractly, can the down-and-out vagrant who steals money to buy a much-needed meal be held less morally blameworthy than the student from a privileged background who steals a similar sum from her college 'just for kicks'?

Desert theorists do acknowledge that there are enormous practical difficulties in attempting to legislate for 'just deserts in an unjust world' if this means creating a system of formal justice predicated upon an assumption of equality before the law within a socio-economic system which perpetuates substantive material inequality (von Hirsch, 1976: ch. 17; 1993: ch. 10; Carlen, 1989). Nonetheless, most desert theorists, while gradually conceding more importance to the problems of social justice, have continued to insist that, on balance, disadvantaged offenders will be better served under a desert scheme than under a utilitarian one since the former at least generally rules out the sort of predictive or deterrent sentencing that the latter might allow. Responding to his critics on this point, von Hirsch, for instance, has argued that while the widespread existence of social injustices may strengthen the argument for some reduction in punishment levels overall, it does not diminish the harmfulness to their victims of the common 'victimising' crimes (von Hirsch, 1993: 107–8) nor does it take away the liability of an individual to be punished for their own actions in having violated the law (von Hirsch, 1976: 148). This argument is persuasive, however, only in as far as people *are* autonomous, free-willing individuals with moral responsibility for their own actions (Lacey, 1988: 190).

One does not have to embrace a full-blown determinism to see the force in the argument that the sort of 'freedom of action' which bears on an individual's criminal liability is a contingent social good rather than an essential property of all sane individuals (Duff and Garland, 1994: 30). Or, to put it in the more direct and colourful language of one recent text on probation work, the range of choices and the moral context in which choices are made are not the same for the company director as for the young person living in the broken-down car on the forecourt of his parents' home in a run-down inner estate, and therefore, by implication, neither is the level of culpability attached to their respective criminal behaviours (Drakeford and Vanstone, 1996a: 107). Such an approach is not entirely inimical to desert theory, for, as Andrew Ashworth has argued, personal circumstances like extreme need and deprivation or the evidence of a deprived childhood or physical abuse leading to a discernible character defect might indicate a reduction in culpability 'in extreme cases' (Ashworth, 1994: 9). But the room for such compromise is limited since desert theories are founded upon the basic philosophical premise that those who commit offences are *in general* responsible for their own wrongdoing and, hence, are deserving of blame. From a desert theorist's point of view, the proper response to the problem of a social system that is more or less unjust is to call for a general reduction of all sentences *pro rata* rather than on a case-to-case basis and, within those parsimonious constraints, to impose sentences that are proportionate to the seriousness of the offence.

Advocates of a more individualised approach to sentencing, on the other hand, argue strongly that penal systems must engage in just this sort of beneficial discrimination, since any failure to adjust assessment of culpability to reflect social disadvantage merely serves to perpetuate the vast over-representation of the economically marginal within the carceral system (Carlen, 1983; Morris and Tonry, 1990; Tonry, 1994b). As we shall see in Chapter 4, one of the dilemmas presently faced by many practitioners within the probation service is how to square their commitment to a philosophy of this kind with the demands of a service which has found a new role as an integral part of a criminal justice *system*, oriented towards just deserts in sentencing and being driven increasingly by punitive sentiments.

Can desert theories set limits on the overall severity of sentences?

Given these difficulties in arriving at a workable definition of 'commensurability', some philosophers of sentencing have been content to settle for 'proportionality' between offence and punishment. Again, however, the precise meaning of 'proportionality' can be hard to pin down. For some (e.g. Cross, 1975: 120; Christie, 1995: 27) there is no question of being able to find a precisely correct sentence for each offence in isolation from all others. Rather, proportionality is in essence merely a comparative quality which exists between various punishments themselves so that, as long as those whose offences are serious are punished more severely than the authors of mere peccadilloes, the demands of proportionality and hence commensurability have been satisfied. Others, however, find such a pragmatic definition of proportionality unsatisfactory and unnecessarily limited.

Andrew von Hirsch, who is probably the leading proponent of modern desert theory, distinguishes, for instance, between two forms of proportionality, which he terms 'ordinal' and 'cardinal' (von Hirsch, 1986; 1990a; 1993: 15–19). 'Ordinal' proportionality relates to comparative punishments in much the same way as has just been outlined. Its requirements are both positive and negative in the sense that it demands that persons convicted of crimes of similar gravity should receive punishments of like severity, while persons convicted of crimes of differing gravity should receive punishments correspondingly graded in their degree of severity. These requirements are explained primarily on the basis that since punishing one crime more severely than another expresses greater disapprobation ('censure') of the former, the increase in severity can only be justified to the extent that the first crime is more serious. 'Cardinal' proportionality, on the other hand, provides a series of benchmarks or anchoring points to which ordinal scales of sanctions may be 'tethered'. As such, cardinal proportionality serves as a constraint upon the absolute limits of severity to which a range of punishments, all neatly stacked according to principles of ordinal proportionality, may soar.

Whether considerations of cardinal proportionality also set *lower* limits on the severity of punishments (i.e. ruling out certain sanctions as just too lenient for a particular offence) is more problematic. In as much as the institution of punishment is 'about' the communication of censure, or morally based disapproval, one must be able to conceive of levels of punishment, at least in theory, which were so low that few objective people would consider that they conveyed sufficient disapproval of the criminal act to which they related. Following his Swedish colleague Jareborg on this, von Hirsch has recently come to accept that it is only considerations of inadequate prevention (i.e. consequentialist reasons), not considerations of cardinal desert, which set the lower limits of acceptability and he could envisage, albeit in an ideal world, a system of censure with only token impositions (1993: 38). This seems a difficult premise to sustain, however, particularly given von Hirsch's own insistence that censure also addresses *the victim,* for surely censure accompanied by only a token punishment comes perilously close to the sympathy-and-little-else response which von Hirsch himself regards as insufficient (1993: 10).

Notwithstanding this difficulty with justifying the setting of lower limits, some stipulation of absolute or 'cardinal' principles seems necessary for a thoroughly worked-out desert theory. If all that commensurability and proportionality required was that various punishments displayed some sort of internal rank-ordering and relative spacing among themselves and some reasonably coherent linkage with similarly ranked levels of offending, then desert theory would be shown to be essentially relativistic and would provide no coherent safeguard against tyrannical escalations in (neatly stacked) sentences. In fact, this is just the sort of accusation that has been levelled against modern retributivist theories, including von Hirsch's version (Hudson, 1987; Carlen, 1989; Walker, 1992), and if desert theory is to deflect this criticism, some further step towards an objective referent for the validity of sentencing is clearly needed.

An objective basis for proportionality?

In response von Hirsch has argued that, while there is no intuitively consensual yardstick and no credible external standard that can be applied to set an absolute amount of commensurability for particular crimes, this does not imply that all conceivable sentencing conventions are equally valid. Limits on the severity of sanctions can – indeed, should – be imposed by reference to other values so that the direction of sentencing policy is towards progressive *pro rata* reductions in sentence severity, a decremental strategy as von Hirsch calls it (1993: ch. 5).

The most important of these values is *parsimony*, which may be defined as an ideological commitment to keeping state-inflicted punishment to a minimum. This commitment, moral or ethical in nature, would exclude the opportunistic 'optimising' of crime prevention through exemplary or deterrent sentencing, since in the von Hirschean model prevention must always be seen as a 'supplementary prudential disincentive' achievable by 'rather modest sanction levels', almost – but not quite – a byproduct of the censuring process itself.

'Censure', and indeed retributivist theories more generally, find their roots in a classical model of human nature which involves treating individual citizens as 'moral agents', 'responsible' and reasoning people who can be persuaded, but never coerced, away from law-breaking behaviour (von Hirsch, 1993: 43). Thus, while, as we have seen, penal law serves two interrelated functions – it communicates disapproval of criminal behaviour and, by threatening unpleasant consequences, it also seeks to discourage such behaviour – these two functions are not equals, in von Hirsch's view, and he asserts that the preventive element must always be considered secondary or 'supplementary' to the censuring function. Changes in sentencing convention, he concludes, which were faithful to this principle would inevitably cause graded penalties to move downward *pro rata*, rather than upwards as his critics allege, since the overarching principle would be that the preventive function of punishment should not loom so large as to coopt or displace the normative message. Indeed, in those jurisdictions which have enacted 'three-strikes-and you're-out' style legislation aimed at persistent offenders, it could logically be argued that it has been the very denial of proportionality requirements which has led to enormous rises in prison populations (von Hirsch, 1992: 215).

From a desert theorist's point of view, therefore, what prevents the use of non-custodial penalties for serious offences, for example, is not the *theoretical* constraints of just deserts as such but the *empirical* existence of a sentencing convention, or 'tariff', which sets the 'cardinal' limits at so high a level that even moderately low-ranking crimes are punished by imprisonment (Wasik and von Hirsch, 1988). Sentencing tariffs evolve over many years, 'bolstered', to borrow Andrew Ashworth's phrase, by arguments from analogy and swayed by occasional moral panics (Ashworth, 1995: 98), but they are susceptible to change if challenged on sufficiently compelling grounds, as the experience of other jurisdictions reveals (Downes, 1988; Feest, 1988; McMahon, 1992). And once a sentencing convention has been revised downwards by forcing upon it the claims of more humanitarian values, such as an ethical commitment to parsimony, then *pro rata* changes in all available punishments are achieved without offending the principles of ordinal proportionality (von Hirsch, 1993: 89; von Hirsch *et al.*, 1989: 615–16).

Von Hirsch's stipulation of a quasi-objective basis for cardinal proportionality is clearly contentious. It is based on the proposition that the deterrent effects of punishment must always be considered secondary or 'supplementary' to the censuring function so that 'the requirements of proportionality' are not undermined. This, in turn, is premised on two further presumptions: that human beings are essentially moral, autonomous and rationalising individuals who can be appealed to, but never coerced, into law-abiding behaviours; and that it is an essential element of a democratic society that its basic institutions, including the institution of state punishment, should be designed with a responsible citizenry in mind (1993: 43). Many criminals may, in fact, not be susceptible to moral persuasion alone so that the preventive efficiency of a decrementally-oriented deserts scheme may in practice be less than other approaches might yield. Well, says von Hirsch, so be it: 'The criminal sanction cannot achieve anything near one hundred per cent efficiency, and fulfils its proper function if it helps induce most people to comply' (1993: 44).

To stipulate as much, however, is merely to express a preference among a range of competing ethical values. In the absence of any more objective basis for preferring the requirements of proportionality not to be undermined by, say, considerations of 'decency' towards disadvantaged and marginalised people who have broken the law out of a sense of desperation (Christie, 1995: 21), or considerations of what would be the most *appropriate* mode of punishment to express the necessary censure to a particular offender in a substantive rather than a formal way (Duff, 1996: 62), such a stipulation appears essentially a matter of choice. The assertion that the demands of 'fairness' through desert and ordinal proportionality are more likely to promote the greater well-being of individual

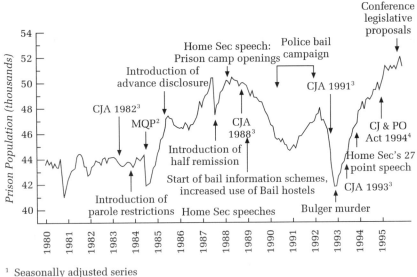

¹ Seasonally adjusted series
² Change of minimum qualifying period for parole
³ CJA = Criminal Justice Act
⁴ Criminal Justice and Public Order Act

Figure 2.1 Prison Population: Policy Interventions 1980–1995
Source: Home Office Statistical Bulletin 14/96.

offenders and of society as a whole than, say, therapeutic interventionism based on a state-obligated model of rehabilitation can certainly be argued (see e.g. Duff, 1996: 11), but it is by no means self-evidently true. Nor does an appeal to 'practical' outcomes add much to this argument. In so far as the justification for preferring a desert rationale is grounded on the assumption that sentence severity is only ever increased for utilitarian, reductivist reasons (von Hirsch, 1992: 228), it is very questionable indeed. Given the ease with which any sentencing system that is based on more or less rigidly drawn guidelines can be manipulated by populist politicians (Christie, 1995: 23; Hough, 1997), there are grounds for fearing an escalation in severity for purely retributivist, denunciatory grounds (as appears to have happened in England in 1993 after the murder of Jamie Bulger and other high-profile crimes illustrated in Figure 2.1 above; and see Currie, 1996 for telling evidence from the United States).

Therefore, while there may indeed be no *necessary* link in theory between desert model penal policies and more severe sentences (von Hirsch, 1993: ch. 10; Hudson, 1993: 42), it is equally the case that desert theory, of itself, is insufficient to ensure the sort of 'decremental' or downward movement in sentencing severity that von Hirsch and other liberal advocates of desert theory seek. To perform this more ambitious but essential task, desert has to be harnessed to and bolstered by some non-intrinsic principle like 'parsimony' or 'restraint' in sentencing. Desert theory, as von Hirsch has acknowledged on more than one occasion, tells us more about comparative punishment than it does about setting the penalty scale's anchoring points (see e.g. von Hirsch, 1990a: 288; 1992: 214). Without some more fundamental ethical principle upward 'hikes' in sentencing levels are perfectly feasible even under a deserts-based scheme. It should be no comfort to those who favour 'parsimony' in sentencing (which is von Hirsch's own position) to know that aberrant severity was being experienced universally; if punishments are 'wrong' because they are too severe, they are not made 'right' by being made equally severe for all.

Applying justifying principles to the choice of non-custodial sentences

Consequentialist justifications

Traditionally, non-custodial options have tended to be justified on essentially consequentialist grounds to do with the reduction of offending or reoffending, whether this was expressed in individual or general terms. The probation order is perhaps the best example of this long-standing association between punishment in the community and the reduction of future levels of offending through reform and rehabilitation. From its inception, as Chapter 3 reveals, the probation order held out the prospect of effecting some positive change in an offender's attitudes and behaviour. The simultaneous rise of criminology as a scientific or *quasi*-scientific discipline (Garland, 1985) seemed to make possible the development of thoroughly effective 'normalising' regimes based upon diagnosis and treatment of the underlying *causes* of crime (Peters, 1986: 29). While this may have transformed the working methods of probation officers, the emergence of scientific criminologies tended to reinforce rather than undermine the reformative zeal of the service itself (McWilliams, 1983; 1987; May, 1994).

By the time the community service order was introduced in England and Wales in the mid-1970s, scepticism about the effectiveness of many therapeutic programmes and the resurgence of other penal objectives were already beginning to challenge the pre-eminence which the rehabilitative ethic had once enjoyed (Garland, 1996). Nonetheless, the presumptive link between non-custodial sentencing and reform was still evident in the 1970 report of the Advisory Council on the Penal System (the Wooton Report) which had originally recommended the introduction of community service as a sentence of the court. While not ruling out other possible aims, the chief attraction of the new order as far as the Council was concerned was 'the opportunity which it could give for constructive activity in the form of personal service to the community, and the possibility of a changed outlook on the part of the offender' (ACPS, 1970: para. 34).

This long-standing, 'common-sense' association between non-custodial sentences and reform or rehabilitation has had both positive and negative consequences for the acceptability of such disposals over the years. On the one hand, it has allowed those who have sought a reduction in the overall use of prison to promote non-custodial sentences as an altogether more optimistic and effective way of reducing reoffending, particularly given the high rates of recidivism associated with imprisonment. However, such direct appeals to 'effectiveness' as a justification for choosing a non-custodial over a custodial disposal immediately give rise to demands for evaluation and empirical proof that, in fact, non-custody 'works' in the terms that have been claimed for it (Home Office, 1959, cited in Bottoms and Stevenson, 1992). Such 'proof' has been notoriously difficult to establish, especially when the expectation was that this superiority could be demonstrated to be inevitable and universal across all manner of offences and offenders. In a sense, the fleeting but significant claims of modernity that the technical application of scientific knowledge could resolve all the problems of society, including the problem of crime, imposed a burden of optimism on rehabilitative sentencing regimes that they were never likely to be able to bear in the longer term (Garland, 1990: 7).

Consequentialist justifications for punishment, with their focus on demonstrable goals and ends, always carry with them the potential to be undone by unfavourable 'evidence' that shows them not to be achieving their stated aims (Bottoms and Stevenson, 1992: 22). This risk is greater when (and this is usually the case) the aims which are stipulated for a non-custodial sentencing option include the reduction of future offending by those who are sentenced to it. The limitations of therapeutic interventions began to be exposed by the results of the very evaluations and monitoring that had been an intrinsic part of the epistemology from which they had sprung. Major reviews of the evaluation literature on criminal rehabilitation programmes, first in the United States (Martinson, 1974; Lipton et al., 1975) and then in Britain (Brody, 1976; Croft, 1978; Phillpotts and Lancucki, 1979), failed to find much consistent or reliable evidence of any appreciable effect on recidivism. Thus, the once optimistic age of 'penal modernism' (Peters, 1986: 29; Garland, 1990: ch. 8) gave way to the soul-searching era of 'nothing works' (which might more accurately have been described as the 'nothing-can-be-shown-to-work-any-better-than-anything-else' era) in the 1970s. The apparent failure of rehabilitation to live up to the claims that had been made for it forced penal policy makers to look for a new rationale which did not depend for its legitimacy upon the proof that utilitarian goals had been achieved.

This is not to imply that the legacy of 'nothing works' has banished consequentialist justifications from the non-custodial repertoire entirely.

Robert Martinson, to whom the phrase 'nothing works' is usually accredited, distanced himself from that gloomy conclusion as early as 1979, following a further review of his own data (Martinson, 1979). With the introduction of new and more powerful statistical techniques in the mid-1980s, so-called 'meta-analysis' or simultaneous comparisons of large numbers of different evaluation studies became possible, producing, in effect, larger experimental samples and control groups than had previously been examined. Several of these meta-analysis studies (e.g. Gendreau and Ross, 1987; Lipsey, 1992) claimed to have detected significant positive effects in reducing recidivism across a range of 'treatment' programmes, directly contradicting earlier reviews of the research literature. One recent estimate suggests that when all the meta-analyses are taken together a 'net effect' of the various treatment programmes studied is, on average, a reduction in recidivism rates of between 10 and 12 per cent (McGuire and Priestley, 1995: 9). This view remains contentious (see e.g. Pitts, 1992, to the contrary) and its proponents concede that scepticism about the positive effects of rehabilitative programmes remains the dominant, 'mainstream' view (see further Chapter 7 on the limitations of evaluation studies of sentencing measures). Nonetheless, there is little doubt that belief in the viability of rehabilitation, which has survived within the probation service despite the earlier pessimistic research findings and the encroaching influence of 'managerialism' with its 'obsession' with 'input measurement' (Raynor et al., 1994: 72), has received a tremendous boost from the revisionist claim that some interventions, at least, 'do work'. Increasingly, the emphasis in working with offenders is shifting towards identifying 'what works' and with whom.

Therefore, as we shall see in Chapter 4, the rehabilitation of offenders remains part of the mission of the probation service and indeed continues to be one of the statutory purposes of the probation order. However, the experience of the 'nothing works' era has led many of those who continue to champion non-custodial sentencing to be more guarded in their aspirations. There is a tendency now, when relying upon utilitarian reasons for choosing one sentencing option over another, to emphasise that a particular approach may work with some specifically targeted offenders in some specified circumstances (what one might call 'goal limitation') or else to emphasise broader measures of success such as an increase in an offender's self-perception, social skills or earning capacities, alongside more offending-oriented criteria ('goal supplementation') (McIvor, 1992, 1993; Raynor et al., 1994: 77–84). Nor should one overlook the fact that, at an institutional level, the rise of 'managerialism' within the service has tended to 'decouple' performance evaluation from external social objectives. Instead of social norms, like rehabilitation and reintegration into the community, or public safety, institutions like the probation service begin to measure their own outputs (e.g. the proportion of pre-sentence reports produced within a given deadline) as indicators of performance (Feeley and Simon, 1992: 456; 1994: 188; Garland,

1996: 458). We shall examine the consequences of this development further in Chapter 4.

This kind of goal sublimation is not universal, however, and the claims of what has been termed 'new rehabilitation' (to distinguish it from the former, discredited variety (Cullen and Gilbert, 1982)) can be heard both inside and outside the probation service, albeit from an oppositional, rather than a mainstream, position in the policy spectrum (McGuire and Priestley, 1995: 5). Among academic commentators, for instance, Pat Carlen has called for the currently perceived obligation on the state to punish offenders to be replaced with an obligation to rehabilitate them (Carlen, 1983: 213; 1989). Expressly rejecting 'desert' theory as a justification for sentencing on the grounds that it is inherently 'punitive', Carlen has argued that denunciation, crime-reduction, rehabilitation, and reconciliation (between community, offender, and victim) should be the major aims of sentencing (1989: 19). Within this framework, rehabilitation becomes an obligation both for the state (which must in every case provide the opportunity for an offender to adjust their behaviour to reduce the risk of future offending) and for the offender, who could be obliged or even coerced into participation in any 'feasible' programme of rehabilitation or regulation. Criticism that such an approach represents a violation of civil liberties (for a summary and further development of this critique see Duff, 1996: 10–12, 47–57) is rejected on the grounds that the criticism is based on an inherently individualistic and anti-communitarian version of rights theory which does not wish to recognise that individuals have 'a fundamental interest in the maintenance and development of a peaceful and just society to which they belong and through which many of their interests are realised and indeed constructed' (Carlen, 1989: 19, citing Lacey, 1988: 172; on the 'primacy of the social' in the construction of personal autonomy more generally, see Lacey, 1988: ch. 8).

Under such conditions both offender and state have a positive obligation to take all *feasible* action to reduce the likelihood of crime in the future since both might be 'more or less responsible' for the breakdown of social relations which had resulted in the crime for which the offender was currently being sentenced. Other commentators have strongly endorsed this call for 'state-obligated rehabilitation', although, as we have seen above, some who are broadly in sympathy with it would prefer to see it located within a 'mixed' or 'hybrid' sentencing model in which limits on the state's right to punish *and to rehabilitate* would be indicated by, *inter alia*, the constraints of proportionality (Hudson, 1993: 168). Although I have previously argued to the contrary (Brownlee, 1994a), I am now persuaded that it is this latter 'hybrid' approach which is more likely to produce outcomes favouring substantive, as opposed to merely formal, justice and to secure greater preventive effects. I accept, however, that this choice is largely an ethical one (von Hirsch, 1992: 226), and I remain open to the possibility that some (possibly many) crime control interventions and rehabilitative programmes might not produce sufficient benefits to justify the departure from the principle of equal treatment implicit in a more individualised approach to sentencing.

Non-consequentialist justifications

Despite the historical tendency to justify non-custodial sentences on utilitarian grounds, there is nothing in theory which prevents reliance on non-consequential principles for this purpose, if it is accepted that a desert rationale addresses only the severity of penalties, not their particular form (Robinson, 1987; Wasik and von Hirsch, 1988: 558; von Hirsch, 1992; 1993: 59). Indeed, the claim of desert theorists is that, in justifying the use of community-based sanctions, recourse to non-consequentialist principles, particularly proportionality, is not only *feasible*, it is *essential* if the wilder excesses of discretionary sentencing are to be avoided (von Hirsch, 1992: 220–1). From this perspective, the consequentialist tendency to assess non-custodial sentences principally in terms of their 'effectiveness' has too often led to a disjunction between the punishment which an offender receives and the actual harm that their offending has caused.

> Imprisonment is obviously a severe punishment, and its manifestly punitive character brings questions of proportionality into sharp relief. Non-custodial measures, however, are also punishments – whether their proponents characterise them as such or not. A sanction levied in the community, like other punishments, visits deprivation on the offender under circumstances that convey disapproval or censure of his or her conduct. Like any other blaming sanction, its degree of severity should reflect the degree of blameworthiness of the criminal conduct. In other words, the punishment should comport with the crime.
>
> (von Hirsch, 1990b: 163)

For those, then, who claim to be defending the rights even of the guilty from those for whom 'doing good' is the prime objective (Allen, 1964 cited in von Hirsch, 1990b; Bottoms and McWilliams, 1979; Bottoms, 1995a: 22–3) the comparative infrequency of considerations of proportionality in writings and initiatives on non-custodial sentencing is a serious neglect. Such neglect is particularly worrying in relation to some of the newer non-custodial sanctions such as curfew orders with electronic monitoring and intensive supervision which can often involve substantial deprivation of liberty. Just because such sanctions are less onerous than imprisonment, does it necessary follow that any amount of them is justifiable, as long as it keeps the offender outside the prison walls? To a desert theorist or to anyone committed at least to the principles of negative retribution, the answer to that question must clearly be 'no' (see e.g. von Hirsch, 1993: 80–1).

Concern with proportionality in relation to the *amount* of punishment does not necessarily prescribe the *method* of punishment, however, provided one accepts the possibility of establishing some principled system of interchangeability or substitution whereby the relative penal 'bite' or penal 'value' of each available sanction can be measured accurately enough to allow the total penal 'bite' deserved for a particular offence to be contributed by any of a range of penalties, not just one (Robinson, 1994). One should not underestimate the practical difficulties of establishing comprehensive sentencing policies which combine prison and 'non prison' into a system of interchangeable punishments, or of persuading politicians to adopt them in the present ideological climate. Nevertheless, there have been attempts to establish at least the theoretical framework for such an approach by both advocates and opponents of desert theory. The idea underlying the whole approach is that while different methods of sanctioning have different punitive effects, they may, nonetheless, be interchanged or substituted on the basis of some agreed assessment of the respective punitive value of each and some sense of 'exchange rates' between punishments (cf. Wasik and von Hirsch, 1998 with Morris and Tonry, 1990 for different approaches to calculating the range of equivalencies, and see von Hirsch, 1992 for a thorough, if somewhat partisan, review of both). It is an important requirement of this approach that non-custodial penalties cease to be thought of as 'alternatives' to imprisonment and become penalties 'in their own right' capable of bearing an identifiable penal value which can then be 'exchanged' for some pre-established calculation of offence seriousness.

In their model of interchangeability, which is designed to be a good deal more flexible and to allow sentencers more discretion in the choice of sanction than those modelled predominantly on 'desert', Morris and Tonry see a distinction between purposes *of* sentencing and purposes *at* sentencing. The former are the general justifying aims and it is these which give guidance on undeservedly severe and undeservedly lenient sentences (the commensurability criteria). Within those boundaries, they argue, there is ample room for 'principled interchangeability of punishment', and once the principle of (in their version, 'rough') equivalence between custodial and non-custodial punishments is accepted, the choice of punishment should be guided by the purposes or 'function' sought to be achieved *at* the point of sentencing in the individual case (Morris and Tonry, 1990: 89–90).

The fact that Wasik and von Hirsch's more deserts-oriented 'substitution' model also envisages the choice between the range of sanctions available within a given band being made 'perhaps even on utilitarian grounds' (Wasik and von Hirsch, 1988: 561) demonstrates the potential which this approach has for providing some accommodation between desert theory and the demands of rehabilitation for individualised sentencing. However, von Hirsch has subsequently made clear his view that within a substitution model based on notions of desert and proportionality the choice of 'interchangeable' sanctions would be considerably more constrained than that envisaged by Morris and Tonry (von Hirsch, 1992: 223): in his view too wide a range of non-custodial options merely adds to the already considerable problem of ranking available punishments in terms of their severity.

The two approaches are not dissimilar, therefore, and may even achieve broadly similar outcomes in particular instances, but they are not the same. In particular, they incorporate two different concepts of 'doing justice'. The deserts model insists on the supremacy of 'formal' justice of administering (as far as we can) equal quanta of censure to equally culpable criminals, while the individualised approach seeks to do 'substantive' justice by finding punishments that are substantively apposite to the offender and his or her crime. These two conceptions are in tension and while this tension can be reduced to a certain extent by, for instance, restricting the role of formal proportionality to a limiting principle and permitting individualised sentences within the boundaries it sets, Duff's conclusion that we cannot totally dissolve the real conflict between the demand for formal proportionality and the demand for substantive appropriateness in the choice of sentence, that we cannot consistently pursue both aims together, seems unquestionably true (Duff, 1996: 62–5). A large part of the difficulty which faces the probation service at the present time (as we shall see in Chapter 4) is that it is attempting to do just that. With the present disinclination to justify sentences on consequential grounds, there is the tendency to attempt to further aims and methods more in tune with substantive, individualised approaches through a rhetorical commitment to the demands of formal proportionality.

The role of 'community' in implementing punishment

So far this discussion of community-based sanctions has proceeded as if the meaning of 'community' itself can be taken for granted. Of course, even a passing awareness of recent developments in sociology would alert the reader to the fact that 'community' is both one of the most ubiquitous and one of the most contested terms in the sociological vocabulary (Bottoms, 1995a: 34; Lacey and Zedner, 1995; Crawford, 1997: ch. 5). Communities may be composed or defined in a number of different ways including spatially, culturally, politically, by reference to a defined range of common values or interests, or by any combination of these and other characteristics. In relation to the current official endorsement of 'community punishment' the sense of 'community' which is being invoked is essentially spatial or geographic. Sanctions are 'in the community' principally because they are implemented outside prisons or similar custodial institutions.

In official discourse, therefore, 'community' is essentially a matter of locale. It is true that, in conformity with the 'multi-agency' approach of the age and as a result of specific requirements on the probation service to foster 'partnership' working (Home Office, 1988b; 1990b; Broad, 1996), many specific community-based sanctions are provided and run by non-statutory bodies such as charities and private companies. While this undoubtedly represents some decentralising of the functions of the state in relation to punishment, it does not (at least, as yet) constitute any significant transfer of responsibility away from formally-structured 'professional' organisations towards informally coordinated local communities (Bottoms, 1995a: 35). Advocates of the 'what works' resurgence of belief in rehabilitation are certainly prepared to argue on the basis of a meta-analysis of research data that, on balance, programmes to reduce reoffending yield more positive outcomes if they are located in the community rather than in custodial institutions (McGuire and Priestley, 1995: 15). However, few additional responsibilities are placed upon local communities by this form of relocation (or 'transcarceration': Lowman *et al.*, 1987) other than the requirement to tolerate in their midst officially classified deviants from whom they might, under other arrangements, be segregated. In this narrowly drawn conception, punishments are *in* the community, but not *of* the community.

At an official level, whatever rationale is offered for community-based sentencing, little credence has been given in recent years to suggestions that crime might have its origins in the chaotic or impoverished social conditions in the very communities to which appeal is being made; in the current climate of mainstream criminology, community is almost invariably presented as a cure, not a cause, of crime (May, 1994: 867). However counter-factual claims to have secured true community involvement in punishment may be in substance (Bottoms, 1995a: 35), the association of the two terms can usually be relied upon to secure considerable formal legitimacy for what may be essentially supply-side driven initiatives in penal policy. This in turn delivers important ideological benefits for hard-pressed governments who wish to be seen to be 'doing something' about crime without thereby increasing the public indebtedness.

Such a limited and passive role need not be the only feasible type of involvement for 'communities' (however they are to be defined in specific instances) in the sanctioning of criminal and antisocial behaviours. A wider conception of 'community' might include a model of the human being, not as an atomised, rights-bearing individual but as essentially a member of a group of 'significant' others whose activities and responses are of fundamental importance in the construction of self and in the promotion of personal well-being. As we have seen in the discussion of state-obligated rehabilitation, such a concept of personhood presents a considerable challenge to the assumptions of classical liberalism upon which the retributivist/just deserts model of punishment is built (Lacey 1988: 172; Bottoms, 1995a: 38).

In recent years John Braithwaite and others have begun to outline the theoretical conditions under which actual members of real communities, so conceived, could be actively involved in censuring and ameliorating deviant behaviour through the manipulation of processes of shame, repentance and reintegration (Braithwaite, 1989; Braithwaite and Mugford, 1994). In grounding his theoretical work, Braithwaite uses concrete examples from modern-day Japan and from contemporary aboriginal societies. Much international attention has also recently centred on the use of 'family group conferencing', originally practised among Maori communities, but now the principal way of dealing with medium-level juvenile offending in New Zealand (Maxwell and Morris, 1993). Approaches such as these promote the merits of 'informalism' over the routinised activities of the formal criminal justice system and seek to encourage non-judicial settlement of disputes through community mediation and reparation between offenders, their victims and the communities in which they reside (Marshall and Merry, 1990; Dignan *et al.*, 1997).

As such, they form part of a wider movement towards 'relational justice' which characterises crime primarily as the manifestation of a breakdown in social and communal relationships (Burnside and Baker, 1994). The essential social task thereafter is not so much punishment as the 'healing' of those fractured relations, a responsibility which is more likely to be discharged successfully by actions (including the imposition of penalties expressing disapproval, where necessary: Duff, 1996: 83) which maintain the offender's position as part of his or her community. Active and immediate participation in the sanctioning of those who break communal rules is also said to contain cathartic and renewing possibilities for the rule-enforcers so that not only the offender but the whole community is 'rehabilitated' through these processes of community-centred justice.

The implications of such a movement for the promotion of non-custodial sanctions are obvious, since it could be argued that the incarceration of an offender removes that person from the possible influence of their family and other significant figures in their immediate environment and thus diminishes the possibility of repairing the social breakdown which, according to the theory, has precipitated the criminal behaviour in the first place. It also has considerable overlap with the 'abolitionist' movement which argues that there is no natural or normative relationship between law enforcement and punishment and that, given the potential – logically and empirically – for other ways of dealing more rationally with wrongdoing, punishment cannot be justified in a just society (de Haan, 1990: 128; Duff, 1996: Section VI). Both abolitionists and 'informalists' more generally call for the 'decentring' of punishment from its conceptual high-point in penal philosophy. Both positions argue, in varying degrees, that social rules, even if they are embodied in criminal laws, might more usefully be 'backed up' by sanctions which do not involve the inflicting of 'hard treatment' or deprivation upon the rule-breaker. Community justice structured along these lines, it is claimed, would be more humane, less coercive and would better restore those communal bonds of social solidarity which are the real and essential bulwarks against crime and criminal victimisation.

Despite the instinctive humanitarian appeal of such views, however, there are those who, although broadly in sympathy with the endeavour to reduce the punitiveness of modern penal systems, caution against the wholehearted adoption of unregulated 'informalism' (Abel, 1982; Fitzpatrick, 1992; Duff, 1996). One has only to reflect upon the violence that can be inflicted on innocent people by vigilante gangs to see the furthermost bounds to which 'informal justice' can go, and even in less extreme forms community-derived penalties can sometimes be at least as harsh as those prescribed by the state (Maxwell and Morris, 1993). Communities can be harsh, hostile and exclusionary and, as Duff argues (1996: 85, emphasis in original), 'the formal apparatus of the state and the criminal justice system can help to *protect* offenders (and others who deviate from the mores of their local communities) against their neighbours'. Perhaps because of this reserve on the left, and almost certainly because the radical philosophy which underpins it is inimical to the essentially conservative neo-liberal theory which currently predominates penal policy making, relational justice type initiatives have been rather marginal to mainstream criminal justice developments (Bottoms, 1995a: 37). Nonetheless, their potential for revitalising the provision of community-based sanctions in the future should not be dismissed, given a more favourable political climate.

Summary

From the discussion above it will be appreciated that the use of non-custodial sentences can be supported on a number of quite disparate philosophical bases. However, this is not to say that the choice of a particular justifying philosophy is unimportant or without significant implication for the type of non-custodial regime that can be sustained in practice. The historic association between community-based sanctions and consequentialist justifications endures, having emerged again, although hardly unscathed, from the decade of 'nothing works'. Anxieties about the 'Trojan horse' effects of rehabilitative programmes (see further Chapter 7) have not been overcome entirely, though, even if the 'dispersal of discipline' thesis is no longer uncontested (Bottoms, 1983; Matthews, 1987). Some consequentialists still call as an act of ethical commitment for the reductivist doctrine to be further entrenched in the recognition of an obligation on the state to rehabilitate rather than to punish. For many within the consequentialist camp, however, the need to demonstrate that 'something works' has led to a narrowing of objectives and to more attention being paid to the careful targeting of therapeutic interventions on a selective range of offenders. Further, because the dominant 'justice' model of punishments has increasingly been colonised by populist politicians, there have had to be compromises with the punitive language of official discourse and a preparedness, if not exactly an enthusiasm, to portray non-custodial programmes as an integral part of a punishment-oriented justice system, rather than as an alternative to it.

While this accommodation may have preserved vital space in which non-custodial initiatives can not only survive but also produce new and innovative ways of working (ISTD, 1997), it has also provoked considerable debate within the probation service and elsewhere about how well penal measures that were once undoubtedly therapeutic in intent can fit within a sentencing system predicated upon retribution and punishment. (The terms of this debate are explored further in Chapters 3 and 4, below.)

Meanwhile, proponents of 'just deserts' continue to argue that, despite recent appearances to the contrary, there is nothing inimical to leniency or the use of non-custodial sanctions in their approach, once the principle of 'punishments in their own right' is accepted and the specifics of ordinal and cardinal proportionality and of interchangeability or substitution have been enunciated. These arguments have had effect, as the application of the principle of 'just deserts' to community penalties in the Criminal Justice Act 1991 demonstrates (Newburn, 1995: 118). More generally, proportionality in sentencing is held out both as a feasible objective and as a necessary safeguard against the over-intrusive expansion of social control through punishments, including non-custodial sanctions, predicated upon welfare or reductivist principles.

Desert theorists continue to attract criticism, however, from those who allege that the promotion of 'equal treatment' as the principal objective of sentencing, rather than 'appropriateness' or actual outcome, lends itself all too conveniently to the needs of populist politicians building reputations for toughness through the promotion of ever more draconian sentencing regimes. Despite consistent denials that there is any necessary link between the primacy of desert and a 'hike' in sentencing severity, there remains a deep suspicion that in the real and sometimes premodern world in which actual sentencers live and move, 'deserved' punishments are going to be equated with severe punishments for a long time to come. Recent history both in Britain and the United States suggests that it is the law-and-order rhetoric of populist politicians, feeding off the anxieties of large swathes of the population and fed back in turn through the information-loop of an over-compliant or manipulative news media, rather than adherence to any particular philosophy which sets the anchor points of that range, driving up the severity of sentencing as a result (cf. Bingham, 1997: 2). Those who witnessed the then leader of the main opposition party in Britain declare in the dying days of the 1997 election campaign that 'the prisoners should be those who commit the crimes, not those who are the victims of crime' (Blair, 1997) cannot be entirely confident that the sentencing climate is about to change dramatically, although we must obviously await the publication of more detailed policy proposals before we pass any final judgement.

And waiting in the wings, as it were, are the abolitionists and other champions of 'informal' or communitarian models who wish to challenge the primacy of punishment as the principal aim of the justice system. Espousing this stance, or some variety of it, would call into question the very definition of crime itself , knocking down established notions of the fixed and absolutist nature of that concept and putting in its place a model of crime as a social construct and the product of myriad social decisions. Once such a deconstruction had taken place, the whole nature of the punishment system, indeed its very *raison d'être*, would be vulnerable and susceptible to the most radical changes. At present, however, such a revolutionary change seems too utopian to be within reach and in any case there are, as we have seen, contrary arguments to suggest that the practical implementation of such visionary thinking might not produce the wholesale social benefits that its proponents claim.

So, in practice, what we are left with in the trial courts is a generally eclectic approach in which a series of compromises between the demands of retribution, at least as a limiting principle, and the common-sense or intuitive desire on the part of sentencers to pass sentences that will 'do some good' provides some working justification for the continued use of non-custodial sentences on a day-to-day basis. Against this somewhat pragmatic (in the common, rather than technical, sense of the word) philosophical background we now turn to examine the range of community-based penalties that are available in England and Wales. Given the central position of the probation service in the provision and administration of community sentences, it is sensible to start with an account of the history and development of the service and this begins in Chapter 3.

Chapter 3

The Changing Role of the Probation Service (1): Missionaries in the Age of Welfare

Plus ça change...

The observation that the probation service in England and Wales is in 'a period of transition' at present has become something of a cliché. Depending on one's viewpoint, the extent of change involved in the present transitional process can be described variously as presenting the service with a challenge, a dilemma or even a crisis. Over the last decade or so considerable quantities of time, ink and paper have been consumed in thinking about, planning for and either commending or (probably more often) condemning the enforced changes in both the philosophy and practice of probation. This chapter reviews the early history of the probation service in order to illustrate the principal influences on the development of the service's distinctive ethic. In Chapter 4 we continue to chart the service's development, outlining the origins of the latest transformation, pointing out the continuities and departures from probation's traditional values contained within the process of transition and suggesting the possible consequences of change for the future direction of those community penalties provided by, or through, the probation service. Together, the next two chapters will provide illustrations of how the range of philosophical approaches outlined in Chapter 2 have been translated into practice and how the contours of the various penological debates discussed there have shaped the non-custodial landscape.

...Plus c'est la même chose?

In some senses the probation service in England and Wales has always been an organisation 'in transition', in as much as its origins and development bear witness to processes of evolutionary change and adaptation rather than anything more instrumental and preconceived (Haxby, 1978:

15). This is not to deny the agency of government departments and parliamentary committees in that earlier evolution, nor the influence that significant individuals and external organisations have had upon the direction in which the service has developed. But 'the service' (if one may use that collective noun to describe 55 separate organisations in England and Wales) has always displayed an acumen for recognising that neither the role which probation fulfils in the sentencing agenda nor the methods which its practioners employ is unchanging. In the history of the probation service, therefore, one has the sense of an organisation gradually defining and then redefining itself as it adapts, with the need to explain its purposes and their utility to a series of constantly changing audiences. But the latest turn in this evolutionary cycle *is* different, both in terms of the extent of the change that it is demanding from individual officers and from their organisations and, perhaps more fundamentally, in terms of the depth to which it has challenged the central values around which the service has traditionally been organised (Drakeford and Vanstone 1996a: 1). In order to appreciate the magnitude of these changes, it is helpful to have some sense of the history of the service and of the origins of its original legitimating principles.

The probation service and the sense of 'mission'

Conditional release on 'probation' entered into the judicial repertoire in the first part of the last century as a development of the medieval common-law doctrine of recognisance. A recognisance was a bond entered into by an accused person before the court to do, or to refrain from doing, some specified act or other, often simply to 'keep the peace'. Sometimes, although not invariably, entering into a recognisance involved depositing money with the court against future behaviour. The consequence of the court agreeing to accept a recognisance was that the accused would be released without punishment or, indeed, sometimes without trial, subject only to their continuing to be of good behaviour.

By the early nineteenth century this procedure was being used to deal with young and petty offenders both in England and in some of the States of New England, enabling the courts of the day to mitigate in appropriate cases the severity of penal regimes that were, in most instances, extremely harsh. This early procedure shared many of the features of a modern probation order, including the possibility of revocation if any of the conditions set upon the freedom of the accused were violated, but in its earliest days it lacked the element of supervision which is the defining characteristic of probation today (Dressler, 1959: 9). By 1841, however, the practice of requiring at least some of those who had entered into recognisance to subject themselves to the supervision of persons approved by the court had developed, almost simultaneously, in both the United

States and Britain. In both jurisdictions this development had come about through the pioneering activities of philanthropic individuals rather than as a result of any initiative by the courts or other official bodies. (Further details of the earliest experiments with 'probation' in both England and the United States may be found in Bochel, 1976 and McWilliams, 1983.)

During their period of reformation the released offenders were 'on probation' (in its original sense of 'testing'), to see whether their self-professed willingness to be reformed would actually result in sufficient amelioration in behaviour to render further prosecution unnecessary. The procedure for placing offenders on probation was put on a statutory basis, at least as far as juveniles were concerned, in the Juvenile Offenders Act 1847, but, in contrast with the American experience, expansion of the practice of supervising those conditionally released by the courts came about in England not through official appointments but rather as a result of the evangelising activities of religious organisations, principally the Church of England Temperance Society (CETS).

As part of its general mission to save the souls of those addicted to alcohol, the Society was persuaded by yet another businessman philanthropist, Frederick Rainer, to send 'missionaries' into the lower criminal courts (then known as 'police courts') to minister to, and 'save' those (and there were huge numbers of them) whose criminality arose, it appeared, primarily from their drunkenness. The first two court missionaries were dispatched to the Police Courts in Central London in 1876 and further appointments gradually extended the mission to other courts and other petty sessional districts (Harris, 1996). The objectives of these first missionaries were, as their title suggests, essentially religious. By preaching, distributing tracts and encouraging abstinence, they sought to save the souls of individual drunkards appearing before the summary courts (McWilliams, 1983: 134). In order to give effect to their work the missionaries would appeal to the magistrates to bind over into their charge those for whom moral 'restoration and reclamation' through 'grace' was thought to be a reasonable possibility.

The evolution of probation work

The presence of the CETS missionaries in the courts was quickly recognised as providing magistrates with an additional sentencing resource through which (in petty cases) they could mitigate the undoubted severity of the generality of punishments. The Summary Jurisdiction Act 1879 had extended the range of offences that could be dealt with by magistrates' courts and thus had greatly inflated their workloads, but it had also extended the statutory basis for the taking of recognisances in lieu of sentencing petty offenders other than juveniles. This provided the courts with a sort of 'safety valve' and they soon began to involve the court missionaries in the supervision of offenders released on recognisances. That it also presented the possibility of avoiding the use of a custodial sentence was, even in the 1870s and 1880s, attractive to the government on cost grounds (McWilliams, 1983: 130).

Although the supervision of discharged offenders was thought by some in the Society to be a diversion from the primary objectives of the Mission, the involvement of missionaries in work akin to that of modern probation officers expanded rapidly to the point where by 1884 work with offenders had become their principal duty (McWilliams, 1983: 135). By the time the Probation of First Offenders Act was passed in 1887 court missionaries were also undertaking social enquiries about offenders on behalf of the courts to assist in identifying those for whom 'probation', as it could now be called, was the appropriate disposal. It is important to remember, however, that it was not until 1908 (with the coming into force of the Probation of Offenders Act 1907) that any of the missionaries became publicly paid officials of the court. In the early days the CETS missionaries and others like them, useful though their functions may have been to the courts, were recruited and funded not by the state but by religious and philanthropic charities.

Several important themes emerge from this early history. First, one may note the incremental nature of the way in which the practice of probation and, eventually, the probation service itself emerged in England and Wales. This sets the present 'transitional' phase in which the service finds itself in a historical context which suggests that the current process may represent something of a continuity (in form, if not necessarily in magnitude) as well as a break with the past. More importantly, the early history demonstrates most clearly the rehabilitative, welfare-oriented and non-punitive philosophy on which the practice of probation was originally built. As Rumgay has observed, it was the 'unpalatability' of an unrelievedly punitive criminal justice system which 'spawned' the probation service in the first place (Rumgay, 1989: 185). McWilliams, too (1983: 137), sums up the relationship between the court missionaries and the courts in which they served in terms of 'mercy':

> Mercy is the concept which provides the key to understanding the missionaries' place in the courts and in particular their social enquiry practice. Mercy stood between the offender, the missionary and the sentencer, and it was mercy which made sense of their relationships.

This same ethic of rehabilitation through clemency and individual example survived the transformation of many of the court missionaries into employed probation officers. The 1907 Act was explicit that the role of the newly created 'probation officers' was 'to advise, assist and befriend [the person under supervision] and, when necessary, to endeavour to find him [sic] suitable employment' (Probation of Offenders Act 1907, s. 4(d)). About a half of all those who took up the new statutory posts had been court missionaries, and dual control over the direction and philosophy of the service between the CETS mission to the courts and the petty sessional probation committees endured until 1936. In that year, following a recommendation from a Home Office Departmental Committee investigating the role of the social services in the lower courts (Home Office, 1936), the activities of the Court Mission were merged into the statutory service. The merger did not alter, however, the basic purpose of the organisation or its members. Although dual administrative control of the service may have been abolished, the same humane conception of its purpose was to persist 'for many years'. As McWilliams succinctly puts it, 'it was the *Mission* which was to be rejected, *not* missionary zeal' (McWilliams, 1985: 270–1), and May was later to observe that throughout the history of the service its members did share one common bond: a missionary and humanitarian approach to the administration of criminal justice (May, 1991a: 20).

Care and control in probation work

To that observation, however, one must juxtapose another characteristic of this history of emergence. Alongside the more voluntaristic aspects of the relationship between probation officer and probationer there has always existed the possibility of coercion. The court missionaries were of use to the magistrates because their willingness to exercise control over those who were discharged into their care provided a more politically acceptable disposal than the complete and uninhibited release of those for whom imprisonment was thought excessive. And despite, or perhaps because of, their reformative objectives the missionaries were under no illusions about the possible need for compulsion to be used against those who stubbornly refused to remove for themselves the 'stumbling blocks' to their own redemption (McWilliams, 1983: 141). Formalising the arrangements for supervision by making the carer an officer of the court and the conditions of probation the subject of a formal court order (as happened with the passing of the 1907 Act) merely increased these coercive possibilities, as the Home Office Report on the working of the Act recognised:

> The formality of making the order, the regular visits and reports, the knowledge that supervision is not merely by the agent of a philanthropic society but by a person who is, in addition or alternatively, a legally appointed officer of the court, the imposition of definite conditions clearly stated in black and white – all of these thing have a powerful influence on the minds of probationers – gives us a much stronger hold over the offender.
>
> (Home Office, 1910, cited in McWilliams, 1985: 259)

The gradual introduction into the service of more 'scientific' methods of working and the increasing emphasis on 'diagnosis' and 'treatment' of offenders did not reduce the possibility of coercion, it merely altered the form of interventions with which it might be associated (McWilliams, 1986: 257). No matter how altruistic and humane the motives of an individual officer, the probationer is inevitably under threat of further or renewed sanction for failure to comply with the requirements of the order and this imputes at least the threat of coercion into a relationship which, despite a sort of collective denial on the part of some officers, has always been ultimately about *control* in some form or other (Cohen, 1975: 83; Harris, 1995: 33–4; Haxby, 1978: 102). So, although much of the current controversy about the proper role for probation revolves around the extent to which it should be promoted as a means of restricting the liberty of offenders, it should not be forgotten that the issue of control has always been accepted as an integral part of probation work (Mathesion, 1992: 146).

This is not to imply that the distinction between 'care', 'control' and 'punishment' is unimportant or a mere matter of semantics. Clearly, the degree to which each of these potential functions is incorporated within the aims and practices of the probation service is of fundamental importance in determining what sort of organisation it will become. Nor can it be thought that making the choice between these potentially conflicting values will be easy or without some human and political cost. Merely to talk, as some do, in terms of striking the 'right balance' between 'care' and 'control' is probably disingenuous given the differing consequences that might now be assumed to arise from each of them in the present political climate. But the point of locating the present debate in the wider history of the probation service is to demonstrate the extent to which the service has always operated with a range of contradictory aspirations involving, as Harris puts it, 'care *and* control, liberation and constraint, calling offenders to account *and* demanding social reform' (Harris, 1992: 154, emphasis in the original). This continuity with one aspect of the traditional characteristics of the service suggests that in the current debate no one particular outcome is necessarily preordained, and that all is to be argued for.

Probation and the petty offender

One final characteristic of the earliest forms of probationary practice should be noted for comparison with more modern developments. Probation, or supervised conditional release from punishment (or conviction in the United States), was never meant to be a universal benefit. Rather, it was to be used *selectively*, 'targeted' in the modern jargon, upon those who by reason of their age, previous good character or triviality of offending, taken together with considerations of the influences by which they would be likely to be surrounded in future, seemed both deserving of mercy and 'promising subjects' for reformative intervention. In this, the primary impulse was to save offenders from their own bad ways rather than from the pains of imprisonment *per se*. In other words, the earliest objectives had to do with reformation and rehabilitation, not reduction in the use of imprisonment, although clearly that additional outcome might be associated with the use of probation orders, provided that any potential 'net-widening' effects (see Chapter 7) were contained. And allied to this is the observation that probation originally targeted the *petty* offender and those thought most susceptible to rehabilitation; work with 'heavy-end' and recidivist offenders is, by comparison with that tradition, a relatively new priority.

The appliance of science – probation, professionalisation and modernity

From these philanthropic and evangelical beginnings the probation service in Britain gradually transformed itself from the 1920s onwards into a bureaucratic and professionalised organization dedicated (chiefly) to remedying the offending behaviour of those individuals entrusted to it by the courts through the application of its officers' social work and psychotherapeutic skills. This 'second age' of probation, probably best characterised by reference to the concept of 'diagnosis', was ushered in by the gradual reception of the so-called 'medical model' as the basis and justification for its practice. The history of this period in the development of the probation service has been extensively documented and discussed elsewhere (see e.g. McWilliams, 1985; 1986; May 1991a; Newburn, 1995).

In keeping with the advances of scientism elsewhere in society, a new conception of law was emerging, one which emphasised law's role in the protection of society through the correction and resocialization of the offender (Peters, 1986: 27). The era was marked by an ideological reconstruction of the 'criminal' and a concomitant shift in emphasis in probation practice from saving the souls of the 'wicked' to identifying and treating the pathologies of the 'sick' (May, 1994: 863). And, as in so many outposts of 'modernity', these 'humanizing' and 'individualizing' tendencies in the penal system rested on more profound shifts in the relations of power between those who operated in this particular 'field', shifts which were mediated through the claims to specialised knowledge being made by the newly emerging 'scientific' social workers in the probation service (Garland, 1990: 138). Therefore, the transformation towards diagnostic methods also involved a subtle but none the less significant alteration in the relationship between probation officers and the courts, whereby the former gradually elevated themselves from the position of supplicants for mercy on behalf of their clients to that of 'experts', able to guide and 'educate' the magistrates into identifying the 'correct' disposal in the interests of 'objective' science (McWilliams, 1986: 257).

This new ideology is best exemplified by, and in turn helps to explain, the changing use of the social enquiry report, which was transformed in character and content from a special plea for mercy to an 'objective'

professional appraisal (McWilliams, 1986: 241). In this diagnostic framework, report writing came to assume an ever greater importance in the
probation officer's role and to constitute an increasing proportion of the
workload of the service as the courts gradually moved away from 'tariff'
sentences towards greater consideration of the social and domestic circumstances of the offender (Bochel, 1976: 193–6).

The beginnings of professionalism

Along with the rise of 'the diagnostician' this period also witnesssed the
blossoming of the new service's professional aspirations. McWilliams sees
these two processes as 'inextricably mingled' (McWilliams, 1985: 260). As
probation officers became more thoroughly 'scientific' in their outlooks
and practices, so they sought, as a sectional interest group, to achieve
'proper' recognition for their increasing professionalism. From their earliest days probation officers had had the opportunity to join a representative body, the National Association of Probation Officers (NAPO), which
had been established in 1912, initially as much in the nature of a learned
society as a trade union. By 1935 NAPO could claim as members 96 per
cent of full-time officers and, as the main pressure group concerned with
probation issues, it campaigned both to secure better pay and conditions
for its members and, more generally, to influence government policy on
probation matters (Bochel, 1977: 117–21). As such, it was instrumental
in leading the drive towards recognition of the professional nature of
probation work.

Although, as we have seen, religious charities continued to play an
important part in the recruitment and organisation of probation officers
even in the 1930s, the drive towards professional status involved a gradual
shift away from the traditional view of the probation officer as being
qualified chiefly by the possession of a religious vocation or calling towards the idea that he or she was the member of an organised profession
for which one was selected on aptitude and prepared by training and
professional socialisation (McWilliams, 1985: 260–1). The reception in
the 1940s and 1950s of psychologically based 'casework' modelled on
practice in the United States as *the* method of working with clients served
only to intensify the clamour among probation officers and their representatives for recognition of their aspirations to professional status.

During this 'diagnostic' period progress towards professional recognition was marked by a greater emphasis on academic and professional
training which leading figures in the service saw as necessary to counteract
the connotations of 'amateurism' previously associated with probation
work. This innovation was the culmination of a slow change in government thinking over the previous decade to the point where 'the breadth
of view afforded by a liberal education' (Home Office, 1927: 59) was seen
to be as desirable a quality as 'missionary spirit' in a probation officer.
Six years later the Departmental Committee on the Social Services in

the Courts of Summary Jurisdiction (Home Office, 1936) recommended that there should be no appointment of probation officers without prior training. Although the implementation of this recommendation was to be delayed, principally on cost grounds, for almost forty years (and its fullest implementation was to last, ultimately, for only 25 years), it represented an important acknowledgement by government at the time of the direction in which the nature and role of probation was developing, and it set the tone for further advances in professional education and training in 'scientific' methods over the next two decades.

The growth of administrative controls

This emerging professionalised self-characterisation was accompanied by and, in part, legitimated upon the standardisation of administrative controls and the introduction of bureaucratised forms of management, which, perhaps more than any single factor, was responsible for the first major 'transition' in the nature and philosophy of probation work. These developments, centred on important legislative changes in 1925 and 1948, have been discussed in detail elsewhere (May, 1991a; 1994; Newburn, 1995).

To summarise, the Criminal Justice Acts 1925 and 1926 made it *mandatory* for each petty sessional division to employ at least one probation officer, and probation areas were restructured into uniform boundaries using the petty sessional district as the basic unit but providing for the creation of combined areas where populations were small. Probation was also made available as a disposal for judges in the higher courts as well as after summary conviction. Of especial significance in the 1925 restructuring was the provision of additional regulatory powers to the Home Secretary to 'secure the efficient provision of probation services' in recognition of the granting for the first time of central government funding for local services. These new powers (under section 8 of the 1925 Act) included the ability to fix the salaries of probation officers nationally, set the levels for expenses and superannuation and prescribe the qualifications necessary for permanent appointment as an officer. Reflecting this increase in control and the partial shift of power from local to central government which it represented, the third edition of the Probation Rules which were issued in 1926 Acts was greatly expanded and more detailed than those of 1908 or 1923 had been (Bochel, 1977: 101). Among other things, the 1926 Rules created the conditions for the development of a hierarchical management structure by establishing for the first time the grade of principal officer, although the possibility of making such appointments was not taken up universally for some time (Bochel, 1977: 54, 109).

Taken together, these statutory changes laid the basis of a more formalised and bureaucratised probation service with standardised methods of organising the provision of services across the country, a pattern that was reinforced incrementally as the century matured and the age of the welfare state began. The 1925 legislation also formalised the tension between local and central provision for and control of probation services, which was to continue to be an important issue in the emergence and transformation of probation and in the governance of criminal justice services more generally, right down to the present time.

Building probation's empire: the expansion of roles in the age of welfare

The expansion of probation 1950–1965

Following the interruption caused by the Second World War, policy and practice developments in the probation area accelerated as the 'warfare' state (Garland, 1996) gave way to the welfare state of the 1950s and 1960s. 'Case working' based on 'scientific' principles of the diagnosis and 'treatment' of individual offenders took a firm hold on probation practice, seriously weakening, but not entirely extinguishing, the influence of missionary zeal and religious inspiration upon the ethos of the service (McWilliams, 1986; 1987). The range of offenders with whom the service worked also changed in ways which altered its relationship with the rest of the penal system. The Criminal Justice Act 1948, which provided a new statutory framework for probation and increased the level of funding from central government to 50 per cent, also greatly extended the possibility for early release on licence from prison of various categories of offenders.

In order to cope with the anticipated increase in the amount of compulsory 'after-care' that would be needed, the Probation Rules 1949 included after-care among the duties of probation officers. At first the contribution of the probation service to the after-care of prisoners was carried on under the auspices of a non-governmental organisation, the Central After-Care Association, which also coordinated the activities of other charitable and non-statutory bodies working in this field. By 1968, however, following upon the recommendations of the Advisory Council on the Treatment of Offenders (Home Office, 1963), the probation service had assumed responsibility for all prison, borstal and detention centre after-care and at the central level an expanded Probation and After-Care Department at the Home Office became responsible for the overall development of the system.

This additional responsibility, which was generally welcomed by the service as recognising its especial expertise in dealing with offenders in the community, gradually transformed the nature of the probation caseload so that an increasing proportion of clients (one tenth in 1951, one quarter in 1971: McWilliams, 1987) came to be supervised as a result of *having been* imprisoned rather than having been diverted from imprisonment. Although the same aims of rehabilitation and reintegration which informed probation practice with the unsentenced offender applied equally in after-care work, this extension of the probation officer's role undoubtedly altered the balance of the service's work and brought it into closer contact than ever before with the custodial elements of the penal system. It also changed the nature of the service's 'clientele' (as well as increasing it in size) by bringing within it a greater proportion of older and more experienced offenders who were likely to prove to be more committed recidivists than most probationers (Bochel, 1976: 185, 191). From this point, the probation service began to move 'up-tariff' and, once begun, this trend was cumulative.

The gradual transfer of the post-release supervision function to the probation service also raised the question of how this element of 'treatment' might best be coordinated with welfare work *within* prisons designed to prepare the prisoner for release and after-care. Prison welfare work had traditionally been the preserve of a number of voluntary bodies, but in keeping with the professionalising ethic of the time the Advisory Council on the Treatment of Offenders had recommended that social workers in prisons who would need 'essentially the same qualities and skills as a probation officer' should be members of a centrally organised prison welfare service under Home Office control (Home Office, 1963: 23–4). After lengthy consideration and consultation the government decided against the perpetuation of a separate service and determined instead to extend the role of the probation service once more by providing for the secondment of probation officers to fill prison welfare posts on a fixed-term basis. This scheme, which had the backing of NAPO and the Principal Probation Officers' Conference, came into effect in January 1966 and it marked both a further expansion of the service's role and another stage in its incorporation into what NAPO, in its evidence to the Advisory Council's enquiry into after-care provision, had called 'the unity of the correctional services' (Bochel, 1976: 222). With it, the service's traditional antipathy towards prisons was compromised and first-hand experience of working in the custodial regime became routinely a part, at least, of most probation officers' careers (Haxby, 1978: 242; May, 1991a: 17).

The intimate connection between the probation service and the rest of the penal system that was now more clearly emerging was further emphasised by its involvement in the system for general parole introduced by the Criminal Justice Act 1967 and by other new responsibilities which arose in the late 1960s and early 1970s as a consequence of the search for alternatives to custody discussed in Chapter 1. As we have seen in Chapter 1, part of the government's strategy to relieve the pressure on the prison regime revolved around the introduction of a range of measures, including community service, designed to deal with more offenders 'in the community' while maintaining some element of control and restriction of liberty over them in the interests both of public protection and retribution. Although it had always been envisaged that voluntary and other non-statutory bodies would play a major role in providing specific programmes of work, the general administration of the community service system and the responsibility of investigating the suitability of offenders for CSOs were entrusted to the probation service.

Further innovations in the Criminal Justice Act 1972 which added to the workload of the service included the normal requirement for magistrates' courts to obtain and consider a social enquiry report before imposing custody on someone under 21 or a first custodial sentence on an adult. The one major exception to this general expansion came with the Children and Young Persons Act 1969 which, in keeping with the holistic approach advocated in the Longford Report and the Labour government's thinking on children, families and juvenile offending (Home Office, 1965), transferred the principal reponsibility for the supervision of young persons under 17 from the probation service to the social service departments of local authorities. This reduction in role was never fully implemented due to a change of government (May, 1991a: 18) and it was, in any event, out of keeping with the general tendency towards an expansion of probation's responsibilities.

The emergence of the professional 'manager'

During the post-war period, therefore, the probation service experienced a time of continual growth, both in the numbers of offenders entrusted to it and in the size and complexity of the organisation itself. In 1951, just over 55,000 offenders had been supervised by the probation service in England and Wales. By 1971 this figure had risen to more than 120,000 (McWilliams, 1987). During the same general period the numbers of probation officers of all grades increased from 1,006 in 1950 to 5,033 in 1976 (Haxby, 1978: 51) although growth slowed down considerably after this. This significant expansion obviously made the case for increased funding of the service irresistible, and the extended range of responsibilities which individual officers carried also assisted in their long-running campaign for improved pay and conditions and better career prospects. Significantly, too, the ratio of supervisory to mainstream grades also increased in this period from 1:6 to 1:3 (Haxby, 1978: 34). The increasingly hierarchical structure that this statistic represents provided the platform upon which later changes towards a more centralised and managerialist approach could be developed (May, 1991a: 20–1).

This latent consequence of expansionism provides a clear example of the way in which broadly liberal reforms to criminal justice policy in the age of welfare stimulated the formation of a professional class of criminal justice managers whose presence facilitated the institutionalisation of strategies that were eventually to supersede welfarism (Feeley and Simon, 1994: 191). For at the heart of the incremental expansion of the functions of probation and of the service itself lies a paradox by which, Trojan-horse like, the rhetorical claims of welfarism introduced the necessary conditions for a more correctionalist alignment. Expansion in the 'diagnostic phase' (of which these developments form a part) was undoubtedly predicated on the centrality of welfare and treatment to the service's work and legitimated by the service's acknowledged expertise and experience in social casework with offenders.

So, for instance, while the Wooton Report appreciated that the supervision of offenders on suspended sentence might represent a departure from the traditional understanding (at least in Britain) of what probation was for, it was nonetheless prepared to recommend this extension on the grounds that such offenders would then receive the sort of welfare intervention hitherto reserved to probationers and those on licence or parole (Bochel, 1976: 238). The expansion into parole, similarly, had been justified on the basis that it fell into 'the broad band of social casework which probation officers can appropriately undertake' (Home Office, 1962: 44). And generally in the 1960s, as the report of the Morison Committee on the Probation Service demonstrated, the probation service continued to be viewed officially as a welfare-oriented organisation, sharing common aspirations, skills and practices with other forms of social work (Home Office, 1962: 23).

Yet, the closer the work of the service was integrated into the general activities of the wider penal system, the more anomalous and less satisfactory that welfarist justification appeared to those whose responsibility it was to determine and implement policy for the criminal justice system as a whole. The effect of these additions to the responsibilities of the service, as Haxby argued as early as 1978, was to lay the ground for a major shift in the focus of the service in which the traditional tension between welfare and control (which, as we have seen, had always been an issue for probation officers) would be resolved more and more in favour of correctionalism, first at an institutional level and then more pervasively throughout the service.

The contrast between this increasing correctionalism and the early exculpatory ambitions of the service should be noted. Nor should one overlook the substantial workload which probation officers carried in relation to civil cases involving matrimonial and child care issues which continued to demand the exercise of 'traditional' social work and caring skills. The resultant tension between care and control in the exercise of the probation function was succinctly summarised in the report of the Morison Committee in 1962. Having identified the close similarity in both outlook and approach between probation officers and other 'social caseworkers', the committee went on to observe that:

> It must be added that while, as a caseworker, the probation officer's prime concern is with the well being of an individual, he [*sic*] is also *the agent of a system concerned with the protection of society* and as such must, to a degree which varies from case to case, and during the course of supervision, seek to regulate the probationer's behaviour. He must also be prepared, when necessary, to assert the interests of society by initiating proceedings for

breach of the requirements of the probation order. This dichotomy of
duties . . . is one [of] which the probation officer cannot cease to be
conscious, and the probationer's recognition of him as a representative
of 'authority' will affect the casework technique that the officer employs.
(Home Office, 1962: 23, emphasis supplied)

The beginnings of bifurcation

If this statement represents a position somewhere near the centre of balance of the continuum between care and control, clear indications of
how far the emphasis shifted, at least in official thinking, during the next
twelve years can be found in the 1974 report of the Advisory Council on
the Penal System (the Younger Report) on Young Adult Offenders (Home
Office, 1974). In some senses this was a progressive document which, while
acknowledging that the demands of retribution might sometimes rule out
the use of a non-custodial sentence, endorsed in general the superiority
of supervision in the community over custody in tackling reoffending
(Home Office, 1974: 56). But, in order to bridge what it saw as a lack of
confidence among sentencers and the general public in the alternatives
to custody then available, the majority on the Advisory Council recommended the creation of a 'new and stronger' non-custodial sentence for
young adults, to be known as the 'supervision and control' order. Under
such an order, which, unlike a 'standard' probation order, would not
require the offender's consent, the supervising officer was to have a wide
discretion to impose any of a range of requirements, such as a condition
of residence or a prohibition on visiting specified places, as he or she
thought necessary. In addition, and most controversially, in the event of
a breach or even a *contemplated* breach, a supervising officer would have
had a power to have the supervisee detained for up to 72 hours on application to a magistrate (Home Office, 1974: 91–8). This last suggestion was
unacceptable to at least four of the Council's members, who signed a
note of dissent on the point, and, given what has been said above about
the service's traditional ethos, it was hardly likely to find much of a welcome among probation officers. In fact, many probation officers reacted
to the proposed new order with horror, claiming that it would turn them
into 'screws on wheels' (Haxby, 1978: 162).

What the Younger Report was urging its various audiences (including probation officers) to accept was that liberal policy aims (reducing
reliance on custodial sentencing) could best, indeed perhaps only, be
achieved through embracing what many would instinctively feel were 'illiberal' means. This approach has important echoes for succeeding policy
developments, as we shall see. The following year the Home Secretary
reinforced this line of thought in seeking to defend the proposed new
order at the annual conference of NAPO. In words which now seem strikingly prescient, he defined the problem that confronted penal policy
makers and the probation service as one of finding the best way of

encouraging the courts and the public to accept the use of non-custodial sentences. And to this question the Home Secretary proposed an answer which foreshadowed much that was to emerge in Conservative criminal justice policy in the next two decades. Rather than propose any drive to educate or to challenge the attitudes of the magistracy, judiciary and the public on the issue (as he perceived them to be), he asked the conference to consider whether non-custodial sentences should not become generally more correctional in nature, so as to 'meet reasonable expectations of the amount of control to be exercised' (Haxby, 1978: 27). The fact that the Home Secretary of the day happened to be a member of the Labour Party merely serves to illustrate how the drift towards a more punitive and control-oriented criminal justice system represents deeper 'pre-political' thought that cannot easily be associated with conventional party labels (Feeley and Simon, 1994: 190). In the end the particular proposals in the Younger Report were resisted by what Raynor has called 'arguments based on traditional social work commitments and values' (Raynor, 1988: 3), but it is now clear from these exchanges that the age of 'punishment in the community' and of the probation service's involvement in it, had already begun (May, 1994: 870).

From this point forward one can mark a significant change in the philosophy which underpinned sentencing policy and which as a consequence has had an enormous effect on probation practice. The chronology of this paradigmatic shift has been sketched out in Chapter 1 above and its theoretical commitments were outlined in Chapter 2. The next chapter fleshes out those general comments and relates their influences directly to the changes that have taken place in probation practice over the last decade and a half.

Chapter 4

The Changing Role of the Probation Service (2): Probation in the Age of the Actuary

The new penology

At this point we must leave the intimate history of probation for a little while to focus on broader socio-political theories that help to explain the shape not just of the probation service but of the wider criminal justice system and much else in the government sphere at the present time. These broader themes also contribute to our understanding of how the various penal philosophies which we examined in Chapter 2 have been implemented, and in some cases subverted, in practice. A good place to start this wider enquiry is with an important review of current trends in criminal law in an essay by Antonie Peters, a Dutch sociologist and criminologist, published in 1986. In this important contribution to the sociology of punishment Peters identified three different schools of thought which have successively dominated conceptions of criminal law and penal practice over the past 100 years.

The first of these, the Classical School, with its emphasis on legality, individual responsibility, proportionality of punishment and above all on the *restraint* of law's power to intervene in the lives of private citizens, characterised Western legal systems in the late nineteenth century (Peters, 1986: 23). Readers can, no doubt, recognise the links between this intellectual movement and the retributivist philosophy which underpinned it. The classical concept of law was superseded from about 1900 onwards by what Peters calls 'The Modern School of Criminal Law' in which the dominant legal ideology is of law as an instrument of social protection against criminals (1986: 26–9). Under the influence of Modernism, which lasted until at least the 1950s, the prevention of crime and treatment of offenders became the overriding concern of criminal justice. At its zenith the Modern School was animated by a

> universal belief in the possibility of a scientific understanding and mastery of the world, including the world of crime and criminals. . . . Thus traditional

legal concerns made way for the scientific, or pseudo-scientific, categories of psychiatry and criminology. In the words of Michel Foucault, punishment ceased to be a moral lesson and became a technique for the coercion of individuals.

(p. 29)

It is easy to recognise in such a conception of law the necessary conditions for the emergence of the sort of diagnostic practices discussed in Chapter 3 above which came to characterise the probation service in Britain and elsewhere during the first half of this century. However, Peters was able to identify a new paradigm which he claimed had already replaced the Modern School as the dominant way of understanding and directing criminal justice. For want of a better name, he called this new philosophy the 'School of Social Control' and he identified its dominant concerns as 'policy, planning and organisation' (1986: 31). The emerging model was one which parallels the rational organisation of an ideal-type industrial enterprise in which the various departments work together in a well-coordinated fashion towards the same institutional goals.

In this model of criminal justice the essential requirement is to pull together the activities of the different agencies into a rationally coordinated and centrally accountable system in which law makers and law enforcers are seen as participating jointly in a common social enterprise. Increased 'systematisation' (to use a rather ugly neologism) facilitates increased financial control in the interests of greater efficiency, as criminal law is seen increasingly as only one of a range of formal and informal forms of social control from which one has to choose in a rational way, unhampered by moral considerations. The idea that the problem of crime can be eliminated or even brought under complete control has been abandoned and attention has shifted from individual wrongdoers to general policies directed at types and volumes ('aggregates') of criminal behaviour. In this new model the maintenance of the system itself and the continual striving for ever greater efficiency of operation become *the* inherent values which are to be pursued. Wider social or ethical values, legal norms and constitutional principles are excluded as

> many of the earlier humanitarian ideals have been lost in a drift towards business-like, centralized, bureaucratized and efficiency-oriented policies in which financial and quantitative considerations loom larger than the philosophy of resocialization.

(Peters, 1986: 33)

Peters is by no means alone in offering this description of modern criminal justice *systems*. Feeley and Simon, for instance, have offered a broadly similar analysis of the paradigm shift in American penal ideology and practice over the last twenty years (Feeley and Simon, 1992; 1994). They argue that the changes which have taken place in the discourse, objectives and techniques of the penal process have multiple and independent origins and are not reducible to any one reigning idea, nor has what they identify as 'the new penology' (yet) reached an overarching position of hegemony over all other possible penal strategies (1992: 449–51). Nonetheless, the new penology has had considerable influence on penal practice primarily because it provides penal administrators with a viable way of meeting the objectives set by the policy makers *within existing resource allocations.* The task of the new penology is managerial, not transformative, and its discourse is characterised by an emphasis on systemic integrity and on internal evaluation based on formal rationality, rather than on external social objectives such as the elimination of crime or reintegration into the community. Consequently, it is concerned less to diagnose and treat individuals than to identify, classify and manage unruly groups sorted by dangerousness (cf. McWilliams, 1987: 104; Mathiesen, 1983: 139).

Underlying the latter objective is the creeping influence of the law and economics movement (Feeley and Simon, 1994: 188) which, while not synonymous with the new penology, has helped to import the actuarial techniques of 'risk management' from economic theory into criminal justice policy. The imperatives of the new 'actuarial' penology are to manage a permanently dangerous segment of the population (the 'underclass' of permanently excluded, irredeemably dysfunctional deviants) while maintaining the system at a minimum cost. Its goal is not to eliminate crime but to make tolerable the twin burdens of crime and crime control through systemic coordination.

Where this new penology holds sway, the forms of control which it legitimates 'are not anchored in aspirations to rehabilitate, re-integrate, retain, provide employment, or the like. They are justified in more blunt terms: variable detention depending upon risk management' (Feeley and Simon, 1992: 457). According to this analysis, intermediate and non-custodial sanctions are just as susceptible to this new actuarial rationale as custodial sentencing:

> Similarly, probation and parole have assumed new functions. Once conceived of as 'half-way' stages whose aim was to integrate offenders back into their communities, parole and probation are now simply alternatives to custody for lower-risk offenders. 'Supervision' consists of monitoring levels of risk as determined by several indicators, most prominently drug testing. Moreover, with large portions of the non-incarcerated population in some of the poorest and most crime victimised communities in the country, probation, parole or some form of community supervision are becoming a lower cost alternative to traditional justice.
>
> (Feeley and Simon, 1994: 180)

Cost-effective crime control

The reference to cost-effectiveness as a component of this new paradigm in criminal justice serves to link this particular policy development to more deep-seated political, sociological and cultural transformations in Britain and elsewhere. These transformations were associated with changes in the nature of the global economy and the decline of the sort of inclusionary/integrative strategies that flourished just after the Second World War because of the fiscal crisis that such strategies helped to produce (Bottoms, 1995a: 47). From the late 1960s onwards, deteriorating economic circumstances provoked a crisis of legitimacy (Habermas, 1976) for many Western governments as it became ever harder to deliver the sort of expanded welfare state which had been at the core of the compromise between capital and worker that facilitated the growth of corporatist economics in the post-war period (Unger, 1976). Different responses to this crisis may be identified in individual countries but certain common themes emerge.

Globally, there occurred a realignment of fiscal and economic policies which sought to reassert the interests of capital and to protect profit margins in order to stimulate economic activity and enterprise. This produced a common tendency to bear down on social welfare and other centralised costs in an effort to reduce the proportion of gross national product consumed by government activity. This tendency was necessarily associated with a pressure to repudiate overtly collectivist policies and the ideologies which sustained them. As governments (of whatever particular political hue) found it ever more difficult to continue the welfarist project of providing for the needs of their people 'from cradle to grave', so it became increasingly convenient to emphasise individual personal responsibility again in a wide range of policy areas.

It is certainly possible, even without adopting a position of economic determinism, to discern in these globalised economic trends sufficient motivation for much of the transformation in criminal justice policy which has already been described in Chapter 1. In straitened fiscal circumstances the complete eradication of poverty became an unrealistic aspiration even for economies more resilient than Britain's. This pointed to the more or less permanent exclusion from economic prosperity of a proportion of the population, with all the criminogenic consequences which that implied.

Under such economic conditions, too, both rehabilitation and deterrence cease to make much sense as sentencing objectives, at least in respect of those consigned to society's margins. As suggested in Chapter 2, rehabilitation, or any kind of reintegrative strategy, rests upon the assumption that society is built on a 'common normative universe' – involving essentially middle-class values derived from the labour market – into which ex-offenders can be resocialised. Permanent economic marginality renders the prospect of such reintegration illusory for significantly large groups in most modern societies (Feeley and Simon, 1992: 468; Christie, 1993). Similarly, deterrence relies in the end on the existence of alternatives through participation in the labour market and cash economy for the population being deterred (Feeley and Simon, 1994: 189). When rehabilitation and deterrence are rendered inoperative, prevention through incapacitation becomes the only realistic sentencing objective for a size-able minority of offenders. The task for the criminal justice system then becomes one of differentiating on the basis of an actuarial calculation of aggregate risk between various groups of offenders in terms of who might be rehabilitated or deterred and who would not, and of providing appropriate and affordable levels of incapacitation according to that assessment of risk.

In this indirect way the fiscal crisis of the late 1960s and 1970s pro-moted the search for alternatives to imprisonment in the form of 'com-munity penalties', the very name evoking a nostalgia for older forms of social organisation in a period marked by what Bottoms, following Giddens, calls 'increased disembedding of social relations from traditional contexts' (Bottoms, 1995a: 47). Alongside the gradual introduction of the so-called 'managerialist' solutions to the problems of crime and crime control, with all the 'actuarial' assumptions which underpin that approach, this rediscovery of 'community' as a 'cure' rather than a 'cause' of crime was another significant intellectual shift that has helped to shape current sentencing policy, including the policy of non-custodial sentences, since the mid-1970s (Bottoms, 1995a: 18). As the government endeavoured to increase the 'systemic' integration of the various criminal justice agen-cies in pursuit of 'a common purpose and common objectives' (Home Office, 1986: 38–9; Faulkner, 1989) the probation service came to be iden-tified as an appropriate 'sub-system' for the management of offenders who, although guilty of more serious offences than had traditionally been the case with probationers, might nonetheless be dealt with more cost-effectively 'in the community' rather than in prison.

Talking tough on probation: the justice movement 'kicks in'

At the same time as these economic and ideological shifts were taking place, the philosophical debate between rehabilitation and retribution outlined in Chapter 2 was gradually but inexorably being won by those who argued that giving offenders the 'just deserts' of their offending would be more likely to promote the interests of justice than sentences based on notions of treatment and cure. Without reiterating completely the discussion in Chapter 2, above, we can remind ourselves that the 'just deserts' movement as it emerged in the United States in the 1970s had essentially liberal ambitions. The classical, retributivist model of human nature which underpinned it was at odds with the soft-determinist con-ception that had informed penal policy during the ascendancy of what Peters (1986) calls 'The Modern School', which included the diagnostic period of social casework in probation. Locating itself in earlier classical philosophies, the new retributivism embraced a model of the human agent as an individual fully responsible for both their own criminal wrong-doing and their own reformation. The first characteristic made them liable to punishment on moral grounds, the second ruled out any question of coercive rehabilitation which infringed the individual's status as a bearer of fundamental human rights. Conveniently, this neo-classical conception was more in accord with the sorts of shift towards greater individualism in economic and cultural spheres discussed above and it came, quite soon, to dominate official discourses about the proper role of punishment.

One of the chief objectives of the just deserts movement was to re-duce what it saw as unacceptably wide disparities in the sentences which were passed when courts tried to match their punishments to the sup-posed therapeutic needs of individual offenders. In this, desert theorists had qualified support (for different reasons) from the conservative right, who saw therapeutic sentencing as a 'soft option', and the radical left, who tended to characterise social welfare interventions as merely the 'soft end' of a continually expanding apparatus for social control. The effect of this 'unholy alliance' was to reduce considerably the intellectual re-spectability of rehabilitation as an aim of sentencing, precisely at a time when, as we have seen, unfavourable or inconclusive evaluations of a range of therapeutic disposals had raised serious doubts about the feasibility of rehabilitative sentencing, on empirical grounds. As a result, talking about 'punishment' rather than 'treatment' in discussions of the aims of sen-tencing became both more intellectually respectable (even humane) and more politically acceptable.

As Chapter 2 concluded, none of these intellectual developments, of themselves, *necessarily* implies greater punitiveness in sentencing. The adoption of a just deserts model, it has been argued, could in theory be associated with a *reduction* in the overall level of punishments if the an-chor points of cardinal proportionality were set at sufficiently tolerant levels (see again Chapter 2, where this argument is articulated and criti-cised). However, there is little doubting that *in practice* each of these shifts in the intellectual climate which underpinned changes in sentencing policy took place against a background of increasing punitiveness in most countries, including Britain.

One has to be careful here, as has already been suggested, to distin-guish between 'populist punitiveness' in government policy and heavily punitive attitudes in popular opinion (Bottoms, 1995a). The complexity of the relationship between the two concepts excludes any simple or automatic equivalence although, obviously, there must be points of con-tiguity between them. It has been argued, for instance, from a Gramscian marxist position that, in order to buttress themselves against any popular resistance to the sort of economic realignment required by the fiscal crisis of the late 1960s and early 1970s, the British government succeeded in introducing more authoritarian forms of rule by first inducing or collud-ing in the creation of a climate of 'populist authoritarianism' engendered by carefully nurtured 'moral panics' and unrealistically high levels of fear of crime (Hall *et al.*, 1978; Hall, 1980). While this thesis has been criticised as overly instrumentalist and at odds with some of the facts (Downes and

Rock, 1995: 292–4), there is little doubt that the success of the Conserva-tive Party in 1979 was due in large measure to its strong law-and-order rhetoric; and it was only when the Labour Party completed its slow con-version to a law-and-order party that it could seriously hope to defeat the Conservatives electorally. In such a punitive climate, as Chapter 2 con-cludes, justifying sentences in terms of 'punishment' rather than 'reha-bilitation' is unlikely to result in a general reduction in severity.

And so it proved in the 1980s and 1990s. Politicians 'talking tough' on law and order had more than rhetorical significance for the probation service. The systemic integration of the probation service into the wider penal process, coupled with the supremacy of 'just deserts' over rehabilita-tion as a sentencing principle and the centrality afforded to terms such as 'tough' and 'demanding', as well as 'punishment' and 'control' in the language of policy formation, all of these developments sent a clear mess-age about the purposes which the government saw community-based sentencing fulfilling. More than at any time in its history the probation service and the non-custodial disposals that it operated were being ex-plicitly linked to the concept of punishment and, thus, to the infliction of pain (Rumgay, 1989: 177). The problem, from the government's point of view, was that even as the age of punishment in the community began, a large and well-organised section of the probation service membership, as resistance to the Younger Report (discussed at the end of Chapter 3) had shown, were committed to preserving the service's traditional human-itarian ideals and welfare-oriented working practices (May, 1994: 871; McWilliams, 1986: 257). This situation was perceived as particularly trouble-some because of the considerable degree of professional discretion that had hitherto been afforded to individual officers in their day-to-day work-ing relationships with probationers. Such wide discretion made the spe-cifics of 'service delivery' unpredictable and led, in turn, to the variable implementation of community-based sentences across the country. To a managerialist-driven Home Office, which was now providing 80 per cent of the cost of probation services, such a state of affairs was unacceptable, and the pursuit of uniformity in practice became the dominant theme of subsequent policy developments (May, 1994: 870–2).

Internally, too, probation service managers had a powerful incentive to change. In the face of the apparently damning and certainly disheart-ening evidence of the 'nothing works' era, there was a real danger that if the probation service continued to define its role primarily in terms of the 'scientific' rehabilitation of offenders it would simply be abandoned as 'irrelevant to the major problems faced by the courts' (Haxby, 1978: 148). This fear provided a powerful motive for those responsible for the direction of individual probation services to accept the need for a new focus for probation work, one which welded the service more closely to the aims and activities of the rest of the criminal justice system, including the reduction of pressure on the prison population. As a result, the waning of confidence in the treatment model of probation was accompanied by the emergence and speedy development of 'the idea of *policy*' to the point where, as McWilliams puts it, 'it has become impossible to understand the service other than as an instrument of government policy' (McWilliams, 1987: 103–5).

Resetting the probation agenda: 1979 and all that

Having contemplated the wider horizons, as it were, it is time to relate these broader themes to the history of developments within the probation service which we began in Chapter 3. McWilliams has identified the beginnings of the demise of 'local customs and traditional arrangements' in probation practice and their replacement by a national policy as early as 1961 in the recommendations of the Report of the Interdepartmental Committee on the Business of the Criminal Courts (Home Office, 1961), and he argues that from that point forward a change to a 'bureaucratic-managerial model' in the organisation of probation services 'just happened' without any deliberate and careful planning (McWilliams, 1987: 107).

However accurately that analysis may describe the gradualism of the 1960s and 1970s, there can be little doubt that the election of the right-wing Conservative administration in 1979 introduced a radical new agenda for the governance of Britain which has had profound implications for the way the entire public sector, including the probation service, is structured and run. In a real sense the neo-liberal 'Thatcherites' were merely responding to the sorts of wider socio-economic developments discussed earlier in this chapter. Indeed, it can be argued that the outgoing Labour administration had already departed from the supposed post-war social democratic consensus under the demands of successive fiscal crises and in line with what Feeley and Simon (1994: 190) have called 'pre-political thought'. Whatever the origins of its rhetoric, however, the Conservative government which was elected in 1979 made a positive virtue out of the necessity to rein in public spending and downgrade the 'social' aspects of government policy. In place of welfarism and interventionism, the virtues and the values of 'the market' were extolled as a panacea for both the country's economic and its social failings.

As the pace of the change foreshadowed in this rhetoric gathered momentum, the dismantling of state-owned enterprises and the mechanisms of corporatist economic planning were supplemented by a gradual 'hollowing out of the state' in which the responsibility for the day-to-day provision and administration of public functions was shifted onto non-governmental organisations and agencies 'at arm's length' from central government (Rhodes, 1994; 1996). At the same time, central government took new and extensive powers to enable it to set national policies in a range of areas such as education, health and criminal justice and to allow for the extent to which those policies were being implemented locally to be more precisely monitored from the centre. This distinction between policy setting and policy implementation, or between 'steering and rowing' as it has been characterised (Osborne and Gaebler, 1992), is one of the key developments in government policy since 1979 which has enabled successive Conservative administrations to claim that they were reducing the scope of government intervention in civic life, however counter-factual that claim may have been (Rhodes, 1994: 139–40).

We have already noted that the decentralised structure of the probation service in England and Wales – a network of local probation committees each responsible for the provision of probation services in its area – has never precluded direction from central government. The service is a creature of statute, and ever since the establishment of national arrangements for probation in 1907 the Home Secretary has had statutory authority to make rules and to issue guidelines to local area committees and, indeed, to do away with some of them by amalgamating two or more petty-sessional areas into one probation area. Thus, there has always been a tension between central and local control and the precise relationship between the two has gradually altered as the nature of public governance in Britain has evolved. But the changes which have taken place since 1979 have not simply continued the shift towards central control – they have increased it in both magnitude and pace. As a consequence central government has been able to promote a fundamental alteration in the philosophy and practice of probation, and in the whole range of public services, while still preserving (and indeed, within the strict limits of centrally determined budgets, actually increasing) the semblance of local autonomy.

The concept of the 'hollow state' also identifies a new style of public management involving the introduction of methods and philosophies borrowed from the private sector in pursuit of greater discipline and parsimony in resource use (Rhodes, 1994: 144). This 'new public management', or NPM as it is called, prioritises the setting of explicit standards of service and the measurement of performance in terms of how far those standards have been delivered within the constraints of cash-limited budgets. NPM also requires of its exponents a more hands-on, directive and professional management style more attuned to the ethics of the commercial sector (Hood, 1991: 4–5). 'Value for money – VFM' and 'better use of resources' have become the key phrases in policy debates, and 'outputs' have been defined more and more in terms which can be quantified and measured by a range of instrumentally constructed 'key indicators', so as to be susceptible to external audit. As Peters (1986) and others have pointed out, under the influence of NPM extraneous value systems become increasingly marginalised as debate becomes focused on better methods of scrutinising internal efficiencies, in pursuit of the ultimate goal: the '3 Es' of economy, efficiency and effectiveness. So, while its proponents may claim that it has produced some efficiency gains and financial savings (and even that is contested), the introduction of NPM has unquestionably eroded the broader values of the public sector ethos and installed a narrow focus on cost-efficiency at the expense of broader notions of social value and public accountability (Rhodes, 1994; 1996).

New management in the probation service

The probation service has certainly not been immune from the pervasive influences of NPM. Management of any kind is a reasonably recent innovation in the probation service but, as we saw, the service did gradually develop an administrative and supervisory hierarchy during its 'diagnostic' era in response to the expansion and diversification of its roles. This meant that there was already in place a *professional* management structure which could respond to the challenges of NPM and begin to perform more of a planning and controlling function, to formulate policy and set objectives, rather than performing principally as a means of enabling main-grade officers to practise their social work skills. 'Supervision' by principal and senior officers which the Morison Report of 1962 had defined as 'casework supervision' was to become a function of *control* in pursuit of policy objectives (McWilliams, 1987: 106–8 and fn. 9). Once that transformation was complete the traditional 'commonalty' of interests and of experience between officers and those who managed them had become outdated and the way was open for the recruitment of professional managers with expertise in areas outside social work.

Grasping these wider and deeper structural and cultural changes helps us to contextualise and so to make better sense of the bewildering array of Green Papers, White Papers, policy documents and Acts of Parliament which have so utterly transformed the probation service in the 1980s and 1990s. The first of these policy statements was the *Statement of National Objectives and Priorities* (SNOP), issued by the Home Office in 1984. This was a particularly significant document not only because of what it contained, but also because it pointed quite clearly to the direction that relations between local services and central government would take in future. The level of central control over local probation services was increased and the attention of local services was directed to the 'bifurcated' policy objectives signalled in the Criminal Justice Act 1982 of increased diversion of some offenders and new, more punitive responses to others (May, 1994: 872–3; Raynor, 1996b: 244).

Significantly, in line with the emerging actuarial approach to crime control discussed above, SNOP set out new priorities for the service which moved the focus away from assisting minor offenders 'in need' of social work intervention towards working with categories of offenders thought to be a risk to society (Audit Commission, 1989: 2). As such it represented a self-conscious attempt to move the probation service 'up-tariff' and away from the client group which it had historically served, and from other categories of welfare-oriented work, such as after-care and civil family work. At the same time SNOP emphasised the need for local committees and Chief Officers to ensure that probation resources were managed efficiently and effectively in the pursuit of clear objectives so as to secure value for taxpayers' money. The statement of national objectives, together with local statements agreed over the course of the succeeding year, was intended to serve as the basis for applying the quasi-market disciplines of the government's Financial Management Initiative (FMI) to the probation service (Humphrey, 1991). From now on, resources were to determine policy, rather than the other way round, and the introduction of FMI techniques imported a new emphasis on objective setting, performance measurement, delegated resource management and critical scrutinies of the value for money of service provision at the expense, it has been argued, of attention to wider and more substantive social goals.

In the new climate created by these changes the roles of the Audit Commission, the National Audit Office (NAO) and Her Majesty's Inspectorate of Probation (HMIP) in periodically monitoring the 'Quality and Effectiveness' of local services against a standard range of 'key performance indicators' (KPIs) (worked out jointly by HMIP and the NAO but not fully developed until 1994) became increasingly important and pervasive. In addition, there were several attempts at introducing standardised management information systems across the country, although not all of them were successful (Humphrey, 1991). Eventually, in 1992, the funding of probation services changed from an open to a cash-limited system calculated on a national formula rather than on locally determined needs. This crucially altered the central–local balance, elevating the importance of demonstrating cost-efficiency in line with the KPIs and giving even greater significance to efficiency scrutinies of HMIP and of the other external watchdogs (Raine and Willson, 1993).

New working practices for the 1990s

With regard to working practices, the changes foreshadowed in SNOP were realised incrementally by further prescriptive policy documents emanating from central government which were aimed directly at full-time probation personnel rather than through local probation committees. National Standards for Community Service were issued by the Home Office in 1988 and these, in a greatly expanded form, became National Standards for the Supervision of Offenders in the Community in 1992. Both documents, and particularly the latter, emphasised the role that uniformly 'stiff and demanding' (i.e. punitive) community punishments could play in a comprehensive and systematic response to crime. Breach procedures, another punitive aspect of probation work, were tightened up and their importance re-emphasised.

The National Standards document also established a new framework for the writing of pre-sentence reports (PSRs) in which the sort of information to be provided would focus much more closely on the offence and the offender's attitude toward it and less on what might have traditionally been thought of as the welfare needs of 'the client'. A later revision reinforced this emphasis and directed increased attention to the assessment of the risk of reoffending and the risk of harm to the public from the subject of the report (Home Office *et al.*, 1995: 11). (These aspects of probation practice are discussed in more detail in Chapter 5, below.) From a managerialist perspective these changes were designed to align PSRs more closely with the needs of the court in implementing the just deserts requirements of the 1991 Act and wider aspects of sentencing policy. At the symbolic level, however, they also represented a further repudiation of the social work traditions of the service in a conceptual shift which was gradually redefining the historical relationship between officers, the courts and those under supervision.

As we saw in Chapter 1, 1988 also saw the publication by the Home Office of a requirement for local services to draw up 'action plans' which would target non-custodial sentencing options more specifically at those offenders aged between 17 and 21 who were most 'at risk' of custody (Home Office, 1988b). We can now appreciate how the action plan approach emphasised certain key elements which reflect the general shift in the focus of probation then taking place. First, non-custodial disposals were to be made 'persuasive' to the courts on the basis of their punitive character; powers created by the Criminal Justice Act 1982 to attach specific requirements of attendance, compliance and desistence were to be used to 'toughen up' probation orders so that they provided conditions of 'intensive supervision' imposing appreciable levels of restriction of liberty for offenders made subject to them. Secondly, the new non-custodial programmes were to be provided, wherever possible, 'in partnership' with non-statutory agencies and other providers, an aspect which some critics portrayed at the time as the opening shot in the ideological battle to secure the privatisation of the probation service.

Towards a new framework for community sentencing

We have already seen that these policy developments were part of wider currents in criminal justice policy, which was becoming increasingly punitive and centralist in direction. The government had made its views on the future direction of probation abundantly clear in its 1988 Green Paper *Punishment, Custody and the Community* (Home Office, 1988a). Developing the themes of systematisation and bifurcation which had been evident, for instance, in the 1986 working paper on criminal justice (Home Office, 1986), the Green Paper sought to confirm the position of the probation service within the criminal justice system as one of a number of specialist agencies working alongside each other in the provision of a comprehensive set of differentiated responses to criminal behaviour. The particular role of the service was to provide and supervise a range of community-based punishments which would be truly punitive (in the sense that they would involve a graduated restriction of liberty for, and would place various other demands upon, the offender), but which would none-theless preserve the possibility for rehabilitation through the fostering of the sort of increased self-reliance and self-discipline unlikely to be found in offenders sentenced to custody (Home Office, 1988a: para. 1.1). The provision of community punishments of that kind was seen as an essential part of the government's overall strategy of reducing the reliance on prison by preserving its use for only the most dangerous of offenders, a policy which, as we have seen, had been emerging since at least the days of the Younger Report. In order to play the role in diverting from custody those seriously at risk of a custodial sentence the probation service would have to refocus much of its activity by targeting more serious offenders than had been the case.

Very much the same message came from the 1989 Audit Commission report on promoting value for money in the probation service (Audit Commission, 1989: para. 63), which concluded that the service was ex-pending too much of its resources on working with offenders who were at no risk of being sent to prison and who might more cost-effectively be dealt with by a fine or some other less intensive disposal. Significantly too, given its important position within the matrix of organisations which helped to develop criminal justice policy, the Audit Commission iden-tified the survival of what it called 'a tradition of individualism' – of each officer operating as 'an independent practitioner rather than as a mem-ber of a team' – as 'the source of some resistance to recent management initiatives' designed to move the service in the direction desired by govern-ment (Audit Commission, 1989: para. 29). The role envisaged in the Green Paper was held out as a great challenge for the probation service to meet. The foreword to the document spoke of the chance which the service had 'to move centre-stage in the criminal justice system' by fulfil-ling its unique potential for supervising punishment in the community, provided only (and it was no small precondition) that it was willing to embrace the punitive connotations of that policy. On the other hand, both the Green Paper and the Audit Commission report made it clear that, should this challenge be declined, the government did not rule out the possibility of setting up a new organisation to organise punishment.

The message was clear. Either the probation service would have to harness its efforts more closely to central policy objectives based upon the renaissance of punishment and the primacy, in sentencing, of 'just deserts', or it was going to be eclipsed by some more punitive agency (Audit Commission, 1989: para. 7; Windlesham, 1993: 227–8). Either it would have to 'talk tough' on probation or it was in danger of not being heard at all by those who were driving criminal justice policy. Those at the top levels of management heard the message and were willing to react pragmatically to it, as evidenced, for example, by the brief publication of an ACOP paper entitled *More Demanding than Prison* (ACOP, 1988), in which an attempt to move the debate away from prison as the central focus of punitive thinking was phrased in language clearly designed to resonate with that of the punishment lobby (Rumgay, 1989: 181). By this point it is clear that the debate had become firmly fixed within the parameters set by the government's version of a just deserts model. Thereafter, discussions of the various probation roles were to be increasingly conducted in overtly punitive language that stressed the efficiency, effectiveness and economy of community sentences and of the susceptibility of working practices to monitoring and control (May, 1991b: 177; 1994: 875; ACOP, 1996).

Probation as a sentence of the Court

In response to the logic of the ideological transformations just described, the Criminal Justice Act 1991 converted the probation order into a punishment in its own right rather than the alternative to punishment that it had always previously been. The 1991 Act also consolidated probation orders with other non-custodial sentences within a framework predominantly based on the principles of just deserts and proportionality and in so doing created a theoretical hierarchy of punishments in which non-custodial measures were required to 'fill the gap' between offences for which a fine or discharge was sufficient and those for which custody was judged to be required. By this stage another Green Paper, *Supervision and Punishment in the Community*, had already defined the main objective of the probation service as preventing or reducing reoffending by those under its supervision and, ultimately, reducing crime (Home Office, 1990b: para. 2.3). To achieve this objective, the Green Paper said (at para. 3.2, emphasis added),

> probation officers must confront offenders with the effects of their criminal behaviour on their victims, influence their conduct and help them, where possible, to lead a new life. Probation work has never meant an exclusive commitment to the interests of offenders; and probation officers have always had to take account of the requirements of the court and the legitimate concerns of victims and the wider public. However, the changes in the [1990] White Paper *may require a different balance to be struck between these demands.*

The Green Paper, concentrating as it did on the potential of the service for crime control and public protection, emphasised the close symmetry which the government wished to establish between the objectives of the probation service and policy aims of the wider criminal justice system (Windlesham, 1993: 225–31). Although the 1991 Act retained a limited scope for individual rehabilitation in the objectives to be pursued in the making of a probation order (section 2(1)(a) Powers of Criminal Courts Act 1973, as amended), its inclusion within the general deserts-based framework established by the Act make it clear that probation now operates within an offence-focused rather than offender-centred regime of punishments in which retribution is the overriding principle (Home Office, 1990b: para. 3.11). It was also envisaged that under the new arrangements the role of the probation officer would 'broaden' to include assembling, coordinating and monitoring supervision packages provided by others – in other words, a much more managerial role set in the context of greater 'partnership' working and privatised provision. Work with individual offenders would continue, the Green Paper said, but 'programme management in its widest sense' would become increasingly important (para. 3.4).

The subsequent history of the 1991 reforms and the series of counter-reforms since 1993 has been charted already in Chapter 1. That history, with its restoration of the idea that 'prison works', has had the effect of increasing the overall levels of punitiveness in the sentencing framework. More than ever, non-custodial sentences are being required to measure up to that central custodial pillar in terms of their punitive 'bite' and their ideological significance has been diminished as a consequence (Nellis, 1996: 20). Government priorities for the probation service are now set out in a rolling three-year plan published annually by the Home Office. For 1996 (the latest available at the time of writing) the priorities were the provision of tough and demanding punishment which was effective in reducing crime and increasing public protection by enhanced risk assessment, enforcement and management (Home Office, 1996a: para. 7.4): unashamedly punitive and set in the managerialist context of increased quality of service and cost-effectiveness. The distinction in official discourse from the reformatory zeal of the early missionaries could not be starker.

Of course, since the publication of the 1996 priorities, we have witnessed a change in government. Early signals from the new administration are mixed. Ministers apparently see a much bigger role for probation officers, one which would involve them in the welfare-to-work programme of the new government, as well as running compulsory drug treatment programmes and a much expanded electronic monitoring scheme. All of this continues, however, to be articulated in language which points to the persistence of a populist, punitive agenda in which sentencers can only be expected to have confidence in community sentences 'if we can make them tougher' (Home Secretary Jack Straw, quoted in Travis, 1997).

Changing the skills and knowledge base: no more Mister Nice-Guy?

In line with these developments towards a more punitive approach to probation practice, the 1990s have witnessed significant changes in the way that new officers were trained. The early history of academic courses for probation officers has been discussed above in the context of the emergence of a professionalising, diagnostic and welfare-oriented service. Since 1971 the training of probation officers in England and Wales had been conducted under the auspices of the Central Council for Education and Training in Social Work (CCETSW). As its title implies, CCETSW is a generic organisation which is responsible for overseeing and validating all forms of social work training. The incorporation of probation training within this generic framework served to reinforce the social work identity of the probation service and to re-emphasise the similarity between probation and other forms of social work (Haxby, 1978: 113). Officers under training typically attended university and college courses in which the 'streams' with a specifically probation/criminological orientation were part only of a wider, generic syllabus shared with students from other welfare services.

Although the suitability of this generic approach for the specialised employment needs of probation officers had always been a point of some controversy (May, 1991a: 19), it was only with the introduction of the 'punishment in the community' ideology that the CCETSW-based arrangements began to be openly questioned. The 1990 Green Paper *Supervision and Punishment in the Community* (Home Office, 1990b) made it clear that in relation to probation training generic social work principles were no longer to be considered of paramount importance: the need for changes to working methods called for probation officers to acquire new skills in addition to basic social work expertise, including skills in management (Brake and Hale, 1992: 157). Somewhat reluctantly, CCETSW responded by publishing a 'training syllabus' to be followed by probation students on courses leading to the award of a Diploma in Social Work (DipSW) and by specifying that a minimum of 35–40 per cent of 'probation' DipSWs should be devoted to matters relevant to practice in the justice system (Nellis, 1996: 18).

The move from knowledge to skills

All of this was taking place in a wider educational climate in which the emphasis was shifting away from the inculcation of 'knowledge' and 'values' towards the acquisition of 'skills' and 'competencies' across a broad range of vocational and near-vocational courses. This shift was seen to be necessary by a wide spectrum of political opinion in order to make educational 'outcomes' more relevant for the demands of employers and the needs of the economy more generally. However, several critical commentaries have characterised this development as an extension of the Conservative government's desire to subordinate education and training in general to the discipline of the market and to place 'employers in the forefront of any training system' (Issit and Woodward, 1992: 43). On this account competence-based training is linked to the rise of managerialism in a range of settings since the competencies to be acquired are derived from a functional analysis of the tasks required by the organisation rather than any wider concern for personal self-fulfilment. As with all aspects of managerialism, the 'investment' in training must be clearly and demonstrably cost-effective in the extent to which it facilitates the organisational aims and objectives of the body which has paid for it. The competence-based approach, it is alleged, is designed to equip employees for the routinised and uncritical performance of a prescribed and fragmented set of work tasks, rather than for any more demanding role which might require the exercise of professional discretion (Drakeford and Vanstone, 1996a: 5).

As the influence of managerialism grew within the probation service so, by implication, did the demand for uncritical employees and for competence-based practice (Nellis, 1996: 14). Although CCETSW did not embrace the concept wholeheartedly, the structure of the DipSW course clearly reflected what Nellis (1996) has characterised as 'a partial competence model' which represented a compromise between management-influenced statements of practice competencies and a continuing commitment to wider, generic values such as anti-discriminatory and anti-racist practice. This compromise was of temporary effect, however, because by the end of 1993 the resurgence of populist punitiveness discussed in Chapter 1 and Treasury-driven expenditure cuts had combined to redraw the training agenda once more. The commitment to a competence-based approach, already demonstrated in the early pronouncements of the Home Office Probation Training Unit established in 1992 (Nellis, 1996: 19), was further reinforced in an internal Home Office review of training needs initiated in 1994 and designed to align training with newly developed competencies for basic-grade officers (Home Office, 1994b; 1994c).

This was followed in the next year by a consultation document on the future development of probation training in which the government made clear its determination to end the existing monopoly of training by higher education institutions so that in future all training would be employment-based with local area management determining the individual development needs of new applicants, having regard to national standards and local priorities and objectives, and then purchasing specific training to meet those needs (Home Office, 1995b). Defending the proposals in his address to the 1995 National Probation Conference, the then Home Secretary said he rejected an approach to training which equated punishment in the community with 'social work with offenders' (Howard, 1995). Despite considerable and perhaps predictable opposition to these proposals, and against the wishes of ACOP, the Conservative government gave effect to them, claiming thereby to have 'cleared away a barrier to the entry to the probation service of able people by ending the legal requirement that probation officers hold a social work diploma' (Home Office, 1996b: 68).

When the Labour Party came to power in May 1997, however, the new Home Secretary, Jack Straw, moved quickly to reverse this trend, at least in part, by announcing his intention to establish a new qualification called a Diploma in Probation Studies which would be based on a mixture of university teaching and work-based assessment. However, this was only a partial reversal because, in making his announcement, Mr Straw appeared to endorse much of his predecessor's stand on this issue and, in words that clearly echoed Michael Howard's, to distance himself from 'the welfare approach' to probation training. 'New probation officers', he declared, 'should no longer be linked to social work education ... The new diploma will focus on their vital role in protecting the public and reducing crime through effective work with offenders' (quoted in *The Guardian*, 30 July 1997).

Whether this latest reform will result in an increase in the recruitment of probation officers with a military background (the group who featured most prominently in the previous government's rhetorical assault on the pre-existing arrangements) and whether that would necessarily result in the spread of a more punitive culture among officers both remain to be seen. What is more certain is that the culmination of this process of change represents one further shift towards a more intellectually restrictive, competence-oriented and managerial culture which infuses not only the probation service but much of contemporary society (Galbraith, 1992; Nellis, 1996: 25). This cultural shift has in turn both reflected and driven a gradual but inexorable erosion of the traditionally liberal and humanitarian philosophy of probation described at the beginning of this chapter to the point where its core task appears to have less to do with the application of social work skills with offenders in the community and more to do with 'system involvement and offender management' (Harris, 1994: 34; Nellis, 1995a: 28).

Searching for a new soul: probation in the 1990s

By now I hope it will be apparent that the whole history of the probation service has been one of gradual transformation and adaptation. However, the scale of the changes that have taken place over the last fifteen to twenty years and the extent of external compulsion which has accompanied them represent the greatest challenge yet to the value system which underlies the service's work (Drakeford and Vanstone, 1996a). Given the magnitude of this upheaval, it is hardly surprising that the probation service finds itself somewhat confused as to what exactly its core values are and what its essential *raison d'être* should be, as it faces the twenty-first century.

There has been no shortage of advice from informed academic commentators and from well-placed practitioners as to what should properly constitute the values of the service in the decades ahead. Some have called for a return to or a reaffirmation of what they portray as the 'traditional values' of probation which would once more prioritise 'help' for offenders over punishment and coercion. Others have urged the service to seek out new roles in promoting community safety through a range of strategies including, but not limited to, the reduction of present and future behaviour, although, as Drakeford and Vanstone point out, exactly how the probation service working through the agency of individual officers can implement these 'broader strategies' is a matter of 'debate and difference' (1996a: 6). One fairly common theme that runs through much recent writing on 'probation values' is the need for the probation service to engage more cooperatively and honestly with other organisations and with the communities in which offenders live, so as to mobilise the resources, and influence the attitudes, of both (Raynor, 1996a: 20). Harris, for instance, has called for the 'surrender of exclusivity' on the part of the service in return for an emergent role in other areas of the criminal justice system. He argues that the probation service should cease to regard individual counselling or supervisory sessions with 'clients' as its core activities if it wishes to become a more visible and effective participant in the 'fight against crime'. As well as involvement in the 'management of offenders', the service should seek to develop its role in other areas such as work with victims, crime prevention, dealing with fear of crime and community involvement (Harris, 1992: 154, 174).

In a similar vein, Nellis, in an important contribution to this debate, has argued that to avoid being sucked into a wholly punitive role, the service must construct a new value-base around the three elements of anti-custodialism, restorative justice and community safety (Nellis, 1995a: 30). Drawing on ideas from mainstream and critical criminologies, Nellis condemns both the culture of 'managerialism', which he asserts is incompatible with the traditional approach to 'social work' values, but also the common assumption that the compassionate and humanitarian values which, it is assumed, should guide progressive action in the criminal justice arena must inevitably be based upon the principles of 'generic' social work. Progressive and humane values exist independently of 'genericism', and generic values, according to Nellis, have made only a limited contribution to innovation in probation practice in the past. While clearly not advocating the transformation of probation into the sort of community-based 'correctional service' suggested two decades earlier by Haxby (1978: 148), Nellis argues that in order to preserve a space for humane and progressive ideals at the centre rather than the margins of the criminal justice system, the service must resist the urge to 'retreat' into its generic social work identity. By conceiving of itself in future as a 'community justice' agency or even as 'a broadly conceived penal reform body' rather than a 'social work agency' for offenders, the service can preserve sufficient political credibility to be able to continue promoting practices which reduce reliance on the use of custody and promote greater levels of social justice for offenders, their victims and the wider community. The service should recognise, he suggests, that rehabilitation alone is insufficient as a value base for probation, not only because the service undertakes a range of worthwhile activities which are not essentially or primarily rehabilitative (for example, bail support), but also because the placing of offenders' and interests *above*, as opposed to *alongside*, the rights of victims and the requirements of public safety lacks moral justification and, in the 1990s, political credibility.

(1995a: 26, emphasis in original)

Nellis argues that it is only in the context of genuine concern for the needs and experiences of crime victims that concern for offenders (expressed as rehabilitation) will have any political plausibility. He suggests, therefore, that, in addition to incorporating an explicit anti-custodial stance into its philosophy and practice, the probation service has no choice but to expand its involvement in activities which promote 'restorative justice' such as victim–offender mediation and neighbourhood dispute settlement, and to play a much more active role in crime prevention initiatives. These three commitments could, in Nellis' view, form the basis of a new probation value-base, but the critical insights and knowledge base which would be necessary to inform and enable such an expansion of roles are more likely to come from criminology and penology than from traditional generic social work. It is, therefore, in the former rather than the latter paradigm that trainees, practitioners and managers should, primarily, be educated (Nellis, 1995a: 25).

Nellis' position has found generalised support in other contributions to the debate (e.g. Raynor, 1996a: 20) but predictably perhaps, given its radicalism, it has also attracted criticism. James (1995) and Spencer (1995), for instance, endorse Nellis' critique of the impact of 'managerialism' upon the service's traditional value system, but both harbour doubts as to whether the 'stances' Nellis identifies amount to values at all. They could be construed instead as 'aims' from which values could be implied, but as such they would have no privileged status among other possible aims that might equally be pursued by the probation service or by other agencies with whom, increasingly, the service will be required to work (James, 1995: 330). From this point of view, the lack of a genuine and generalisable value-base in the context of an increasingly multi-agency and 'corporatist' system of working leaves open the potential for destructive clashes with representatives from other parts of the criminal justice system over unresolved power struggles and unclarified values and principles (Pratt, 1989; Crawford, 1994a; James and Bottomley, 1994). Spencer also asserts that Nellis' position involves 'altering the value paradigm away from the individual to the institutional' in ways which risk transforming individual probation clients into the 'means' to achieving a decarcerative outcome, rather than 'ends' in themselves (Spencer, 1995: 345), a charge which Nellis rejects (Nellis, 1995b). Some critics also query how far the probation service can focus adequately on the needs of both offenders *and* their victims, two contrasting client groups often with conflicting needs and expectations, without developing a sort of institutional schizophrenia (James, 1995: 331; B. Williams, 1996).

Moving beyond offending behaviour

Somewhere between the two poles of institutional and individual intervention, (if that is, indeed, what the contributions of Nellis and Spencer
represent), Drakeford and Vanstone (1996a; 1996b) call for the probation service to embrace 'a dual strategy' which involves influencing systems as well as individuals. They too castigate much of the management
of probation, in uncompromising terms, for its willingness to embrace
new 'macho' styles and its 'headlong rush to placate, incorporate and at
times anticipate the agenda of an ever more intrusive Home Office'
(1996b: 17). This, they insist, has spelt the end of cooperative working
relationships within the service and between many officers and their
clients and has opened the door to policies which insist on individual
responsibility for offending and have 'no truck with economic, social or
psychological explanations of offending' – a 'bastardised form of moral
scolding', as they so memorably put it (1996b: 19). Rigid standard procedures supported by 'macho correctionalism' and 'radical managerialism'
encourage practice which neglects 'the diversity and complexity of real
life'. With Hudson (1993) and others, they are unwilling to accept the
classical tenet (outlined in Chapter 2, above) that offending behaviour is
the outcome of an individual's reasoned decision-making devoid of a structural context. They contend that without social justice, criminal justice is
impossible and they argue that the specific contribution of the probation
service within the criminal justice system should be nothing less than the
promotion of the conditions of social justice (1996a: 106).

To begin to work towards this end, Drakeford and Vanstone argue
that the probation service must revert to 'ways of working which are rooted
in its own distinctive tradition' and which 're-assert the case for active
and collaborative intervention by probation officers in the social worlds
which their clients inhabit' (Drakeford and Vanstone 1996b: 19). They
are in no doubt that (*pace* Jack Straw) probation practice is about 'social
work' in the criminal justice system and see no contradiction between
that approach and imaginatively helping individuals to change in order
to reduce the harm caused by offending (which is the role that the government has set for the service).

However, they suggest, surely correctly, that a simple return to former
ways of working would be 'ill-tuned' for present conditions. Given the
enormity of the changes to the world over the previous fifteen years, they
say, such a nostalgic gesture would offer the probation service little realistic chance of influencing wider social systems so as to address 'those
elements within an individual's life and circumstances in which . . .
offending is rooted' (1996a: 6). The proper concern of the service for
the chaotic lifestyles of individual 'offenders' (a term they avoid, preferring to speak of 'clients' instead) should be balanced by a concern for,
and a desire to change for the better, the wider social stage on which
those lifestyles are acted out. Their analysis illustrates how this might be
begun by detailing examples of initiatives in various parts of the country

through which the service has shifted its focus 'beyond offending behaviour' to address the structural problems surrounding offenders' lives, such as homelessness, poverty and lack of employment opportunity. However, in order to be able to generalise this approach Drakeford and Vanstone recognise that the probation service will have to loosen what they call 'the shackles of its all too-willing compliance with central government policy-making' so as 'to free itself to increase its lobbying and campaigning activities on behalf of, alongside, the disadvantaged and marginalised people with whom it works'.

While many inside the service (and elsewhere) may empathise with this view, it is difficult to see how such a stance could realistically become the policy position of an institution so heavily reliant on central government for its resources and so utterly dependent on magistrates and judges for its day-to-day 'business'. Nor is it certain that any attempt to move towards such a radical policy against the direct wishes of government and senior probation management would secure either the support of the majority of officers or an immediate improvement in the services offered to probationers, if the result were to be a further deterioration in industrial relations within the service.

Therefore, it seems more likely that for the foreseeable future the philosophy underpinning probation work will continue to evolve in ways which emphasise its role in promoting community safety through the reduction of offending and which can accommodate work with groups other than offenders. This need not be a counsel of despair, however, for even within a remit that is focused on 'punishment' in the community there is sufficient ambiguity in the meaning of that term to allow a variety of methods of working, between the 'simplistically punitive' and the 'simplistically caring' (Harris, 1992: 160). Much will depend upon the extent to which the service as a whole manages to retain a humane and enlightened attitude towards the rights and the needs of offenders and to hold this in balance against the rights and needs of others with a legitimate interest in criminal justice, particularly those who have been or may be in future the victims of crime.

Towards 2001: an odyssey of hope or a journey of despair?

This chapter and the one which preceded it have charted important transformations in the history of probation in England and Wales from its earliest days as a branch of the Church's missionary work among the alcoholic and destitute, through its quasi-medical diagnostic and normalising phase, to its current position as an integral part of a systematised criminal justice apparatus, having special responsibility for the supervision of punishment in the community. We have noted how the probation service has always had two central pillars: welfarist ambitions have been mingled with elements of control, backed up by the threat of coercion, should those on probation breach the conditions of their release from punishment. Gradually, the service has first been encouraged and then required to give ever greater emphasis to the pillar of control, so that the challenge for probation, both at an institutional level and for individual officers, has increasingly become one of preserving legitimate opportunities for continuing to provide social work interventions to those entrusted to its supervision.

More widely in society, the era of social welfare has been superseded by the age of cost-effective crime control with its dominant concerns of policy, planning and coordination and its emphasis on effective management. This 'new penology' has abandoned rehabilitative ambitions in favour of objectives which can be more easily quantified and thus achieved, such as the extent to which internally validated procedures have been complied with. Under the joint imperatives of the new penology and the new managerialism which has accompanied and facilitated it, broader, socially related values have largely been replaced by internally derived objectives and measures of 'success'. The wider criminal justice system harbours little or no ambition to 'rescue' individuals; rather, aggregate populations must be differentiated, according to assessments of varying degrees of risk, and 'managed' through the application of appropriate and affordable levels of incapacitation. Within these wider transformations (which are in turn only fully explicable by reference to the consequences of global changes in the free market economy), the probation service has come to be identified as an appropriate sub-system for the management of offenders whose offences are not considered, on retributive grounds, to be so serious as to justify the full rigour (and expense) of a custodial sentence.

Grasping these wider and deeper changes helps to explain current aspects of probation philosophy and practice. The service has moved 'up-tariff' away from the *petty* offender and those who might once have been thought most susceptible to rehabilitation. Work with 'heavy-end' offenders has meant new pressures (and increased personal risk) for officers which, but for the enduring humanitarianism of the great majority of them, might have persuaded the service as a whole to abandon any belief in the possibility of effecting change in a more seriously recidivist clientele. In this changed world, risk assessment both in the preparation of pre-sentence reports and in evaluating suitability for early release, has assumed a much increased role in the ordinary officer's work. The pressure to demonstrate effectiveness and cost-efficiency has further underlined the need to 'target' interventions more selectively and to monitor and evaluate initiatives, so that future practice can guided by informed decisions about 'what works' and with whom. Partnership working with both the voluntary and profit-making sectors is now relatively established within probation practice and, although partnerships may not yet have delivered all that was expected of them (Broad, 1996), local services seem to have managed to cope with the requirement post-1992 to devolve around 5 per cent of their budgets for such work. Similarly, the requirement for the service to involve itself in non-offender-centred crime prevention work, such as the well-known Kirkholt Burglary Reduction Project coordinated by the Greater Manchester Probation Service, has its supporters and is likely to persist for the foreseeable future, despite doubts that some may harbour as to whether the probation service is the correct agency to engage in crime prevention schemes of this kind (Crawford, 1994a; Gilling, 1996).

Not all of these developments would universally be counted as reverses, of course, at least by objective observers. Radical as well as conservative voices, for instance, have welcomed the greater attention being paid to 'gate-keeping' practices in high-tariff 'intensive probation' schemes which (when they are properly applied) limit the range of interventions and reduce the dangers of 'net-widening'. The cause of anti-discriminatory practice has also undoubtedly benefited from the greater degree of oversight and monitoring made possible by the advance of managerialism (Nellis, 1995a: 29). And, as we have seen, the involvement of the probation service in work with victims and in the promotion of community service initiatives has its supporters as well as its detractors, some of whom argue quite passionately that the service can only survive as a non-correctional organisation by providing criminal justice services to this wider range of clients. For some, the challenge of effecting one further transformation into a truly community-based organisation promoting the principles of restorative justice (or relational justice – see Chapter 2 again) provides some small measure of resources for a 'journey of hope' into the next millennium. But others do fear that the service, particularly in its management grades, has too readily embraced the credos of managerialism and has flirted too convincingly with the new right's discourse of punishment and cost-efficiency. Unless checked, these tendencies will, it is alleged, further erode morale within the service by promoting even greater 'de-professionalisation' and 'deskilling' of the workforce as the relentless pursuit of efficiency, predictability and control produces a de-humanised, rationalised techno-bureaucratic service in which, far from addressing the needs of offenders and their communities, an ever greater proportion of the workforce will spend their time monitoring the work of the rest (Oldfield, 1994).

Given this divergence of prognoses, from the apocalyptic to the benign, the future development of the probation service in England and Wales is hard to predict. Clearly, the service has had to cope with considerable challenges and changes in the recent past and its ability to do so is testimony to both its continuing resilience and its long history of adaptation and reinvention. Of course, the probation service in England and Wales has not yet become a 'correctional agency' (although the latest review of its functions may indeed draw it into closer links with the prison service). Probation officers continue in the main to work for the rehabilitation of those whom they supervise. There are specific examples of community-based programmes which are 'working', in the sense of having an impact on the future offending of those who attend them, and such achievements are to be welcomed, not least from the perspective of potential future victims. But, despite all this, there is a real danger that a service preoccupied with securing compliance and with 'confronting' and 'correcting' antisocial behaviour at an individualistic level will lose sight of the wider vision, 'the social' (Drakeford and Vanstone, 1996b), and will have no further interest in, or purchase upon, the wider social and economic circumstances which frame its clients' lives and in which its clients' offending behaviour is rooted.

These 'decontextualising' tendencies are exacerbated by rapidly increasing caseloads and cuts in resources which constrain even further the ability of those who plan for and implement community penalties to address anything other than the immediate demands of the job. Under such conditions, the prospects of achieving the sort of outcome where those under supervision are fully reintegrated into a society in ways which make reoffending not only unlikely but uncharacteristic are seriously diminished. Additional challenges, doubtless, lie ahead, and in the concluding chapter I shall offer some further thoughts on possible ways forward for the service and for the non-custodial penalties which it administers. More immediately, however, the next chapter will describe in more detail the work of the probation service at the present time, in the provision and administration of non-custodial or community sentences.

Chapter 5

Community Penalties

Community sentences and the 1991 framework

We have seen in Chapter 1 that the Criminal Justice Act 1991 continues to provide the basic legislative framework for sentencing in England and Wales and that in the middle of the hierarchy of the sentences that it provides lie the community sentences, properly so-called (see Figure 1.1 again). From our discussion of 'community' in Chapter 2 we can also appreciate how narrowly the concept of community is drawn in the legislation regarding sentencing, where it is essentially a question of spatial location. A community sentence is defined in section 6 of the 1991 Act as one which consists of or includes one or more of the six 'community orders', namely:

- a probation order;
- a community service order;
- a combination order (i.e. a mix of the previous two types of order);
- a curfew order;
- a supervision order (10–17-year-olds only); and
- an attendance centre order (10–20-year-olds only).

In this chapter we examine in turn what each of these orders means in practice, how they are used and what procedural requirements must be met before they can be imposed. Issues concerning the enforcement of orders are also examined and the chapter contains commentary on the rather anomalous role of the suspended (prison) sentence and certain other miscellaneous non-custodial measures. The discussion is set in the context of the 1991 sentencing framework, which means that it tends to assume a just deserts rationale for the decisions made in relation to the sentences and their enforcement. It will be appreciated, of course, that just deserts is only one of a number of competing sentencing objectives, but since it retains its primacy in sentencing theory in England and

Wales, it provides the focus for the analysis presented in this chapter. Where appropriate, however, attention will be drawn to the different outcomes which would arise if sentencers were to adopt a competing penal philosophy. Readers will also be referred to Chapter 7, where the body of empirical evidence which seeks to evaluate the effectiveness of community sentences is critically reviewed.

To set the present chapter in some sort of statistical context we can note that an estimated 130,000 people were given a community sentence by the courts in 1995 compared to 79,100 who were sentenced to immediate custody. The number of community sentences was little changed from the year before, following estimated rises of 13 per cent from 1993 and 11 per cent from 1992 to 1993. Most of those who receive community penalties are men: 88 per cent of such penalties imposed in 1994 went to men, although women's share of each of probation, community service and combination orders rose in 1994. Two-thirds of women sentenced to a community penalty in 1994 received a probation order compared to about 40 per cent of men (Home Office, 1996g: Table 3.3). The different positions of men and women within the criminal justice system presents a series of problems which criminologists have belatedly begun to address (Heidensohn, 1994). As yet, however, there is no commonly agreed account of the influence of gender on the operation of the system (see e.g. Hedderman and Hough, 1994) although few would now seek to to deny its effect.

Equally contested are the reasons for the disproportionate representation of black and Asian offenders among those who receive community sentences, by comparison with their position in the general population. Although systematic monitoring of ethnic data really only began with the 1991 Act, early analysis suggests that the percentage of people with African or Afro-Caribbean origins starting community sentences is higher than their representation in the general population while the percentage of Asians is lower than the equivalent resident population figure (Home Office, 1996g: 15). Again, the reasons behind these anomalies are by no means obvious and there is litttle real agreement about the extent and the effect of racial bias discrimination in the criminal justice system (cf. Reiner, 1989; Hood, 1992; Smith, 1994). Few impartial observers, however, would accept without stronger evidence than exists at present that the fact that black people are *seven* times as likely to be in prison than white or south Asian people is entirely due to differences in the rate and pattern of offending between the ethnic groups (Smith, 1994: 1088). We return to this important subject again towards the end of Chapter 7.

Finally, at this point, it can be noted that the age profile of those receiving community penalties is shifting slowly upward to reflect the diversion from formal criminal proceedings of younger offenders as well as the demographic shift to an older population. In 1985 half of all community service orders, for instance, went to under-21s; by 1994 this proportion had fallen to a quarter (Home Office, 1996g: 7).

In terms of the costs of implementation, community sentences work out considerably less expensive than custody, even when allowing for administrative and other overhead costs in the probation service. Government estimates in early 1997 put the monthly cost of each probation order at £190; community service orders cost £140 per month each while supervision orders fell in between these two at £180 (NACRO, 1997). These costs are provisional estimates only and must be treated with some caution, since the sort of management information systems which would gather more reliable information of in-service costs are still being developed (Home Office, 1996g: para. 72). Nonetheless, the gap between the cost of community-based penalties and the average net operating cost of an adult male prisoner at £1,776 per month (NACRO, 1997) is clear and ought to be more persuasive than it is in debates on penal policy.

The range of community sentences

As their position in the sentencing framework would indicate, community sentences are intended to punish offences of a middling order of seriousness. Section 6(3) prevents courts imposing both a probation order and a community service order together other than as a formal combination order, the terms of which are laid out in section 11 of the Act (and discussed further below). Apart from this technical restriction (which does not really amount to a restriction at all, provided the right procedures are followed), two or more community orders may be combined and, importantly, community sentences may also be used in conjunction with a fine or compensation order and an order for costs. The general requirement to obtain the sentenced person's consent before making either a probation order, a community service order or a combination order will be abolished if and when the Crime (Sentences) Act 1997 comes into force, although the imposition of a requirement to submit to treatment for a medical condition or for drug or alcohol dependency as an additional condition of a probation order will still require consent.

The intention behind section 6, as appears from the 1990 White Paper, was to permit the 'stacking up' of community penalties to give sentencers a variety of options to deal with a range of offences of differing seriousness. However, as the discussion in Chapter 2 revealed, neither offences nor punishments may be as susceptible to ranking in this way with quite the precision that the rhetoric of the White Paper would suggest, and community penalties, with all their former rehabilitative associations, may present especial problems in this regard. One undesirable consequence that flows from this imprecision is the difficulty of deciding on an appropriate *non-custodial* penalty with which to punish non-compliance with an earlier community order. Lacking clear guidance on the order of severity of the various gradations and combinations of community penalty that are available, courts may be tempted too often to resolve their uncertainty by resorting to a custodial sentence in the case of someone who has breached the requirements of a community penalty, an 'up-tariffing' effect which is discussed further at the end of this chapter.

The government of the day offered some assistance by suggesting that 'punishment in the community' might be an effective way of dealing with offenders convicted of property crimes and less serious crimes of violence, when financial penalties were thought to be insufficiently punitive to represent the offenders' just deserts (Home Office, 1990a: para. 4.3). The graduated restriction of liberty was to become the 'connecting thread' in the range of community penalties as well as custody: the more serious the offence is, the greater the restrictions on liberty which would be justified as a punishment. Beyond this, and some broadly framed guidelines from the Home Office (Home Office, 1991a; 1991b), however, it was left to the courts to develop precise boundaries between custodial and community sentences, and between the various types of community sentences themselves, on a case-to-case basis, in much the same way as before the 1991 Act (Home Office, 1990a: paras. 2.16–17). This they have done with varying degrees of consistency (Ashworth, 1995: 236–40). The problem with this incremental approach is that the Court of Appeal, who bear the principal responsibility for establishing guidelines for sentencers, receive relatively few appeals involving non-custodial sentences. Their impact in this area has, therefore, been somewhat limited and much has been left to the discretion of sentencing courts and to the influence of the Magistrates' Association and, to a lesser extent, of individual probation officers through the writing of pre-sentence reports.

The community sentence 'threshold'

The difficulties inherent in this relative lack of authoritative guidance on the use of community sentences are compounded by the potential for conflict that exists between the various principles (enunciated in section 6 of the 1991 Act) with which a court must comply before imposing a community sentence. The first of these principles is a general 'gatekeeping' requirement contained in section 6(1) which provides that a court should not pass a community sentence

> unless it is of the opinion that the offence, or the combination of the offence and one or more offences associated with it, was serious enough to warrant such a sentence.

This requirement was inserted to give effect to the concept of a hierarchy of punishments in which community sentences would be distinguishable from other penalties somewhat lower on the scale and imposing fewer restrictions on liberty. It operates as a seriousness 'threshold' for community sentences in precisely the same way as the 'custody threshold' provided in section 1(2) of the Act divides custodial sentences off from those penalties which lie below them in the hierarchy.

Having decided that a community sentence is justified, and that it is appropriate to impose one in all the circumstances of the particular case before them, the court must then attempt to achieve two further objectives in relation to their choice of community sentence. The court must select the particular sentence or sentences which are 'most suitable for the offender' (section 6(2)(a)) *and* they must ensure that the restrictions on liberty imposed by the community sentence 'are commensurate with the seriousness of the offence' (section 6(2)(b)). The first of these requirements is essentially rehabilitative in nature, and in attempting to fulfil it the court will usually receive assistance from a pre-sentence report prepared by a probation officer. The second requirement, however, has a just deserts and, hence, retributive purpose and here sentencers are left with very little help other than their own assessment of the facts of the case and 'feel' for the punitiveness of various non-custodial options. Further, it will not always be easy for the courts to reconcile the just deserts and rehabilitative elements of section 6(2), and the Act gives no indication on which is to take preference.

The correct interpretation in keeping with the predominantly deserts-oriented philosophy of the 1991 framework must be that retributive considerations are supposed first to set both the upper *and* lower limits of the range of community punishments which would be acceptable on commensurability grounds; if within that range a choice of sentences is available, then the court should choose between them by reference to the greater or greatest suitability for the offender (Ashworth, 1992: 247). Section 6(2), if interpreted in the light of an overarching proportionality requirement, has the effect, therefore, of relegating to a secondary role the influence of rehabilitation as an objective even of a community sentence. However, given the lack of detailed guidance and the limited likelihood of detailed scrutiny by the appellate courts in cases not involving custody, it may be that local practices vary according to localised sentencing practices and the personalities and outlook of the sentencers involved and that, as a result, some courts are more rehabilitatively oriented in their choice of sentence than others.

The role of pre-sentence reports

By virtue of section 7(3) of the 1991 Act, before making a probation or supervision order with additional requirements, a community service order or a combination order, a court was to obtain and consider a pre-sentence report prepared by the probation service (or social worker where appropriate in the case of a juvenile). The intention behind this requirement was to ensure that the courts had more detailed information about an offender's personal and social background, and their assessed suitability for a proposed community sentence, the details of which would also normally be described in the report. It was certainly not in the government's contemplation that PSRs should promote non-custodial disposals in the face of considerations of commensurability and, in order to rid reports of former tendencies to advocate or to operate as pleas in mitigation, their content and format were closely prescribed by the 1992 version of the National Standards. Nonetheless, it was hoped that giving sentencers more detailed information would lead to the more effective targeting of community punishments, which would, in turn, increase sentencers' confidence in using non-custodial sentences.

Whatever the government's aims, the mandatory requirement to obtain PSRs before passing certain community sentences was criticised by a number of sentencers who felt that this was leading to an unacceptably high rate of adjournments in many cases where the likely sentencing outcome was clear and reports could make no difference in practice to the disposal (Wasik and Taylor, 1994: 18). Partly in response to such criticism and partly in keeping with the more punitive, pro-custodial drift of sentencing policy after 1993 discussed in Chapters 3 and 4 above (and see Smith, 1996: 151–2), the then government amended the 1991 Act by permitting courts to dispense with the requirement for a PSR if the offender was over 18, and if the court was of the opinion that it was 'unnecessary' to obtain a report in the circumstances of the particular case. This relaxation in the former rule took effect from February 1995 and thereafter, although the requirement to obtain a PSR remains in place, its force was considerably diluted. It remains to be seen what effect this relaxation will eventually have upon the use of community penalties, although it may be less than was originally thought. Early monitoring showed that it continued to be rare for either the Crown Court or for magistrates to actually impose a community sentence without having first obtained a PSR (Home Office, 1997a).

The concomitant easing of the restriction on sentencing to custody without obtaining a PSR may, however, have an impact on the use of community sentences since this would certainly permit any pro-custodial bent that might exist among sentencers to come through unchallenged, as it were, by any contrary evidence, if the power to dispense with reports is used in inappropriate cases. Six per cent fewer PSRs were indeed prepared in 1995 than in 1994, and while some of the reduction must have been due to an overall fall in the numbers of sentences passed, some at least was attributable to the relaxation in the PSR requirements. It is therefore of significance that the reduction was greatest in the Crown Court, which makes greater proportional use of custody than the summary courts (Home Office, 1996e). One undesirable possible side-effect of this change, noted by Ashworth (1995: 306), could be a further increase in the proportion of black offenders being sent to prison, since there is evidence from Hood's study of race and sentencing in the Crown Court in the West Midlands of a strong correlation between custody for black offenders and the lack of a pre-sentence report (Hood, 1992: 156).

With these general considerations in mind, let us now turn to examine each of the individual community orders in more detail.

Probation orders

The history and development of the modern probation order was discussed in Chapters 3 and 4. It will be recalled that under the 1991 Act a probation order became a sentence of the court rather than a disposal in lieu of sentencing. In addition, the 1991 Act consolidated earlier powers to attach specific requirements to orders in an effort to 'strengthen' them and to make their effects more punitive. The rationale behind these developments has also been discussed above, in Chapter 1 and to a greater extent in Chapter 4. Probation orders continue to be regulated by the provisions of the Powers of Criminal Courts Act 1973 ('the 1973 Act'), although in this respect the 1973 Act has, in reality, been virtually rewritten by sections 8 and 9 and schedule 1 of the 1991 Act.

Any person over 16 who is convicted by the court may be ordered to be under the supervision of a probation officer for a period of not less than six and not more than 36 months, provided the court is satisfied that the offence or offences for which they are being sentenced satisfy the seriousness criteria for a community sentence. As has been mentioned already, the long-standing requirement that an offender consent to the making of a probation order has been removed by section 38 of the Crime (Sentences) Act 1997, although this change has not been brought into effect at the time of writing. Before choosing to make a probation order the court must be of the opinion that the order is 'desirable' in the interests either of securing the rehabilitation of the offender, or protecting the public from harm from that person, or preventing him or her from committing further offences (section 2 of the 1973 Act, as amended). In coming to this opinion courts will still *normally* have considered a pre-sentence report (PSR) prepared by a probation officer despite the changed requirements introduced by the Criminal Justice and Public Order Act 1994 (Home Office, 1997a).

Conditions attached to probation orders

In making a probation order courts have traditionally added a condition that the offender should be of good behaviour and lead an industrious life during the currency of the order. This tradition was not taken into the new statutory framework created by the 1991 Act, and although some courts may still continue with the practice (as they are entitled to do), the requirement as to an industrious life is increasingly regarded by probation officers as irrelevant to modern conditions in which the great majority of those under supervision will be unemployed (Walker and

Padfield, 1996: 261). The normal *statutory* requirements of a probation order ('straight' probation, as it is sometimes called informally, to distinguish it from an order with additional, special requirements) are that the person under supervision keep in touch with the supervising officer as required and notify any change of address (Powers of Criminal Courts Act 1973, section 2(6), as amended).

In addition to the normal requirements of a probation order, courts have powers, under section 3 of the 1973 Act, to attach additional requirements to a probation order where they are of the opinion that this is necessary in the interests of rehabilitating the offender or for reasons of public protection or preventing further offending by that person (i.e. the same considerations as apply to the making of an order in the first instance). Again, the emphasis is on identifying 'what works' with the particular offender in question. The range of additional requirements that may lawfully be added under this section are now set out in schedule 1A to the 1973 Act. They comprise:

(a) a requirement as to residence either in a probation hostel or in some other approved place;
(b) the requirement to take part in or refrain from specified activities;
(c) required attendance at a non-residential probation centre for up to 60 days (or longer if in connection with a sexual offence);
(d) requirements as to treatment for a medical or psychiatric condition ('a psychiatric probation order'); and
(e) requirements to undergo treatment for drug or alcohol dependency, if either of these have been a factor in the offence for which the order has been made.

The idea of 'strengthening' probation orders by the addition of specific additional requirements was far from new, even in 1991. Apart from the conditions relating to drug and alcohol treatment, all the others had existed in some form or another before the 1991 Act. The requirements to attend a probation centre (formerly a probation day, or day training centre) or to take part in other specified activities, for instance, had been introduced in 1972 and 1982 respectively and their role in helping to move probation up the tariff of punishments has already been discussed in Chapter 4. Similarly, the conceptual linkage between more 'demanding' probation regimes and the reduction of prison populations was also fairly well established, if not always confirmed by research. Intensive probation programmes had operated in this way for some years in the United States (Vass, 1990; Lurigio and Petersilia, 1992) and although earlier experiments in England with this approach had not been very encouraging from a crime control perspective (Folkard *et al.*, 1976), more recent experience of intensive probation with young adult offenders did suggest that such orders could operate to divert high-tariff offenders from custody without thereby increasing their rate of reoffending over those receiving custodial sentences (Brownlee and Joanes, 1993; Mair *et al.*, 1994; Brownlee, 1995; and see McGuire and Priestley, 1995: 20; Oldfield, 1996).

In many senses, therefore, the consolidated provisions of the new schedule 1A represented merely an extension, or reinforcement, perhaps, of existing policy (Raynor, 1996a: 14). Under that policy 'strengthened' probation orders which offered the prospect of 'intensive' supervision involving not inconsiderable restrictions on liberty were held out to sentencers as sufficiently punitive to deal with quite serious offenders who might otherwise have come close to the threshold of a custodial sentence. In other words, 'strengthened' or 'intensive' probation orders were intended to operate close to the top of the sentencing tariff where they might serve to divert at least some offenders who might otherwise be sent to immediate custody.

For this reason intensive probation orders fitted very well into both the reductionist and the punitive aspects of the twin-track philosophy which had originally informed the 1991 sentencing framework (Windlesham, 1993: 221). The 1990 White Paper had been quite explicit that the purpose of including additional requirements in probation orders was to increase the level of discipline exerted by such orders by matching the 'severity' of the restrictions on liberty to an assessment of the seriousness of the offence. In other words, the addition of special requirements, while they might also increase the intensity of therapeutic interventions, were intended by the government of the day primarily to make probation orders more punitive and, thus, more attractive to sentencers (Home Office, 1990a: paras. 4.4–4.5). As the discussion of the 1974 Younger Report in Chapter 1, above, reveals, the harnessing of 'illiberal means' (increased punitiveness) to 'liberal ends' (diversion from custody) had been part of the policy debate for at least fifteen years before the 1990 White Paper was published. What was new was the confidence and certainty with which the Thatcher government of the late 1980s set this philosophy out in its various policy documents, a mood which resulted in part from their apparent political invulnerability but which had a great deal more to do with the paradigmatic shift in penal and criminological thought that had taken place in Britain and elsewhere in the intervening period (see again Chapter 4).

What probation involves in practice

The basic requirement of a probation order is that the person under supervision maintains regular contact with their supervising officer. The National Standards suggest that an appointment for a first meeting should be made wherever possible before the offender has left court and that this first meeting should normally take place within five working days of sentencing. At the first meeting the person under supervision is given an individual supervision plan setting out the purpose, objectives and desired outcomes for the supervision period, together with the methods to be tried and the frequency of contacts. Again the National Standards are prescriptive on the last point: a person on a 'straight' probation order should attend a minimum of 12 appointments – normally weekly – with the supervising officer or somebody acting under his or her direction in the first three months of the order, six in the next three months and then at least one each month until the completion of the supervision. Attending appointments obviously gives the officer an opportunity to work towards effecting some change in the offender's attitude and outlooks and is thus linked to the rehabilitative objective of probation. But the requirement to attend also represents a restriction on the liberty of the person under supervision in line with the idea of a 'connecting thread' which runs through all the penalties in the 1991 framework. This punitive aspect is given emphasis by the strict recording requirements placed on officers and by the attempt in the National Standards to link non-attendance much more consistently to breach proceedings.

During the period of supervision the officer is required to identify the operant causes of the offending behaviour of those under supervision. Antisocial behaviour should be 'confronted' (a tactic prescribed very clearly in the previous government's blueprint for the probation service of the 1990s: Home Office, 1990b: para. 3.2) in an attempt to encourage a greater sense of personal responsibility (including responsibility for their crimes) and discipline, and a heightened awareness of the impact of crimes on victims, the community and those who commit them. In line with the objective of protecting the public, the officer should also undertake an assessment of the risk posed by those under their supervision 'systematically and at regular intervals' and should use these assessments as the basis for 'appropriate action' such as applying to the court for additional conditions to be inserted into the probation order. Supervision of a person on a probation order must be in accordance with a supervision plan which is 'demanding and effective'. In response to several high-profile media crusades against supervision orders which included so-called 'safari holidays' and the like, the 1995 edition of the National Standards requires (in bold print!) that all activities should be carefully assessed to ensure that their location or nature could not give the impression of providing a reward for offending. In particular, the possibility of offenders being sent abroad as part of a probation supervision is expressly excluded without the least consideration of any possible rehabilitative advantage that might arise from such a strategy (Home Office *et al.*, 1995: 20). Clearly, the siren voices of populist outrage have drowned out more sensible or principled debate of the merits or demerits of any particular initiative involving a foreign element.

Supervising officers are also expected to intervene to remedy practical obstacles preventing rehabilitation such as lack of education or skills, homelessness or drug or alcohol misuse (Home Office *et al.*, 1995: 17). Methods to be employed in obtaining these various objectives include individual or group counselling, or referral to a specialist team or facility such as an alcohol or drugs therapy group or an anger-management course, provided either by the probation service or in partnership with the private or voluntary sector. In allocating offenders to different programmes much emphasis is now placed on the need to distinguish between 'crimino-genic' and 'non-criminogenic' circumstances in an offender's life, particularly by those who favour the so-called 'cognitive behavioural' or 'reasoning and rehabilitation' approach (Ross et al., 1988). Cognitive behavioural programmes are designed to help offenders improve their cognitive and reasoning skills as a step towards altering their attitudes towards offending behaviour (see e.g. Raynor et al., 1994: ch. 5; Knott, 1995). Programmes are designed to confront offenders with the con-sequences of their behaviour both for themselves and for others and to stimulate the development of alternative responses to problems within offenders' lives which have contributed directly toward or supported offending behaviour in the past and which place the offender at risk of reoffending in the future (McGuire and Priestley, 1995: 4; McGuire, 1996). On the (by no means uncontested) assumption that such causal relation-ships can indeed be identified with sufficient certainty to provide a basis for remedial intervention, probation programmes are being designed to focus on the criminogenic 'needs' rather than problems which are more distantly related, or unrelated, to offending.

All of this activity takes place in the context of systematic and continu-ing 'risk assessment' by the supervising officer which is, in part, a prevent-ive measure designed to demonstrate the commitment of the service to the maintenance of public protection from those under its supervision. 'Risk' is classified on an actuarial basis, i.e. by relating prior history of offending to statistical tables derived from large samples showing sub-sequent rates of reconviction over time (McGuire and Priestley, 1995: 14). Paradoxically, however, risk assessment also finds a place within the 'revivi-fied' rehabilitation agenda – the 'what works' philosophy so dominant in current rehabilitative thinking within the service. As Chapter 2 revealed, the era of 'nothing works' has by no means extinguished the quest for effective reformative strategies within the probation service, but it has encouraged a greater selectivity in the range of strategies employed and a greater emphasis on targeting interventions on those thought most likely to respond to them. In this context risk assessment can be used to ensure as far as possible that there is a matching between offender risk and degree of service intervention, so that those with a lower risk classifica-tion receive lower or minimal intervention.

Who is sentenced to probation?

Despite the new higher profile given to probation orders in the 1991 sentencing framework and the smack of firmness and resolution that has attended almost every development since then, the attempt to launch probation with a new, tough image has led to only a small increase in its use. The increase has been more marked in the magistrates' courts than at the Crown Court, but, of all offenders sentenced in 1995, 10.9 per cent received a probation order compared to 10.1 per cent in 1990 and 9.9 in 1992 (the first year of operation of the new framework). In real numbers this resulted in 1,700 fewer probation orders being made in the criminal courts in 1995 than 1990, since there has also been a fall in the total number of people sentenced over that period (Home Office, 1996f). Most orders run for one year or less; 61 per cent of all new orders in 1994 were for a period of one year's supervision or less, compared with 36 per cent requiring two years' supervision and only 2 per cent of all orders being for the maximum permissible three-year period.

If there has not been a massive increase in the imposition of probation, patterns in the way that orders are used have indeed changed over the past two decades. Whereas in the mid-1980s half of all offenders starting probation supervision had been guilty of offences of theft or handling stolen goods, these sorts of offences accounted for fewer than one third of all probation 'starts' in 1994. Whether courts have become readier to use probation to deal with the more serious, 'up-tariff' offences in this period, as was the government's intention, is a good deal less clear from the statistics, however. On the basis of returns made by the courts, the proportionate use of probation in cases involving violence or burglary remained constant or decreased between 1984 and 1994, compared with a threefold increase in the use of probation for summary-only offences (Home Office, 1996g). This points to something of a 'down-tariffing' effect although a large part of this apparent movement is attributable to the reclassification of certain indictable offences as summary in 1988 (Home Office, 1992). A different picture emerges if one takes details of offences based on returns by the probation service itself. These figures purport to show a small but significant increase over the same ten years in the use of probation to punish offences of violence against the person and less of an increase, proportionately, in the numbers of probation orders being made in cases of summary offences.

The disparity within the official statistics is unhelpful, to say the least, and although the Home Office indicate that details of offences based on returns by the probation service are considered less reliable than those based on returns by the courts, this still leaves room for considerable uncertainty. Fortunately, another measure of likely sentence severity, the previous criminal history of the offender, provides some additional evidence on the point. Since 1985 the proportion of those commencing probation orders who were known to have served a previous custodial sentence has risen from 30 per cent to 41 per cent in 1995 (Home Office, 1996g; 1997c). This may be taken as a fairly reliable indicator that the probation service is indeed now supervising in the community a greater proportion of offenders who might previously have been sentenced to imprisonment on the basis of their recidivism, although the precise extent of this 'diversion from custody' or 'down-tariffing' effect is notoriously difficult to measure (Pease *et al.*, 1977).

Despite this apparent escalation in the seriousness of the range of offenders with whom probation officers now deal, nearly three-quarters of all probation orders run their full course without breach for reoffending (Home Office, 1996g). Evidence about the effectiveness of probation and other orders in influencing offending behaviour is discussed in Chapter 7 but, to pre-empt that discussion slightly, it would appear from the most authoritative Home Office study available that, while perhaps six out of ten people who are subject to probation orders will reoffend within two years, there is currently no significant difference between reconviction rates for custody and all community penalties including probation (Lloyd *et al.*, 1994; Home Office, 1997c). Indeed, as we shall see later, other more localised studies have produced evidence suggesting that probation, whether strengthened or not, performs at least as well as prison on the measure of reconvictions, particularly if reoffending is tracked over five years rather than two.

Community service

The origins of the Community Service Order (CSO) and the ambiguity that surrounded its purposes when it first emerged have been outlined in Chapter 1 (for further discussion see e.g. Whitehead, 1990; McIvor, 1992). Eventually, it became accepted that the CSO could operate as an alternative to custody for those whose offending was so serious as to merit imprisonment (see *R.* v. *Clarke* [1982] 1 WLR 1090). Although the 1991 Act dispensed with the concept of 'alternatives' to custody (Home Office, 1990a: para. 4.1), the CSO with its associations with hard and demanding work in and for the community fitted easily into the philosophy underlying the new sentencing framework, as a demanding community penalty which is subject to the seriousness threshold contained in section 6 of the 1991 Act. To emphasise its relative position in the hierarchy of sentences the National Standards provide that community service is only available for offences punishable with imprisonment.

The basic power to make community service orders is contained in section 14 of the Powers of Criminal Courts Act 1973, as amended. This provides that the Crown Court, a magistrates' court or a youth court may require a convicted offender over the age of 16 to perform between 40 and 240 hours of unpaid work for the community at intervals over the succeeding 12 months. The prior consent of the offender to the making of such an order had always been taken to be an essential prerequisite in order to avoid the accusation that community service amounted to the sort of 'forced or compulsory labour' forbidden by Article 4.2 of the European Convention on Human Rights. However, as part of its increasingly punitive and authoritarian approach to sentencing policy, the then Conservative government announced in 1995 that it considered such an interpretation of European law 'over-cautious' and a 'derogation from the authority of the court' (Home Office, 1995a: paras. 4.20, 11.1). Ample safeguards existed to ensure that the conditions under which community service was carried out were decent and humane and the due process requirements of the criminal trial meant that its imposition could not be considered unjust or oppressive. The key issue, it was said, was not consent at the outset of the order but willingness to comply throughout the sentence. It was a matter for the courts, not offenders, to decide on the appropriate sentence and, therefore, courts should be free to impose CSOs without the consent of the offender. Once such a sentence was passed, then, as with a fine, it was a matter for the offender whether to comply with the order or not. Consent at the time of sentencing was not considered a very good guide to a defendant's ultimate compliance and, in the then government's opinion, the whole consent procedure could give the impression of hesitancy on the part of the court or that the court was subject to 'the whims' of an offender. The removal of the consent requirement by the Crime (Sentences) Act 1997 was one of the last acts of the Conservative government before its removal from office in May of that year, but the new Labour administration quickly made it clear that they approved of the policy and intended to bring it into force at an early opportunity. This was one of many signals which indicated the extent to which the new government intended to continue with the punitive rhetoric of their predecessors (see, further, Chapter 8).

We have already seen that the absolute requirement for the court to obtain a PSR before imposing a community sentence (save where the case involved an indictable only offence) was removed in 1994. Notwithstanding this liberalisation, it is likely that courts will still ask for a PSR before sentencing to community service in the overwhelming majority of cases, and quite properly so. It is hard to imagine how a court could determine the suitability of such an order without some detailed assessment of an offender's motivation and likely response to the range of work schemes that were available in the local area. Indeed, the previous government's decision to remove the requirement for consent from community sentences was predicated upon the assumption that courts would rely on PSRs for an assessment of the defendant's likely compliance with a proposed order (Home Office, 1995a: para. 11.2). It seems unlikely, therefore, that the high level of PSR preparation in cases resulting in a CSO (which reached 92 per cent in 1994: Home Office, 1996g: 24) will decline to any significant extent.

The organisation of community service

The administration of community service orders is the responsibility of the probation service, although the sort of tasks undertaken will quite frequently involve offenders working under the direct supervision of staff who work for other organisations. As far as is practicable the times at which an offender is required to work must not conflict with observation of his or her religious practices or interfere with paid employment or education. The aim is to restrict an offender's liberty by curtailing their choice of how they spend their leisure, while at the same time affording them an opportunity to experience the possible rewards of contributing to the welfare of others. Unemployed offenders are expected to continue to seek paid work during the currency of their CSO and arrangements under the order should not impede this. The type of work available varies from area to area, but typical examples involve helping the elderly or handicapped with domestic tasks like cooking, decorating or gardening, renovating and maintaining community amenities or working in youth clubs and other facilities for the young or disadvantaged.

Commencement, monitoring and enforcement of community service are all subject to the National Standards, although, once again, actual practices may vary from area to area. In every case an assessment of risk of self-harm and harm to the public should be carried out before a work placement is arranged and this assessment should inform the decision about the sort of placement which would be appropriate. The first work session should take place as soon as possible after the assessment and in any event within 10 days of the making of the order. A minimum work rate of five hours per week is specified in the National Standards, with the maximum being pegged to 21 hours in any one week. Instructions given to those on community service by their supervising probation officer prohibit among other things drunkenness, lack of effort, violent or aggressive behaviour or 'other conduct or language that might reasonably give serious offence to probation staff, other persons under supervision or members of the public' (Home Office *et al.*, 1995: 37). The broad reach of these prohibitions serves to underline the disciplinary role that community service can fulfil, making it a suitable vehicle for the extension of the sort of penal disciplines that Michel Foucault identified into the wider community (Foucault, 1977). This disciplinary function is enforced by strict requirements about investigating non-attendance or other evidence of non-compliance, backed ultimately by the breach procedure discussed at the beginning of this chapter.

Selection for community service

A study of sentencing practice in the Crown Court in the mid-1980s suggested that community service was considered by judges to be a more directly substitutable 'alternative' to custody and, hence, higher 'up-tariff' than other non-custodial sentences (Moxon, 1988). Since then, however, community service may have moved 'down-tariff' by comparison with the 'strengthened' probation order and, more particularly, the combination order (since the latter's introduction in 1992). Certainly, the proportion of those commencing community service who were known to have served a previous custodial sentence fell in that period from 36 to 29 per cent while increases on this measure were recorded for both probation and combination orders (Home Office, 1996g: 7).

Ashworth (1995: 279–80) suggests on the basis of a review of appellate decisions that CSOs might commonly be used to punish young burglars with few previous convictions whose present offences were not particularly aggravated and also in cases of moderate levels of violence where there are mitigating circumstances. He notes, however, that statistically twice as many offenders are sentenced to community service following conviction for theft or handling as for any other sort of offence and, in fact, only about 11 per cent of community service 'starts' in 1994 were connected to offences of burglary or violence against the person (Home Office, 1996g: Table 3.4). The percentages of those in each offence category who are sentenced to community service are broadly similar to those who are placed on probation (*ibid.*), although only a negligible number of sexual offenders receive a CSO. Empirical studies of existing community service schemes tend to point to the tendency for those sentenced to community service to be predominantly white, male, single and unemployed with a few previous convictions but only rarely any previous custodial experience (McIvor, 1992: 35; and see Home Office, 1996g: Table 7.2 on ethnic group). Once more, information on reoffending after CS is discussed in Chapter 7. Briefly, this suggests that, given what we know about the offending behaviour of those who undergo community service, its use certainly cannot be ruled out on grounds of public protection, and may be favoured on other grounds such as reparation, benefit to the general community and cost.

Combination orders

The power to impose both probation and community service in a combined order was one of the principal innovations in the 1991 sentencing framework for England and Wales, although a similar power had existed for some time in Scotland. According to the 1990 White Paper, in introducing the new sentence the government intended to provide courts with an option for dealing primarily with persistent property offenders – those whose offending was of only moderate seriousness but who might, nonetheless, have ended up in prison pre-1991 because their previous bad record had progressively extinguished any possible mitigation they might otherwise have claimed. The new order was therefore clearly intended to have some diversionary effect but, in keeping with the underlying philosophy of the reforms, it was expected to achieve this primarily by establishing its punitive credentials. So, to the reductive, rehabilitative potential of the probation 'element' of the sentence, an element of retributive reparation through compulsory work for the community was added. The combination of the two elements is supposed to create a tough and demanding community sentence at the upper end of the tariff of non-custodial penalties.

The new combination order was created by section 11 of the 1991 Act. Under this section courts are empowered to sentence an offender to the normal range of probation supervision (i.e. between 12 and 36 months) and at the same time to order him or her to carry out unpaid work in the community for a period of between 40 and 100 hours at the determination of the court. The same observations regarding consent and the obtaining of a PSR which have been made in relation to probation and community service obviously apply to this order, which is, in essence, nothing more than a marriage of the other two. It will be noted, however, that the upper limit for hours to be worked is less than the 240 hours permissible under a normal CSO. Such a restriction was necessary, in the government's view, to prevent the combined order becoming 'unrealistically demanding', and as a consequence increasing the likelihood of an offender being 'breached' and perhaps ending up in custody after all.

Similar considerations are, presumably, supposed to temper the court's powers to attach to the probation element of the order all the normal additional requirements which could be attached to any probation order. The 1990 White Paper is silent on this point, however, and the provisions as to the commencement, administration and enforcement of the order as set out in the 1995 National Standards are simply those of the constituent elements without any specific addition or requirement. A combination order may not be further combined with a second probation or community service order for the same offence, for obvious reasons, but, subject to those express exclusions, section 6 of the 1991 permits the addition of other punishments, including a curfew order, a fine or compensation subject to the general principles of desert and commensurability.

The use of the combined order

As courts have become accustomed to using this relatively new order there are indications in the statistics that it is reaching the high-tariff offender at which it was targeted. Of those who commenced a combination order in 1994, 48 per cent had already served a previous custodial sentence compared to 42 per cent of those commencing probation and 29 per cent of those ordered to do community service (Home Office, 1996g: para. 28). Additionally, the same statistics record a slightly higher proportionate use of combination orders among those convicted of offences of violence or burglary than is true of either probation or community service orders alone. The picture is not entirely clear, however, since combination orders are also used proportionately more often for summary only offences than the other two orders. It may well be, therefore, as Ashworth suggests, that there is a need for clearer guidance to be given to sentencers on the proper relationship between the three main community orders to ensure a greater differentiation in their use (Ashworth, 1995: 282). Because of its relative novelty, information on the reconvictions of those who have been sentenced to a combination order is somewhat limited, but details of what is known are given in Chapter 7.

Curfew orders

Section 12 of the 1991 Act gives courts powers to confine a convicted person over 16 to a specified place or places for periods of between two and 12 hours a day for up to six months either as a sentence in its own right or in combination with other community or financial penalties. Although novel in this form, the curfew order is, in effect, an expansion into the adult system of an earlier power, available since 1982, to include 'night restrictions' as part of a juvenile supervision order. The inclusion of such a power among the range of community penalties was intended not so much to confine people more or less permanently at home (as a sort of do-it-yourself imprisonment, similar to some home confinement programmes in the United States: Ball *et al.*, 1988) as to keep specific offenders away from particular places like shopping centres or pubs, at clearly determined times. It was claimed that, if used in this way, curfews could be helpful in reducing some forms of crime such as thefts of and from cars, pub brawls and other types of disorder (Home Office, 1990a: para. 4.20). It is clear from the tenor of the 1990 White Paper and the probation Green Paper that had preceded it (Home Office, 1988a) that although the curfew order was a sentence in its own right, the then government saw its most likely use being in combination with other community or financial penalties, adding the punitive 'bite' of an element of incapacitation to other less restrictive disposals. (Curfews, it should be noted, can also be imposed as a condition of the granting of bail, a factor which tends to confirm that they are more preventive than punitive in nature.)

As with many of the innovations in penal policy adopted by the Thatcher and Major governments, home confinement through curfews was essentially an American idea, the feasibility and desirability of which was already being questioned in its home country by the time that it was imported into Britain. The number of Americans subjected to electronically monitored home confinement had rocketed from less than 100 in 1986 to nearly 12,000 four years later (Renzema, 1992). This dramatic increase had been driven chiefly by a chronic and deepening overcrowding crisis in the country's prisons, and took place despite an emerging evaluative literature which tended to suggest that the incapacitative and public safety potential of the sanction had been overstated by those with an interest in promoting it (Baumer and Mendelsohn, 1992). Nowith-standing this uncertainty, the British government persisted with the intro-duction of the measure in 1991 (and later with its extension to fine defaulters in the Crime (Sentences) Act 1997) in the face of considerable opposition from civil liberty and penal reform groups and many within the probation service (NACRO, 1989; Nellis, 1991).

Objections to curfew orders

Principled objections to the use of curfews emphasise the extent to which such measures impinge upon commonly valued rights of free movement and association within the family and elsewhere, particularly when they are enforced through electronic 'tagging' devices which add what many consider to be an extra element of degradation to the whole procedure. These 'collateral' pains are said to increase the punitive 'bite' of the cur-few order beyond its supposed position in the sentencing hierarchy, on deserts principles. Such objections are not unimportant, but they are susceptible to the counter-argument that home confinement sentences which genuinely divert from custody those who would otherwise have been imprisoned promote, rather than diminish, the liberty of the individual.

However, the issue is not simply an empirical question of how far curfews are actually working in a diversionary fashion (on which point, see e.g. Frost and Stephenson, 1989; Mair and Nee, 1990; Baumer and Mendelsohn, 1992). For even if the empirical evidence were unequi-vocally in favour of the curfew order on this point (which it is not), there remains the normative assertion that the 'anything-but-prison theory' is itself only one version of a wider misconception that an individual can-not complain about how he or she is being punished if something even nastier might have been done to them (von Hirsch, 1993: 80–1). Severity is *one* dimension along which punishments can be evaluated against eth-ical standards, von Hirsch argues, and on this dimension a curfew even with electronic monitoring may be less severe than imprisonment. But 'degradingness' is another dimension in the equation and von Hirsch seeks to make his point against intrusive punishments like 'tagging' by analogy with other, more obviously humiliating practices:

> The stocks may, indeed, be less severe than incarceration; and thus, if
> the person involved has been convicted of a lesser felony, may be less
> violative of proportionality than prolonged imprisonment. The sanction
> is objectionable nevertheless, on the ulterior grounds of its extraordinarily
> humiliating character.

Andrew Ashworth makes a similar sort of objection when he draws attention to the requirements of the European Convention on Human Rights, particularly article 3 (on inhuman and degrading punishment) and article 8 (on privacy), and his conclusion that, despite the existing requirement for an offender's consent, the tagging element of curfew orders offends against both cannot lightly be dismissed (Ashworth, 1995:

276). This point is moot, and is almost certain to be tested in the European Court of Human Rights before long, if the government goes ahead with its commitment to extend the use of tagging.

Practical problems with electronic monitoring

Whatever the force of such objections of principle, considerations of a more practical nature have been behind the failure, so far, to extend the availability of curfew orders beyond a small number of areas which have been involved in 'piloting' the sentence. Given the objectives of a curfew order, its success depends on effective enforcement. A court order, after all, cannot by itself compel a person to stay where they are supposed to be if they do not choose to do so. Some back-up coercion is required and that in turn can only be applied if non-compliance with the original order is first detected. The 1990 White Paper made clear the government's belief that effective electronic monitoring would overcome most difficulties about enforcing curfew orders. With a distinctly modernist air, the White Paper declared that the criminal justice system should take advantage of modern technology 'when it is sensible and practical to do so' (Home Office, 1990a: paras. 4.20–1). Despite the fact that electronic monitoring had been tested in connection with bail curfews with largely negative results, before the 1991 Act was passed (Mair and Nee, 1990), the government chose to press on, its faith in technology apparently undiluted.

In imposing a curfew order, therefore, a court is required by section 12(4) of the 1991 Act to make some suitably authorised person responsible for monitoring the offender's whereabouts during the curfew period. This was allied closely with the additional power in section 13 to secure compliance with the order by the fitting of an electronic device, or 'tag', to an offender, but only if the Home Secretary had certified that suitable arrangements existed locally for this type of monitoring. The extension under section 37 of the Crime (Sentences) Act 1997 of the power to make a curfew order on those who have failed or are unable to pay fines, if brought into force, will be subject to the same restrictions. However, apart from specifying that those who will carry out the monitoring of the order must be approved by the Home Office, the 1991 Act is silent as to whom this responsibility should be entrusted. It is this lacuna, together with the considerable reluctance of the probation service to fill it, which explains why the power to make curfew orders is not yet available throughout the whole country despite enabling legislation in the 1994 Criminal Justice and Public Order Act and the extension to its use in the 1997 Act.

The curfew order has always been a controversial measure, and NAPO have consistently made clear their opposition to any involvement in implementing and monitoring orders. In anticipation, perhaps, of difficulties that might arise because of this, the then government took powers in the 1991 Act to contract out the monitoring of curfew orders to 'other persons', including private security firms. Were a curfew order to be used as a sentence in its own right, it would be the responsibility of the security firm or other agency providing the monitoring to report any violations direct to the court which had made the order, whereas, in situations where a curfew was imposed in combination with a probation order, breaches of the curfew would be reported to the probation service for consideration of what further action would be appropriate under the National Standards (Home Office, 1990a: para. 4.23). This dual responsibility, which appears potentially to give employees of private security firms equivalent 'breach' powers to probation officers, was highly controversial when first proposed and this issue may well excite further hostility if and when curfew orders come into general use.

Further pilot studies were started in 1995 in Greater Manchester, Norfolk and Berkshire and will continue at least until 1988. During the first year of study 83 offenders had been 'tagged' by magistrates as part of a curfew order. Of the 83 orders, 56 (75 per cent) had been completed successfully, seven following breach action. Though there were fewer technical problems than in the pre-1991 pilots, researchers still reported a hesitancy on the part of sentencers to use the new order and a great deal of opposition among probation staff particularly in the early stages of the trials (Mair and Mortimer, 1997). Nevertheless, the new government has made clear its determination to extend the use of electronic monitoring in conjunction with other community penalties in an all-too-familiar attempt to make them 'tough' enough to suit the supposedly punitive instincts of sentencers (*The Guardian*, 23 June 1997; *The Daily Mail*, 28 July 1997). In what appears to have been a pre-emptive and deliberate attempt to 'soften up' probation officers' resistance to this policy, the Home Office (in a move that was largely without precedent) released to the press the results of internal research which showed that one in ten of all murders committed in England and Wales in a year were carried out by someone under probation supervision either as a community sentence or after release from prison (*The Times*, 2 July 1997). The ideological impact of this information was considerable and it laid the ground for the announcement less than a month later of the proposals to extend 'tagging', on the grounds that there could be no expansion of the use of community-based penalties without an increase in the level of public protection afforded by heightened surveillance.

Obviously, it is too early to say when and how far these proposals will be implemented in practice, but experience elsewhere suggests that the capacities of technology might not be so all-encompassing as proponents might hope. As one American study of similar initiatives ruefully concluded:

> In the age of electronics it is not surprising that some have hoped that electronic monitoring would be a technological magic bullet, solving difficult problems with little effort or cost. To those who have seen other new and promising innovations, it comes as no surprise that there is no magic bullet.

(Baumer and Mendelsohn, 1992: 66)

Supervision orders

The most common community sentence given to young offenders is a supervision order (Audit Commission, 1996). A supervision order is to all extents and purposes the juvenile equivalent of a probation order for an adult. Under section 12 of the Children and Young Persons Act 1969, as amended, a youth court or the Crown Court may order a young offender aged between 10 and 18 to be under the supervision of the local social services department (or possibly of the probation service if he or she is aged 13 or more) for a period of up to three years. No minimum period is specified in the statute but in practice most supervision orders tend to be for periods of one or two years (Wasik, 1993). Since a supervision order is one of the designated community sentences under the 1991 Act, courts cannot make such an order unless the normal seriousness criteria and commensurability requirements of section 6 of that Act are satisfied. Unlike probation, the making of a supervision order was never subject to the consent of the juvenile offender, although certain additional requirements could only be added if the subject of the order agreed. The need for consent has been removed by the Crime (Sentences) Act 1997 as far as 'stipulated' intermediate treatment (IT) requirements under section 12A of the 1969 Act are concerned, but it is retained for other additional requirements, such as discretionary IT activities under section 12 or a requirement to submit to treatment for a medical or mental condition.

The aims of a supervision order

The supervision order shares with probation the three purposes of securing the rehabilitation of the offender, protecting the public from harm from the offender and preventing the offender from committing further offences. In addition, the National Standards provide that a supervision order should aim to 'encourage and assist the child or young person in his or her development towards a responsible and law-abiding life, thereby promoting the welfare of the offender'. This distinctly welfarist orientation is a survival of the principle first enunciated in section 44 of the 1933 Children and Young Persons Act that all courts must have regard to the welfare of the child or young person who appears before them, and section 14 of the 1969 Act continues to emphasise the supervising officer's duty to 'advise, assist and befriend' the supervised person.

The continuance, indeed the promotion, of a more caring approach within the official discourse round supervision orders marks a distinction between probation with adults and the supervision of juveniles, and in respect of juveniles the law recognises a duty to assist in the emotional and social development of the individual offender. The Audit Commission investigation into responses to youth crime found that young people on supervision orders are usually required to spend an hour a week with a social worker, often discussing personal problems such as benefit claims, efforts to arrange training or employment, and housing issues (Audit Commission, 1996: paras. 59–65). However, the welfare consideration is a diminishing duty and the older the juvenile, the less the welfare considerations apply. For juveniles aged 16 and 17, where there is a choice of making either a supervision or a probation order, the courts in deciding which order is more suitable will take into account *inter alia* an individual's maturity, level of independence from family, and whether other types of support are needed and being received from social services. The more 'grown up' a juvenile is, the more likely he or she is to be made subject to the adult form of supervision through the probation service.

'Intermediate treatment orders'

Mention has already been made of 'intermediate treatment', or 'IT' as it is almost universally called. This is a generic term which descibes a range of activities including offence-focused individual or group counselling, skill-based work placements or challenging outdoor pursuits. They are 'intermediate' in the sense that while they are still part of a supervision order, they have some of the characteristics of another more restrictive disposal, the care order. Where IT conditions are imposed for periods not exceeding 90 days in aggregate a juvenile may be required to reside at a place determined by their supervisor (such as an outdoor activities centre) and must otherwise follow the directions of their supervising officer (for instance, to present themselves for counselling sessions).

Supervision orders with IT requirements were the precursor of the 'strengthened' probation order for adults, discussed above in Chapter 4. Under the initial impetus of a group of academics from Lancaster University in the early 1980s (Thorpe *et al.*, 1980) a new approach, known as 'systems management', came to dominate much of local and central government thinking on juvenile justice. This approach placed great emphasis on analysing and understanding the relationships which existed between the various agencies involved with juveniles in a local area so that specific interventions could be made at key points in those working relations to reduce the reliance of the system on custodial measures. Part of the strategy involved presenting sentencers with realistic alternatives to custody or care, where earlier interventions had not succeeded in diverting juvenile offenders from prosecution. So, powers of direction available under section 12 of the Children and Young Persons Act 1969 were used to create 'intensive' IT programmes targeted at 'heavy-end' young offenders, i.e. those whose offending behaviour made them prime candidates for some sort of custodial disposal if no viable alternative could be found.

Multi-agency working, effective targeting, detailed advocacy in reports prepared for courts, and monitoring and dissemination of outcomes were all seen as essential parts of this 'secondary diversion' strategy. In order to satisfy complaints by some magistrates that supervisors were being too permissive and undemanding in the directions they gave, the 1982 Criminal Justice Act had introduced a new section 12A which allowed the courts themselves to stipulate the conditions that would be imposed on the juvenile under supervision (hence, 'stipulated' IT). Despite this, IT conditions are more normally included under the pre-existing section 12 ('discretionary' IT) because, as Wasik notes wryly, most magistrates are wise enough to appreciate that the decision whether a particular 16-year-old should be required to learn to canoe or ride a horse hardly seems 'appropriate to the judicial function' (Wasik, 1993: 203).

This general approach found favour with the government, who responded in 1983 with £15 million of funding for local authorities to develop 'intensive' IT programmes as part of a 'systems' approach to managing juvenile offending. The spread of the IT initiative, together with a more progressive approach towards cautioning juvenile offenders (Home Office, 1985) and certain demographic changes, is credited with producing a significant drop in the numbers of custodial sentences imposed on juveniles by the end of the 1980s (Allen, 1991). Whereas in 1981 some 7,700 young males were sent to custody, by 1990–92 the figure was less than 1,500 (Cavadino and Dignan, 1997: 258). Equally significantly, this reduction in the use of custody had been achieved without any evidence of a surge in youth crime (Home Office, 1990a: para. 3.6). The government's firm, if temporary, endorsement of the approach came in 1988 when it announced that it wished to see the availability of IT-type programmes extended to the next oldest category of offenders, those aged 18–21 (Home Office, 1988b).

Although this whole approach was effectively undermined by the punitive counter-reforms of 1993 discussed in Chapter 1 above, the Labour Party have signalled their intention to revive government interest in intensive community sentences for young offenders within a new legal framework involving multi-agency Youth Offender Teams in each local authority area (Labour Party, 1996: 13). There is currently no shortage of working examples on which to base future good practice (ISTD, 1997) and much effort has already gone into the evaluation of IT projects and the identification of good practice (NACRO, 1987; Bottoms, 1995b; Utting, 1996), although not all commentaries have been so sanguine about the desirability of this approach (see e.g. Pitts, 1988).

Parental responsibilities and supervision orders

One of the central focuses of the 1991 Act was on securing greater parental responsibility for the delinquent acts of children through the imposition of penal sanctions on the parents of young offenders who came before the courts. So, for instance, section 58(1) of the Act places an obligation upon the court to bind over the parent or guardian of an offender under 16 if it is satisfied that to do so would be desirable in the interests of preventing further offending by the juvenile. The wisdom and practicality of such a coercive approach may be questioned, particularly since offending behaviour is in many instances a product of dysfunctional family lives in which relationships of control and influence have already broken down.

Nonetheless, a further power was inserted into section 58 by the 1994 Criminal Justice and Public Order Act whereby a court which has passed a community sentence, including a supervision order, on a young offender can bind over his or her parent or guardian requiring them to ensure that the juvenile complies with the conditions of the order. The new Labour government have also committed themselves in their pre-election policy documents to securing an increase in the level of parental responsibility, but through different avenues, such as compulsory counselling and guidance, which do not penalise parents directly for the non-compliance of their offspring with court orders (Labour Party, 1997a: 5). It is therefore possible that the powers to punish parents for the failure of their children in relation to supervision orders may shortly be replaced in practice, if not in law, by more positive initiatives to strengthen and rebuild damaged families.

The use and impact of supervision orders

The supervision order is the most commonly used community sentence among young male offenders aged 14 and under 18 at the present time. In that older age group some 18 per cent of males and 20 per cent of females dealt with by the courts in 1995 were made the subject of a supervision order. This amounted to a total of 7,200 new orders (6,300 males and 900 females). For both male and female offenders this represents a significant increase in proportionate use over the previous decade, although fewer orders were made in real terms, reflecting a general decrease in the numbers of young people sentenced by the courts (Home Office, 1996h: Table 7.9). A similar picture may be found in relation to those aged over 10 and under 14, with similar percentages receiving supervision orders but smaller numbers involved.

Of those supervision orders commenced in 1994, just over a quarter (28 per cent) were imposed for theft and handling offences and just under a quarter (24 per cent) for burglary. The pattern is similar for earlier years, although the precise figures vary and the order of magnitude has been reversed in several years within the last decade. About three-quarters of the orders terminated in 1994 had run their full course, while termination for failure to comply with requirements or because of conviction for another offence occurred in only 14 per cent of cases (Home Office, 1996g). Given that a good many of those on supervision will have been within the peak age range for offending, this completion rate represents a solid achievement, although it should be pointed out this does not guarantee an absence of reoffending, just an absence of breach proceedings. Surprisingly, perhaps, the effectiveness of different kinds of community sentences in terms of reoffending is not measured on a regular basis in many parts of England and Wales, a gap that the Audit Commission highlighted in their recent report on youth crime (Audit Commission, 1996: para. 68).

Attendance centre orders

The final community order provided by section 6 of the 1991 Act is the attendance centre order. Under this power, juveniles and young adults up to the age of 21 can be ordered to attend specified locations for short periods, usually three hours on alternate Saturday afternoons (often to coincide with the home matches of the local football team), up to a maximum of 36 hours (or 24 hours for those under 16 years of age). The age range for which the order is available has been extended by the Crime (Sentences) Act 1997 to 25 where the order is made because of a failure to pay a previously imposed fine, but this provision had not been brought into effect at the time of writing. Activities at attendance centres include physical training and instruction in such topics as first aid and motor vehicle maintenance. Attendance sentence orders were first introduced by the Criminal Justice Act 1948, and the regime of 'constructive diversion' and instilling self-discipline through physical exertion smacks somewhat of an earlier, therapeutic ideal. Nonetheless, the proportionate use of such orders has remained relatively constant despite the increasingly punitive climate of the last ten years, although overall rates have never been high. In 1994 only 5 per cent of sentenced 14–17-year-old males and one per cent of females were given an attendance sentence order (Walker and Padfield, 1996: 307).

Other community supervision orders

Adult offenders can also be ordered to be under the supervision of the probation service either as a result of being given a sentence of imprisonment which is then suspended, or to ensure the payment of a financial penalty. The latter type of supervision can also apply to juveniles or young adults, but since there is no power to suspend a custodial sentence imposed on a person under 21, it follows that suspended sentence supervision orders are of no relevance to that age group.

The supended sentence is an anomaly within the post-1991 sentencing framework, as the 1990 White Paper conceded. Since what is being suspended is a sentence of imprisonment, courts cannot pass such a sentence unless they are satisfied (in the words of section 1(2) of the 1991 Act) either that the offence or offences for which it is imposed are so serious that only a custodial sentence can be justified or, where the offence is of a violent or sexual nature, only a custodial sentence would be adequate to protect the public from serious harm from the offender. Despite having come to this conclusion, however, provided the appropriate length of sentence is not thought to exceed two years, the court may proceed to suspend the operation of the sentence for a period of between one and two years if they find that there are exceptional circumstances which justify such a decision. The effect of this is that someone whose 'just deserts' indicate that a prison sentence would be appropriate is nonetheless released into the community, there to remain unless he or she reoffends within the 'operational period' during which the original sentence is supended. Chiefly because of its anomalous position and the clear guidance from the Court of Appeal that the circumstances which would justify its use must be truly exceptional, the proportions of offenders receiving suspended sentences at the Crown Court (where the bulk of custodial sentences are passed) has fallen dramatically from 16 per cent in 1991 to 2 per cent in 1995.

Some of those who do receive a suspended prison sentence are also made the subject of a suspended sentence supervision order (SSSO), imposed under section 26 of the Powers of Criminal Courts Act 1973. The SSSO is intended to be a therapeutic measure designed to offer those kept out of prison by the suspension of their sentences the same opportunity for beneficial contact with the probation service as those dealt with in the community. It can only be associated with suspended sentences of six months or more, taking it beyond the ordinary sentencing powers of magistrates and reserving its use almost entirely to the Crown Court. Since it is not really a punishment in its own right, the SSSO cannot be 'strengthened' by the addition of any condition beyond the normal requirements of keeping in touch with the supervising officer and notifying any change of address. Breach of an SSSO can lead at most to a fine, not to the resentencing of the offender, although someone who commits other offences while on a suspended sentence will normally find that their original prison term is 'activated' in any event. The use of SSSOs has declined in line with the dramatic reduction in the use of suspended sentences to the point where in 1995 only 300 SSSOs were made, compared to 2,400 in 1990.

The money payment supervision order (MPSO) is available to courts under section 88 of the Magistrates' Courts Act 1980. Under an MPSO the responsibility of the supervising officer is to advise and befriend the offender who has been fined or ordered to pay compensation 'with a view to inducing him [sic] to pay . . . and thereby avoid committal to custody'. No specific requirements are placed on the supervisee and there is little that the supervising officer can realistically do to influence payment. Fewer than 40 per cent of such orders which terminated in 1994 were as a result of supervised payments being completed. The use of the MPSO, although always more extensive than SSSOs, had also been declining, numbers having fallen in every year since 1989 (Walker and Padfield, 1996: 270). However, following significant changes in fine-enforcement practices (discussed in greater detail in Chapter 6) there was a huge rise in the number of MPSOs made by the magistrates' courts: 80 per cent more MPSOs were made in the first quarter of 1996 than in the same period a year earlier (Whittaker and Mackie, 1997: 39). For reasons discussed in the next chapter, this trend looks set to continue.

Bans and prohibitions

For completeness, it may be noted that there are a range of other court orders which place restrictions on the liberty of offenders while leaving them in the community. When sentencing people convicted of violence or threatening violence on licensed premises, a court may also make orders excluding them from entering specified premises for between three months and two years, under the Licensed Premises (Exclusion of Certain Persons) Act 1980. Sections 30–7 of the Public Order Act 1986 also enable the sentencing courts to make exclusion orders prohibiting offenders convicted of football violence from attending designated football matches in England and Wales. This power of prohibition was extended in effect to matches played abroad by the Football Spectators Act 1989, under which persons convicted of violent offences at football matches may be ordered to report to a designated police station in England or Wales on days on which specified matches are being played abroad. It was originally intended that the power to make restriction orders under the 1989 Act would supersede the relevant part of the 1986 Act, but the repealing sections of the 1989 Act were never brought into force with the result that the two Acts continue to exist alongside each other.

Given their various derivations and their lack of inclusion in section 6 of the 1991 Act, these various bans and prohibitions are clearly not community sentences properly so called and are not, therefore, subject to the seriousness threshold contained in that section. Nonetheless, such an order can have serious implications for the liberty of an individual subjected to it, and these can endure for up to five years in the most serious case. Failure to comply with orders or with conditions attached to them is invariably an offence punishable by custodial sentences of varying lengths depending on the precise order involved, a consideration with potentially 'up-tariffing' effects for the defendant who was not imprisoned for the original offence.

These bans and prohibitions owe their origins in the main to a particular period of contemporary history during which the government of the day sought to tackle symptoms of civil unrest and disorder with an array of measures characterised chiefly by their repressive effects. Ranging from the extended police powers contained in the Police and Criminal Evidence Act 1984 through the Public Order Act 1986 to the anti-trespass, anti-'rave' and anti-traveller provisions of the Criminal Justice and Public Order Act 1994, these measures give some substance to the thesis (discussed briefly in Chapter 4) that in response to a crisis of legitimacy Britain has been drifting gradually towards a more authoritarian form of rule (Hall, 1980). All remain on the statute book and many were passed with at least the acquiesence, while in opposition, of the Labour Party. How these particular measures are used in the coming years and whether they are repealed or, alternatively, supplemented by new, equally restrictive powers will be another of the acid tests of the new administration's attitudes to law and order. Early indications that the government is considering powers to confiscate offenders' passports and impose driving disqualifications for non-motoring offences suggest that the days of the authoritarian response may not yet be ended.

Responsibility for enforcing community sentences

Clearly, punishments of the kind discussed here bring with them the element of supervision and 'discipline' that proponents of the 'net-widening' thesis already alluded to (and discussed further below) associate with the 'dispersal' of punishment into the community. For the most part the task of supervision falls to the probation service. Certainly, the first three community orders, probation, community service and combination orders, are each enforced by the probation service, although day-to-day implementation of some orders may be delegated to persons other than probation officers if, for instance, an offender is attending a special rehabilitation programme offered in partnership with a voluntary or other non-statutory agency.

A supervision order may require a person between the ages of 10 and 17 inclusive (a juvenile) to be under the supervision of either a probation officer or the local authority social services department, although, if the juvenile is under 13, the supervisor must be the local authority unless another member of the juvenile's family is already in contact with the probation service. Both probation and supervision orders are subject to the National Standards (Home Office *et al.*, 1995) and these require *inter alia* that local probation services and social service departments should draw up formal agreements for the supervision of young offenders and make these arrangements known locally to sentencers. Attendance centres, on the other hand, are normally run by police officers in civilian clothes assisted by civilian teachers, and their conduct is governed by the Attendance Centre Rules 1958 and 1992. It is the responsibility of those who run individual centres to see that an order is implemented and to return to court those who repeatedly fail to comply with it or commit a breach which is so serious that it canot be dealt with under the Attendance Centre Rules (Wasik, 1993: 200). The remaining order, the curfew order, is in a separate and somewhat anomalous position which has been discussed above.

The effect of breaching a community order

Part of the government's strategy in trying to encourage sentencers to make greater use of community-based punishments involved making enforcement procedures stricter and more predictable. The research literature had pointed to considerable variations across the country in the procedures which followed breaches of the conditions of an order (Willis, 1981; Audit Commission, 1989; Ellis *et al.*, 1996) and these inconsistencies arose, it was felt, from the considerable discretion formerly afforded probation officers in the way in which they conducted their working relations with those under their supervision. Probation officers, it was felt, had often been reluctant in the past to take enforcement action against their 'clients' because of deeply ingrained preferences for the caring rather than controlling aspects of their professional duties. Due to the wide discretion involved in breach decisions, much turned on the attitudes and tolerances of individual officers, which led to much inconsistency and criticism (Lawson, 1978; Humphrey and Pease, 1992). In order to introduce greater consistency of approach and to encourage the spread of what it considered 'good practice' (which meant, essentially, dispelling any tendency to laxity and ensuring a uniformly disciplinarian approach), the government used the 1991 Act to consolidate and overhaul existing legislation for enforcing community-based sentences. The new powers are contained in schedule 2 of the 1991 Act and are backed up by a strict code of practice in the National Standards which places greater emphasis on the protection of the public through a much tougher response to non-compliance with the conditions of a community order (Home Office *et al.*, 1995; Ellis *et al.*, 1996: Annex II).

Under the 1995 National Standards officers are required to record and investigate every failure to attend a supervisory session or perform community service work. If no satisfactory explanation is forthcoming then the incident must be formally recorded as a failure to comply with the relevant order. Breach proceedings can be begun forthwith and without prior warning if the failure to comply is considered serious enough. If no breach action is taken then a formal written warning *must* be issued. The National Standards provide that at most two warnings within any 12-month period of the order may be given before breach proceedings are instituted. Proceedings are commenced by the laying of an information before the local magistrates' court, which may deal with the matter itself or remit the case to the Crown Court if the original order was made there.

What happens as a consequence of a breach being proved depends, unsurprisingly, on the seriousness of the breach itself. In the ordinary run of cases, the court has the choice of three alternative punishments. It may choose to leave the original order in force and either impose a fine of up to £1,000 or make a community service order of up to 60 days on top of the existing community sentence. Or it may choose to revoke the order and sentence the offender again for the original offence. Somewhat confusingly, commission of a new offence while subject to a community order (as distinct from a suspended prison sentence) is not *in itself* a breach of the order although, subject to certain arcane restrictions, it does provide grounds for revoking the original order if the court so decide.

Revoking an order should not normally put an offender at risk of a custodial sentence, at least in theory. Since the court which first dealt with the original offence did not find that the criteria for custody had been met, the second court dealing with it should also normally choose another community sentence. Where a more serious breach is concerned, however, and the court dealing with it is satisfied that the offender has 'wilfully and persistently failed to comply' with the original order, it may revoke that order and impose a custodial sentence by virtue of section 1(3) of the 1991 Act (as amended by the 1997 Crime (Sentences) Act).

There is, therefore, no statutory prohibition on the use of custody in breach proceedings, and while courts are required to take into account the manner in which the offender has otherwise complied with the order, there is clearly a danger, as the 1990 White Paper indeed recognised, that if courts dealing with breach proceedings are not scrupulous in observing the custody threshold, offenders who were not otherwise at risk of custody might find themselves in prison (Home Office, 1990a: para. 4.18). This potential leads some critics of community sentences to allege that their ultimate effect is often to increase the penetration of relatively minor offenders into the penal system by amplifying the punishment their original level of offending actually merits ('thinning the mesh', in Stan Cohen's memorable phrase). Some of the arguments and evidence relating to this controversy will reviewed in more detail at the end of this chapter and in Chapter 7, below.

It might also be noted at this point that a probation order can also be 'discharged' by a court on the application of either the supervising officer or the probationer where it appears that the probationer has made good progress and no longer requires supervision, or where the supervising officer considers the order is inappropriate and the probationer should be resentenced (section 11 of the 1973 Act). Around 10–11 per cent of probation orders are terminated 'for good progress' each year.

Different penalties are provided under section 15 of the Children and Young Persons Act 1969 (as amended) for dealing with the breach of a supervision order. Basically, breaches by young persons under 18 can be dealt with by a small fine or an attendance sentence order, whether or not the supervision order continues. If the supervised person has reached 18, then the court may also discharge the order and impose some other penalty which would have been available for the original offence. In these circumstances, the range of possible penalties does not include a custodial sentence unless the court which originally dealt with the young person stated that it was imposing the supervision order in lieu of a custodial sentence.

Summary and conclusions

This chapter has outlined the wide range of non-custodial sentences available to courts in England and Wales to punish offences thought too serious to deserve merely a fine but not serious enough to warrant custody. Such an extensive range of options may not necessarily be an unquestioned advantage, at least if strict proportionality and equality of treatment are considered to be the most important criteria of justice. Ashworth, for instance, believes that the proliferation of community-based punishments is one of the principal impediments to achieving fairness, consistency and efficacy in the 1991 sentencing framework. Out-and-out consequentialists and hybrid theorists, who, as we have seen in Chapter 2, tend to favour a much more individualised approach, might be less concerned with sentencing disparities. Ashworth, on the other hand, because he is broadly an advocate of the just deserts rationale, argues (1995: 288) that, without much more specific guidance on the relative severity of the myriad non-custodial possibilities (rules, for example, comparing 100 hours community service with a probation order with requirements, in terms of severity), it is difficult to guarantee anything approaching true proportionality within and between different courts.

Plans by the former government for a single 'generic' community sentence composed of elements of existing community penalties 'picked and mixed' at the discretion of the sentencing court would undoubtedly have added to the disparities and inconsistencies but these were abandoned after consultations found less than enthusiastic support for them among practitioners. It remains to be seen whether the Labour government's manifesto commitment to implement 'an effective sentencing system for all the main offences' (Labour Party, 1997b) will successfully address this problem, although as their plans seem to depend on guidelines from the Court of Appeal and since that court has relatively little to do with non-custodial sentences, one may have some doubts on this score.

A further problem is the danger that in an effort to make non-custodial disposals appear convincingly punitive by 'stacking up' community penalties in ever more demanding combinations, sentencers will create the conditions under which failure and breach are more likely than not. Any tendency, then, among sentencers to resort to punishing non-compliance with custody rather than another community-based penalty would propel an offender further into the penal system than their original offending was deemed to deserve.

This is part of Stan Cohen's famous 'net-widening' thesis and it refers to the process by which the 'mesh is thinned' and offenders who might otherwise have escaped custody are propelled 'up-tariff' by failure to complete an over-demanding non-custodial sentence successfully and thus are subject to a greater degree of 'intervention' than they would have been under other pre-existing non-custodial options (Cohen, 1979: 347, and see further Chapter 7, below). Although there are doubts as to the *inevitability* of such a process (McMahon, 1990; Bottoms, 1983, 1995b), the possibility that such undesirable escalation *could* take place cannot be denied (Blomberg and Lucken, 1994). Indeed, the rhetoric of the 1990 White Paper and the fact that section 6 of the 1991 Act removed most of the pre-existing limitations on combining penalties suggests that the architects of the 1991 framework were prepared to run this risk in an attempt to make non-custodial sentences more attractive to the allegedly punitive instincts of the judges and magistrates.

Therefore, while the danger of 'up-tariffing' cannot be discounted, in dealing with breaches of community sentence (which is one of the points at which up-tariffing could occur) courts in England and Wales do seem to be exercising restraint in the use of custody. The latest statistics available at the time of writing show that while there has been a considerable increase in the numbers of breaches reported to the courts (as one would expect, given the strict requirements of the National Standards), there has also been a substantial reduction in the proportionate use of custody to deal with breaches both of probation and community service orders.

In 1985, 56 per cent of those in breach of a probation order and 41 per cent of those in breach of a CSO were given custody; by 1995 these percentages had fallen to 34 and 19 respectively (Home Office, 1996h: Table 7.25). Despite the increased level of reporting of breaches, these proportionate decreases have resulted in a fall in the actual numbers of those who are being sent to custody for breaching community orders. Altogether 2,200 fewer people suffered that fate in 1995 than ten years earlier. Magistrates, it appears, recognise that the National Standards will inevitably result in more and earlier breach proceedings being taken and so are more willing to 'give it another crack', at least on a first breach, if the supervising officer recommends continuance (Ellis *et al.*, 1996: 48). Research also reveals that enforcement practices continued to vary both within and between areas, despite the introduction of National Standards, with some officers less rigorous in their recording and enforcement practices than others and new and more covert ways of subverting strict enforcement practices being devised (Vass, 1990: 168; Humphrey and Pease, 1992: 39). The combined effects of these two sets of circumstances may help to explain the apparent resistance of community sentences, at least in this aspect, to conform to the 'net-widening' tendencies of earlier 'alternatives' to custody such as the suspended sentence (see Chapter 1, above).

Yet, for all of that, it is inescapable that for some time now the use of custody has been rising *alongside* an increase in the use of community sentences. Magistrates' courts' use of community sentences for indictable (i.e. more serious) offences increased steadily between 1990 and 1995 from 20 per cent to 28 per cent of all sentences passed. At the Crown Court the proportion of community sentences reached 34 per cent in 1993, and although it fell back somewhat to 30 per cent in 1995, this was still 5 per cent higher than in 1990 (Home Office, 1996h). But the use of immediate custodial sentences has also been increasing, and the total of 79,100 such sentences imposed in 1995 was the highest since 1985. In other words, although the courts – particularly, but not exclusively, the magistrates' courts – are making more use of community penalties, this has not had the reductionist consequences that many had hoped. Nor has the availability of a range of community 'alternatives' contributed to a reduction in the distortions along lines of social class, gender and (particularly) race which are so evident in the way that custody is used in this country.

There is no simple mathematical relationship either between crime rates and the size of the prison population or between the use of custody and the number of alternatives to it that are available. As we shall see in Chapter 8, the prevailing political climate has considerable influence on the nature of each of those relationships. At the time of writing the prospects for a radical change of direction are uncertain. Little revealed in the Labour Party's election manifesto suggested that the insistence on 'tough' sentencing would be modified or that the accompanying explosions in prison populations would be halted, at least in the short term (Lloyd, 1997; Straw, 1997a). Such circumstances, however, need not pertain for ever since there is no *a priori* reason why punitiveness need always triumph over rehabilitation, given the necessary political will. Certain indications did begin to emerge in the early days of the new administration that it wished to break with the prevailing pessimism at the heart of penal policy and to give renewed encouragement to community-based punishments, (although these were also mixed with signals of a continuing reliance on the language of punitiveness).

Such a shift in emphasis, if it does materialise, makes economic as well (it is submitted) as moral sense, for a government which inherited less extensive resources than it needs to implement all its priorites. The net cost of building the next three privatised prisons in England and Wales is estimated to be £643 million over 25 years (NACRO, 1997). Even diverting a proportion of that planned expenditure into the provision of properly planned and delivered community-based programmes would not only send a different kind of signal to sentencers, but would be likely to advance meaningful attempts to reduce the reoffending by persistent offenders more effectively than the present incarceration policy ever will

(Audit Commission, 1996: para. 56 and Appendix I). In Chapter 8 I shall attempt to sketch out the sort of conditions under which alternative approaches with different outcomes might be possible. First, however, we must turn to consider the remaining non-custodial penalties that are available to the courts under current arrangements.

Chapter 6

Financial and Nominal Penalties

Introduction

Despite a gradual reduction in use since 1979, the fine continues to be the most commonly imposed criminal penalty in England and Wales (unlike the United States, where probation is 'the sanction of choice' (Byrne and Pattavina, 1992: 281)). In 1995 75 per cent of all those who were dealt with by the courts were fined, amounting to not far short of a million people. Fines are the standard way of dealing with summary offences including motoring offences, but in law fines can be used to punish almost every indictable offence as well, and in 1995 14 per cent of those convicted of offences against the person and 29 per cent of those convicted of theft or handling were fined. Fines, therefore, form a broad platform just below community sentences in the hierarchy illustrated in Figure 1.1 above. For the most part, as we have seen in Chapter 5, fines and community penalties are separated off from each other by the seriousness threshold in section 6 of the 1991 Act. However, the Crime (Sentences) Act 1997 (at section 37(3)) provides that courts can impose a CSO, a curfew order or (if the person is under 25) an attendance centre order on someone with insufficient means to pay a suitable fine or who already had an outstanding fine, 'notwithstanding anything in section 6 of the 1991 Act'. In other words, in the circumstances outlined in the 1997 Act, the normally strict relationship of proportionality between seriousness of offence and severity of punishment will be relaxed to allow sentencers greater latitude to choose between a fine and a community sentence. This particular section of the Act has not yet been brought into force, but the rationale behind it will become apparent when we discuss the sometimes undesirable effects on the prison population of fine-enforcement procedures.

There are other measures at this level, too, which the courts can employ. Compensation orders may be imposed, either as punishments in their own right or in conjunction with other penalties, to effect some financial reparation towards the victims of crime. Courts also now have quite extensive powers to confiscate the proceeds of drug-trafficking offences and certain other specified offences and to order the confiscation of property used in the commission of crime. Below this again are found what might be termed 'nominal' penalties: powers to discharge defendants, either absolutely or subject to certain conditions, and the ancient common-law power to 'bind over' a defendant to be of good behaviour or forfeit a sum of money in default.

We shall examine these measures, both financial and 'nominal', below and the chapter will also touch briefly on a small cluster of special powers used in connection with public order offences. The bulk of the chapter, however, will focus on the use of the fine and its relationship with the rising prison population through the problem of default of payment, including the controversy over proportionality in fining which came to a head in the sudden demise of the unit fines scheme originally contained within the 1991 Act. Our discussion of financial penalties, moreover, will be located in the wider economic context of employment and unemployment so as to pose questions about the relationship between the demands of punishment and the maintenance of minimum standards of life that may be thought a requirement of a just society.

Fines

The uses and limitations of the fine

As we have just seen, fines may be ordered in both the Crown Court and the magistrates' courts. There is no statutory limit on the amount of fine which can be imposed by the Crown Court. In the magistrates' courts, on the other hand, maximum limits are imposed: fines are arranged into five bands, depending on the seriousness of the offence involved, with an overall maximum fine for any one offence currently set at £5,000. Fines can also be combined in both courts with a wide range of other penalties including an order to compensate the victim and pay all or part of the costs of the prosecution. Once ordered, a fine becomes payable immediately, but in practice most defendants are given time to pay and the courts have a frequently used discretion to allow payment by instalments. Where payment by instalments is ordered the normal maximum allowed to clear the fine is 12 months (see *R. v. Knight* (1980) 2 Cr. App. R. (S) 82), although a longer period would not be unlawful provided this did not impose an undue burden on the offender or amount to too severe a punishment (*Olliver and Olliver* (1989) 11 Cr. App. R. (S) 10).

Compared to other non-custodial sentences the fine is pre-eminently retributivist, in the sense that it is about putting a penal value on *past* offending rather than seeking to secure any rehabilitative or other individualised reductive effects for the future. Indeed, in his famous critique of Cohen's 'dispersal of discipline' thesis, Bottoms (1983) combines the observed rise in the use of the fine with the lack of any element of 'training' or post-sentence supervision associated with it to question the adequacy of Cohen's theoretical framework – the Foucauldian 'punitive city' – and the universality of the thesis that developments in modern sentencing policy all point towards the extension of 'indefinite discipline' into ever wider reaches of social life. On the contrary, Bottoms sees the increasing use of the fine and of compensation orders as evidence of what he calls 'a juridical revival' – the re-emergence of the classical approach to sentencing, at least in some parts of a 'bifurcated' penal system.

Unlike 'carceral' punishments, which seek to secure the future obedience of the subject through the inculcation of an all-pervasive regime of discipline or 'coercive soul-training', juridical punishments are essentially fixed in duration, calculable in advance, unarbitrary and proportionate to the offences for which they are imposed. When completed, they requalify the 'juridical subject' as a full member of society with no further restriction but, perhaps, with a more focused appreciation of the sort of disadvantage that would be risked by any future decision to reoffend. Once this distinction in Foucault's own typologies is grasped, Bottoms argues, the fine can be seen as clearly more of a classical than a disciplinary punishment. Whatever other changes are being wrought in the nature of social control by the transformation to a post-modern or late capitalist society, the fine remains essentially an exemplar of classical penality, a retributivist rather than a consequentialist sentencing option.

As such, the fine accords with the essentially retributivist and punitive values of many, if not most, sentencers (Young, 1989), a factor which may help to account for its considerable use. It is also a cost-efficient measure, raising revenue by its imposition rather than consuming additional resources in being implemented as, say, a community service order or probation do. The fine exists, therefore, at the point at which ideology converges with administration, to use Peter Young's phrase, enabling sentencers in the vast majority of cases to satisfy their dual mandate of inflicting punishment (and the majority of Sheriffs in his Scottish study saw the fine as a purely punitive measure) and securing the efficient administration of justice. Fines are also associated with lower rates of reoffending than other measures (Phillpotts and Lancucki, 1979). While Bottoms' observation (1973) that this merely reflects the fact that courts tend to use fines for those who have lower risks of reoffending anyway is undoubtedly correct, a commonly-held belief among sentencers in the penal 'efficacy' of the fine reinforces these other positive incentives which in combination explain why the fine is the most frequently used sanction.

There are, however, important social and ideological limitations on the extent to which fines can be used at any particular point in the economic cycle. Where unemployment rates are relatively low, the levels of fines that can be imposed are not artificially depressed by people's inability to pay. The fine, therefore, maintains its reputation with sentencers as an efficient and effective penalty which can impose appreciable levels of punishment through the imposition of sums which are generally recognised as significant. When unemployment increases, however, offenders more routinely lack the means to pay the sorts of fines which sentencers consider to be commensurate, and in such circumstances the use of the fine is partially displaced by other measures which may be either more or less punitive depending on the views of the sentencers involved. A tendency of this kind undoubtedly explains, at least in part, the reduction in the percentage use of fines for adult offenders (both men and women) witnessed in the 1980s during a period of economic recession.

On one view the substitution of other non-custodial sentences for fines under such circumstances is merely common sense. What is to be gained by decreasing still further the financial resources of those for whom deprivation may have been a precipitating cause of offending in the first place? Where fines are replaced by more punitive measures such as community service or probation (or even custody in some cases: Crow *et al.*, 1989), however, varying degrees of 'up-tariffing' take place. In the short term this may not seem so draconian because, subjectively, the impact of, say, a shortish community service order may appear less onerous to an impecunious offender than a financial penalty. But if any subsequent offences are punished on the basis that the particular offender has already 'graduated' beyond financial penalties on previous sentencing occasions, the original decision against fining assumes altogether more serious consequences.

The problem of fine default

A variety of other problems associated with the use of fines within a sentencing regime which is intended to be driven primarily by considerations of just deserts or commensurability should be recognised. One is the problem of how the magistrates' courts, whose responsibility it is to enforce fines, should deal with those who are in default. The court, having enquired into the financial circumstances of a defaulter may decide to remit (i.e. cancel) some or all of the amount outstanding or it (or the court's enforcement staff) may extend the time for payment. In cases which are seen as less deserving, various forms of coercive enforcement, including seizure of personal belongings, or attachment of earnings and (since 1992) welfare benefits, are available. Ultimately defaulters are liable to be committed to prison or a young offenders' institution if either the offence they were fined for is imprisonable and they appear to have the money to pay, or the court is satisfied that their default is due to 'wilful refusal' or 'culpable neglect' and that no other method of enforcement would work. Prison statistics show that there were 32 receptions into prison for fine default for every 1,000 persons fined in 1994, although this figure dropped sharply in 1995 and 1996. Not surprisingly, the use of custody in this context is controversial, particularly as numerous studies have shown that until very recently the courts have been making little use of any enforcement method other than custody, although the operation of commitment has characteristically been suspended upon condition that the fines were cleared (Morris and Gelsthorpe, 1990; Whittaker and Mackie, 1997).

From a purely administrative point of view it must be conceded that commitment to prison (where it actually occurs) is not at all a cost-effective response to the problem of fine default. Apart from the expense of writing off the fine itself, the rest of society must bear the costs of imprisonment (£465 per week for an adult place in 1995) and any associated costs of providing for dependent children where the imprisoned person is a lone carer. To put the cost of imprisonment in the context of one type of offence with which it is commonly associated, Wall and Bradshaw (1994) have recently calculated that the approximate average cost of detecting, prosecuting and eventually imprisoning a single parent of two children for the non-payment of a television licence was about £2,130 in 1994, roughly 25 times the cost of the original licence itself. Those committed for default rarely spend more than seven days actually in prison, and while this means that their contribution to the prison population on any particular day is quite small (for instance on 30 June 1995 it was 1.3 per cent of the sentenced population, Home Office, 1996i), the rapid succession of admission and discharge procedures associated with such short sentences imposes considerable administrative burdens on an already overburdened local prison system.

The use of imprisonment for fine default also seems objectionable on at least two more fundamental grounds. First, in as much as it results in the imprisonment of a not inconsiderable number of people whose original offences were not thought serious enough to justify even a community sentence, let alone a custodial one, this reliance on a custodial sanction defies the logic of the deserts rationale which is supposed to underpin the existing sentencing framework. Secondly, although there may seem to be some justification in punishing a wilful refusal to comply with a court order, the line between 'can't pay' and 'won't pay' is notoriously hard to define, and what may appear to magistrates as wilful refusal can be viewed subjectively by the fine defaulter as the only rational response to multiple debt problems threatening the very continuance of their family. Fines may be used to punish the rich as well as the poor, of course, being combined with imprisonment, for instance, to deprive the career criminal of illicit profits. But most fine defaulters do not even approximate to this description. Empirical studies of fine enforcement have consistently demonstrated significant correlations between unemployment and imprisonment for default (see Penal Affairs Consortium, 1995 for a recent summary) to the extent where it may be argued that fines and their enforcement exhibit an institutional bias against the poor and particularly against poor women, who are proportionately more likely than men to appear in an enforcement court (Shaw, 1989; Walker and Wall, 1997; Whittaker and Mackie, 1997: 21). In one study of unemployment and sentencing in 1987, for instance, Crow and Simon commented on

> The great extent to which defaulters were in a state of financial muddle and mismanagement, very often against a background of unemployment and other problems . . . Many had hire purchase commitments they could not meet, and put fines at the bottom of the list. Some owed rent and fuel bills, and tried to juggle their debts or else to ignore them as long as they could.

More recent Home Office research (Moxon and Whittaker, 1996) confirms that the picture has changed little in the intervening decade. In a sample of 210 fine defaulters in custody during one week in July 1995, 77 per cent were unemployed and dependent on benefit at the time they were imprisoned. The problems of inability to pay are exacerbated where a persisitent offender has accumulated fines over a number of appearances. Even if each individual fine has been set with scrupulous attention to their means, it is possible for repeat offenders to accumulate very large fines over a number of appearances which eventually they cannot pay (Moxon and Whittaker, 1996). Although not always recognised as such, the issue of the differential enforcement of fines is part of the wider question of whether we can ever secure 'just deserts in an unjust world' (see Chapter 2, above) and empirical findings like those above suggest again that desert based sentencing alone (i.e. when it is not harnessed to some over-riding principle of restraint) may not always produce substantive outcomes that are inherently 'just'.

Equality of impact in fines

Even if the consequences of enforcement practices are put aside, there remains the difficult problem of how to secure proportionality in the use of fines in the first instance. This raises the contentious issue of *equality of impact*. Most people would accept that any assumption of formal equality before the law masks stark and undeniable social inequalities which mean that, in reality, some people are better placed to withstand the impact of being fined than others. Since the reality of this disparity is easier to demonstrate than, for instance, the assertion that some people suffer greater pains in being imprisoned, the argument that imposing exactly the the same fine on two offenders of differing means may be unjust commands support more readily than other, similar arguments about other types of penalties. Once this inequality of impact is acknowledged, the assumption of 'like-situated offenders', which lies at the core of desert theories, is seriously challenged and the difficulties of scaling non-custodial penalites in terms of commensurability of severity are exacerbated.

Before 1991 judicial guidance on the use of fines in England and Wales did not really address this desert consideration satisfactorily. Although the need to mitigate the levels of fines imposed on less well-off offenders had long been recognised, the appellate courts had been steadfastly opposed to the corollary, namely that the level of a fine could be *increased* purely on the grounds that an offender happened to be wealthy (see, for instance, *R.* v. *Fairbairn* (1980) 2 Cr. App. R. (S) 315). Increasing fines on such grounds was said to be unjust *per se*, but it was also felt that such a practice was objectionable on the grounds that it give the appearance that those of means were able, by the payment of large fines, to buy themselves out of being sent to prison (cf. *R.* v. *Marwick* (1953) 37 Cr. App. R. 125 with *R.* v. *Reeves* (1972) 56 Cr. App. R. 366).

The life-history of the unit fines system: reason and betrayal

In order to reverse the comparative decline in the use of financial penalties and to tackle the associated problems of fine default and equality of impact, the architects of the 1991 sentencing framework proposed to introduce a system of unit fines similar to the 'day fine' procedure already well established in what was then West Germany and in a number of Scandinavian and Latin American countries. Some kind of unit fines system is a necessary adjunct to a deserts-based sentencing framework, if the problem of substantively unfair outcomes described above is to be addressed. The aim of such systems is to provide a mechanism through which fines could be set at levels which are both appropriate to the seriousness of the offence being punished yet realistic when the individual means of particular offenders are taken in account. While the first objective seeks to achieve commensurability and ensure proportionality between offenders of differing culpability, the second is seen as necessary to secure higher levels of payment and, thus, to reduce the need to rely on more coercive means of enforcement, including imprisonment, to the detriment of the basic proportionality principle.

The key to achieving both of these objectives simultaneously is a conceptual separation between the attribution of moral blameworthiness and the fixing of a monetary value to that level of blame. In day fine or unit fine systems an offence is said to be 'worth' so many units, or so many days' pay, depending on the sentencer's view of its seriousness; only after the calculation of blame has been made and announced does the court (or an administrator in some systems) go on to translate that measure of culpability into a monetary figure, usually by calculating how much disposable income a defendant actually has and deriving the value of each unit in their particular case. The traditional practice of simply announcing a single monetary value to be imposed as a fine conflated the sentencers' assessment of the seriousness of the offence with their feeling for how much the offender could reasonably afford to pay without distinguishing between the effects of these two distinct calculations. Overall levels of fines are also usually constrained by localised notions of 'the going rate' for particular offences, and the result of this largely discretionary process was all too often inconsistency and disparity between different courts within and across different localities (Young, 1989), a feature which is of particular concern to desert theorists with their predilection for formal equality of treatment.

In order to secure the deserts principle in relation to fines as well as community sentences, section 18 of the 1991 Act established a unit fines system for operation in the magistrates' courts (but not the Crown Court) in England and Wales. Under this scheme the culpability of a defendant was to be expressed in terms of a number of units from 1 to 50. Determining the number of units of 'blameworthiness' was, in essence, the total extent of the judicial function, because the actual amount of money to be paid as a result of that adjudication was then to be determined through an essentially administrative procedure, in which a calculation of one third of an offender's net disposable weekly income after the deduction of certain allowable living costs produced a 'multiplier' which determined the monetary value of each unit. Courts were required to announce in open court both the total amount of the fine and the number of units which it had imposed on the offender.

Since the unit value could vary according to means between a statutory minimum of £4 to a maximum of £100, the result of applying the system in an extreme case could be that two offenders who were adjudged to have committed offences of equal seriousness (taking 20 units as an illustration) could end up paying fines that differed by up to £1,920. Clearly, the more serious the offence and the greater the disparity in disposable income the wider the divergence in fines as between equally culpable defendants might become. Provided that seriousness of offence was conceptualised only in terms of the number of units announced, however, the potential difference in eventual outcome was not at all incompatible with the just deserts rationale underpinning the rest of the sentencing framework. Indeed, it was in order to facilitate such differences that section 18 of the 1991 Act expressly established the principle that a fine should be increased if the offender was well off (Home Office, 1991c: para. 2), reversing the effect of the previous case-law on the matter.

The unit fines system came into force on 1 October 1992 along with the majority of the 1991 Act. As well as the international experience, the experimental implementation of pilot versions of such a scheme in four magistrates' courts in England and Wales in the late 1980s provided evidence that a unit fines system could be made to operate successfully even if some of the magistrates were less than enthusiastic initially (Home Office, 1990a: para. 25; Gibson, 1990; Moxon et al., 1990). Unit fines were only ever mandatory in magistrates' courts, Crown Court judges (who make much less proportionate use of the fine, in any event) being left with their discretionary powers to impose a fine of any value.

Although it was greeted with hostility by a minority of magistrates who saw it as an unacceptable restriction upon their judicial discretion and independence, it appears that during its short life the unit fines system began to achieve much of what was intended for it. Data from a special monitoring exercise by the Home Office showed that in the period immediately after implementation the proportionate use of the fine amongst unemployed offenders rose from 30 to 43 per cent while the average value of the fine imposed on those who were unemployed fell from nearly £90 to under £70 (Home Office, 1993; 1994a). The combination of these two figures suggests that the previous reluctance to use fines for the unemployed because of the small monetary values involved was being overcome. As a result courts participating in the monitoring exercise recorded large rises in the numbers of unemployed being fined, producing a rise in the proportionate use of fines overall. At the same time the average fines imposed on those in and out of employment began to diverge quite sharply, suggesting that another of the system's objectives, securing equality of impact, was beginning to be met.

The statutory unit fines system was not without its failings, principal among which were the complexity and seeming rigidity of the regulations which governed the calculation of disposable income and the uncertain relationship between unit fines and fixed penalties applicable in many of the minor road traffic cases. Many magistrates, even some of those who were broadly in sympathy with the principle of equality of impact, found the statutory scheme unduly prescriptive and would have preferred at least some latitude to adjust the final figure produced by the formula to take account of locally derived 'going rates'.

There was also a sense among magistrates that the rubric in which unit fines were handed out diminished the denunciatory effect of the sentence. Under the statutory scheme the court's view of the seriousness of the offence was indicated first by the announcement of so many units. This index of harm and culpability was then converted into a monetary sum by the operation of the means-related formula described above and this sum was then also announced in open court. For many magistrates the conversion process detracted from the moral, denunciatory dimension of the sentencing exercise because the visible outcome, the monetary sum derived from the means-based formula, had no direct correlation with the opprobrium expressed at the earlier stage of the judgment. Since denunciation was seen as an important, even crucial, element of sentencing, the perceived diminution in expressive effect of the fine as a result of the new system was deprecated by many who had to implement it (English, 1997).

This perceptional problem was also shared by sections of public opinion, conditioned to thinking in terms of a direct and transparent relationship between the size of a fine and the moral opprobrium attached to the behaviour for which it was imposed. Undoubtedly, there were going to be 'presentational' difficulties for any new and radical system which was intended to replace a widely understood and generally accepted one. It did not assist the cause of the unit fines system in this respect that the 1991 Act simultaneously increased the maximum permissible fines on each level of the standard scale, producing an overall upper limit of £5,000 where previously it had been pegged at £2,000. This had the effect of producing a sudden dramatic increase in the levels of fines which were being handed down and much wider differentials in the level of fines imposed on offenders with different income levels than had been the case in the pilot schemes.

The unpopularity that these two circumstances engendered among sections of the public was inflamed by the almost universally hostile reporting in the press (particularly in the populist *Daily Mail*) of cases in which ostensibly middle-class or wealthy defendants were fined more than unemployed people for similar offences, and by the furore over the infamous 'crisp packet case' in which a defendant was originally fined £1,200 for dropping an empty crisp packet in the street. In fact, in the latter case the fine resulted from the defendant neglecting to disclose his income to the court and as a result having the maximum unit value of £100 imposed by default. When his financial circumstances were eventually disclosed the original fine was reduced to a more appropriate level, but by then the propaganda value of the case had been exploited to the full by critics of the statutory scheme.

None of these problems was entirely unforeseen (Home Office, 1990a: para. 5.2) nor insuperable by a government with the political will to drive its policies through. The Magistrates' Association were not opposed to unit fines in principle and were willing to reach a compromise on the implementation of an amended scheme which preserved the basic principles of the 1991 arrangements. Alterations to the value of the units and the introduction of a sliding scale of allowances to reflect better differing levels in the middle income band might have mitigated some of the more glaring disparities (Gibson and Levy, 1993). A good deal more could also have been done to counter the dark propaganda in the media and to educate the magistrates and (particularly) the public in the underlying rationale of the scheme, including the ultimate justness of the principle of equal impact.

Instead, on this and on a range of other reforms, the Conservative government of the day responded to its own deepening legitimation crisis by reverting to its punitive instincts after nearly a decade of more self-confident penal liberalism. After a short period of apparent indecision during which he allowed his support for the principle of linking fines to disposable income to be reported in the press, the then Home Secretary Kenneth Clarke announced in the House of Commons on 13 May 1993 that he proposed to abolish the whole statutory scheme for unit fines altogether. The Magistrates' Association, who were even then working on a set of reforms to improve the existing system, were taken aback. It was soon to become apparent, however, that this stunning reversal of a particular aspect of penal policy was but part of a wider political campaign to restore the Conservatives' flagging electoral prospects through an appeal to what Tony Bottoms was later to term 'populist punitiveness' (see Chapter 1 again). In the specific area of fines the government was prepared simply to abandon an approach which had been the product of careful planning, incremental development and successful piloting and which, moreover, was in full accord with the wider sentencing agenda as it was then understood, rather than risk the adverse publicity of being seen to be at odds with a vociferous minority of the law-and-order establishment and out of step with an orchestrated media campaign.

As a result, the statutory system of unit fines was abolished after only seven months of operation. In its place the Criminal Justice Act 1993 stipulated two broad principles which were to guide sentencing practice in both the magistrates' and the Crown Courts, namely that the amount of any fine should reflect the seriousness of the offence (section 18(2) of the 1991 Act, as amended) and that in fixing the amount of the fine the court should take into account, among other things, an offender's financial circumstances 'so far as they are known, or appear, to the court' (section 18(3)). Subject to those statutory requirements (and to non-binding but persuasive guidelines from the Magistrates' Association or local 'tariffs'), the specific amount of a fine falls once more to be determined at the discretion of the sentencer and financial penalties are once again expressed in terms of monetary value only. The magistrates in particular have been given back the flexibility to fix the levels of fines 'in the round' without having first to perform mechanical calculations of disposable income according to prescriptive formulae.

Fines after 1993

The 1993 Act therefore represents a substantial return to the pre-1991 situation, although it should be noted that the amended section 18(5) expressly provides for fines to be increased as well as decreased on the basis of an offender's financial circumstances and thus reverses the earlier law on this point. Despite this concesssion to just deserts, however, it seems that the sorts of fines imposed after the 1993 Act have not reflected the principle of equal impact as well as those imposed under the statutory unit fines system, at least as far as this can be discerned from the Home Office's monitoring exercise carried out between July 1992 and December 1993. The average amount of fines levied at the magistrates' court in the survey on those who were currently employed was much lower after the 1993 Act than it had been shortly after the coming into force of unit fines (down from £233 to £158). For the unemployed the converse was true, with average fines rising from £66 to £78 (Home Office, 1994a).

Clearly, the trend that had begun to be established under the unit fines system towards greater differentials in fines according to difference in income levels has been reversed, and in the immediate aftermath of the 1993 counter-reforms many commentators feared that the extension of discretion and flexibility could result in the re-emergence of a situation in which sentencers consistently failed to adjust fine levels to take

proper account of means, resulting in a resurgence in default and commitment to prison. As Andrew Ashworth (1995: 265) observed wryly of
this possibility,

> There is a particular danger that poor people will be fined too much: fines
> that magistrates or newspaper editors may regard as 'derisory' may have
> a severe impact on those with a low income. The middle class militancy
> which presaged the demise of the unit fine is unlikely to be repeated to
> protect those on state benefits from excessive financial penalties.

In the event, however, not only do the worse consequences of an unfettered discretion seem to have been avoided, but real progress appears
to have made in reducing the reliance upon suspended and immediate
periods of custody in fine-enforcement procedures. The number of fine
defaulters received into prison in 1996 was 8,555, less than half of that
recorded in 1995 and nearly 60 per cent down on the figure in 1994.
Among women fine defaulters the reduction between 1995 and 1996 was
even more marked: the figure of 461 receptions in 1996 was almost 70
per cent lower than the year before. Overall, fine defaulters contributed
10 per cent of all receptions into prison in 1996, again less than half of
the equivalent statistic for the year previously and the lowest proportion
since 1985 (Home Office, 1997e).

Several factors have contributed to this advance. It is clear, for instance,
that a substantial minority of between 17 to 25 per cent of magistrates'
courts have persisted with their own version of unit fines and that these
courts continue to graduate fines reasonably consistently in accordance
with defendants' incomes. Not only do these courts demonstrate more
consistency in their sentencing decisions and vary fines more sensitively
in accordance with offenders' incomes than other courts who have not
persisted with a unit-based system, they also perform better on a range of
measures of indices measuring the efficiency of their fine-enforcement
practices (Charman et al., 1996).

In addition, there has been a good deal of press and parliamentary
interest in fine default and a succession of pronouncements since 1993
regarding the use of custody in this area which have taken an undeniably
reductionist stance. Most importantly, perhaps, in a test case on the use
of custody for young adult fine defaulters (R. v. *Oldham Justices and Another ex parte Crawley* [1996] 1 All ER 464), the Divisional Court reminded
magistrates of the statutory requirement to state clearly their reasons for
believing that other enforcement measures were not appropriate before
committing a person to prison for default. Although the applicants in
that particular case were not successful in securing their own immediate
release, Lord Justice Simon Brown began the judgment of the court with
the express opinion that 'offenders generally and young offenders in
particular ought not to be locked up for non-payment of fines unless no
sensible alternative presents itself' and he concluded by saying that detention really must be 'a last resort'.

This clear articulation of a presumption against commitment appears to have contributed to a different climate in which many courts have been led to revise their enforcement procedure, notwithstanding a later decision in the Divisional Court which had the effect of confining the express obligations under *Crawley* to cases involving defaulters under 21 (see *R. v. Stockport Justices, ex parte Conlon, R. v. Newcastle and Southwell Justices ex parte Keenaghan* (Penal affairs consortium, 1995). The requirement to give reasons for declining to use each of the other forms of enforcement was encapsulated in a model pronouncement produced jointly by the Magistrates' Association and the Justices' Clerks' Society for magistrates who were committing a defaulter to prison. This procedure, reinforced by guidance on the need for good practice in enforcement from the Lord Chancellor's Department's Working Group on the Enforcement of Financial Penalties, concentrated the minds of magistrates on the range of options open to them before they had to resort to committal. Even the Home Office, not otherwise noted at the time for its reductionist tendencies, began to consult over alternatives to custody for fine defaulters in early 1996, moved, no doubt by the need to free up valuable prison space for the consequences of the 'prison works' philosophy that the government were concurrently promoting in relation to almost every other category of offender.

The combined effect of all these different factors may be seen in the number of receptions into prison for fine default, which has more than halved since the *Crawley* case. There is also some tentative evidence that magistrates are making more use of other enforcement measures such as MPSOs and attendance centre orders (Whittaker and Mackie, 1997), and while it is uncertain at the time of writing exactly how much of the Crime (Sentences) Act 1997 will be brought into force, the provisions in Part III of the Act extending the availability of non-custodial penalties as direct alternatives for detention for fine default, if activated, can only serve to reinforce the reductionist tendency of recent years.

The need for further reforms

Welcome as these developments may be, it should not be supposed that they represent a complete resolution of the problems associated with the use of fines in an essentially deserts-based regime. Although part of the purpose behind the 1991 sentencing reforms was to increase the use of the fine, its proportionate use for more serious offences continued to decline from 40 per cent in 1985 to 30 per cent a decade later. Noting that immediate custody and other higher-tariff non-custodial sentences showed increases of between 3 and 7 per cent in the same period leaves open the question as to where on the tariff those who might previously have been fined have been displaced. Given the proportionality constraints of the 1991 framework, one would not now expect the fine to be displacing custody to anything remotely approaching the extent it apparently did in the period between 1940 and 1965 (Bottoms, 1987: 181).

However, there must be a considerable number of offences of middling seriousness for which a fine would be a more appropriate disposal than a community penalty, and it is here that any reluctance to impose what may appear by the sentencers' own standards comparatively small fines most impedes the cause of restraint, or parsimony, in sentencing. The great strength of the unit fines system was its potential to overcome this reluctance through the strict separation of penal value from monetary value and it remains to be seen whether any of the various approaches which have succeeded the statutory system will be anything like as effective in promoting confidence in the use of the fine.

Of course, fines must represent an appreciable loss to the offender if they are to accord with commonly held definitions of punishment; but fines which threaten complete impoverishment are more likely to be ignored or resisted than those which leave the possibility of subsistence and survival. From this point of view the latest (1997) edition of the guidelines issued by the Magistrates' Association is to be welcomed as a step towards reinstating some of the logic and consistency that was removed with the abolition of unit fines. Determination of a fine, the new guidelines state, should be influenced by 'equality of hardship rather than equality of monetary penalty . . . The just deserts principle means that each offender should experience the loss of spending power which his or her offending behaviour merits, and levels of fines should always be set with this principle in mind.' In order to give effect to this, the guidelines provide not simply a single suggested 'entry point' for fines in relation to targeted offences, but three bands graduated according to income. Under the guidelines, for instance, non-payment of a TV licence fee would result in a £90 fine for low-income offenders, compared with £225 for average earners and £540 for high earners (reported in *The Guardian*, 7 April 1997). So it appears that neither the experience nor the philosophy of unit fines has been banished entirely, despite the politicial expediency that dictated an end to the statutory scheme. Further developments of this kind are needed, however, to reinstate fully the levels of fairness, equality and consistency of sentencing that could have been delivered by the unit fines system, once its initial shortcomings had been remedied.

As far as the enforcement of fines is concerned, major difficulties remain. Observation studies by Moss (1989), Allen (1989) and others graphically reveal the level of abject poverty and desperation to which the majority of those in default have sunk by the time they are faced with the prospect of commitment to prison. For many, if not the majority, lectures from the bench on the need for better financial management and on ordering their affairs and their priorities more responsibly must seem like utopian cant. The overwhelming majority of those who appear in the default courts (four out of five men and nine out of ten women according to the latest studies) are without employment and dependent on state benefits for income. Female defaulters are typically caring for children on their own: four out of five women in Whittaker and Mackie's sample were lone carers, although this fact did not appear to affect the likelihood of imprisonment (1997: 25). Any form of enforcement, be it deductions from benefits that are already inadequate, seizure and sale of family possessions, or especially imprisonment, that is not mitigated by positive intervention and assistance in other areas of life can only serve to reinforce existing patterns of social inequality in the criminal justice system.

Magistrates are neither blind nor, for the most part, indifferent to genuine hardship, of course. There is almost universal agreement on the need to remove as many fine defaulters as possible from the prison regime for both humanitarian and administrative reasons. On the other hand, there is a deep-seated, common-sense conviction among magistrates, court officials and penal policy makers that the possibility of imprisonment is a vital deterrent without which what is usually described as 'a hard core' of persistent defaulters would simply never pay their fines. Although challenged on the basis that some other countries seem to manage without imprisonment for default and by empirical evidence in this country that raises serious questions about the taken-for-granted effectiveness of imprisonment in increasing the rate of collection (e.g. Moxon, 1983: 39; Shaw, 1989: 43), it seems likely that this pessimistic view 'from the sharp end' will continue to influence the penal policy debate (see, for instance, the views of the Chair of the Magistrates' Association quoted in Walker and Wall, 1997: 183). Given this, there is little prospect that the custodial option will be removed entirely in the foreseeable future and it is, therefore, imperative that the current policy of encouraging the use of means of enforcement other than custody is maintained and that it is successful.

Compensation orders

Fines are not the only financial penalty that a criminal court can impose. Apart from the possibility of having to pay some or all of the prosecution costs, those who are convicted are also liable to pay compensation to their victims for any injury, distress or anxiety caused or for any loss or damage occasioned by their crimes. Concern with the victim of crime has become a powerful motif in contemporary Western societies' responses to crime (Bottoms, 1983: 172), and the ordering of compensation is one very practical way in which the courts can demonstrate their commitment to this ideal. Limited powers to make such orders have been available in England and Wales since 1907, but the modern approach really began with the provision of much more extensive powers to make compensation orders covering injury, loss or damage in the Criminal Justice Act

1972 (Ashworth, 1986). These provisions are now included in section 35 of the Powers of Criminal Courts Act 1973, as amended. For the first ten years compensation orders were supplementary to other penalties, but in an effort to increase their use the Criminal Justice Act 1982 gave courts the power to order compensation without imposing any other penalty. The 1982 Act also stipulated that where a fine and compensation were ordered together, the compensation order should have priority in enforcement procedures if the defendant had insufficient means to satisfy both. Further impetus came with the Criminal Justice Act 1988, which requires a court actively to consider making a compensation order in every case involving injury, loss or damage, and to state its reasons for not doing so in any such case.

In principle, these developments seem largely unobjectionable. The criminal justice system *should* be concerned with securing more for victims than merely the punishment of their transgressors, important though that latter objective is in symbolic terms. In coming to decisions on whether to order compensation and how much to order courts must be careful to observe the requirements of due process and avoid arbitrariness. Subject to this, the granting of power to the court to require an offender to make some form of financial reparation to the person who has suffered, either on application by the injured party or of its own motion, must be counted a positive and progressive development.

From a victim's point of view the main advantage of a compensation order is that it can avoid the need to take separate civil proceedings and, in theory at least, the sum awarded – up to a maximum of £5,000 for any single offence – should be more secure since it is the court, not the individual victim, which bears the responsibility for enforcing the order. We shall see shortly that the enforcement process is not as effective as it might be, but in principle this mechanism for securing state-directed reparation is entirely in keeping with the wider interests of justice.

To facilitate the making of orders without unnecessarily prolonging summary proceedings the Magistrates' Association have issued guidelines as to reasonable amounts in cases of violence resulting in bodily injury, where quantifying compensation would often be very difficult without the assistance of expert evidence. A court has power to order what it considers to be an appropriate amount even when the precise quantum of loss or damage has not been proved or agreed, but considerations of due process make courts reluctant to make orders in cases where there is a definite dispute as to value. In such circumstances, unless the prosecution can establish the extent of loss or damage by evidence, magistrates' courts will usually prefer to leave it to the parties to settle the dispute by a civil suit for damages.

Suggested reform of the compensation order system

This is one practical restraint on the application of compensation orders, and other factors also serve to restrict their effectiveness. The most obvious

limitation is that without a successful prosecution there can be no possibility of any award, and this excludes not only those crimes (the majority) for which no one is ever brought to book but also most of those for
which a caution is issued since, in the absence of specific arrangements
for pre-prosecution reparation (Marshall and Merry, 1990), the question
of compensating the victim would not normally arise. The possibility of
compensation can also be overlooked when offences are 'taken into consideration' rather being separately charged, particularly as many victims
of crime still appear not to have been properly advised of their rights in
this regard, despite the good intentions of the Victim's Charter. Perhaps
as a result of these difficulties the proportionate use of compensation
orders has been falling from the peak it reached shortly after the Criminal Justice Act 1988. Just 20 per cent of offenders in the magistrates' courts
and 8 per cent in the Crown Court were ordered to pay compensation to
their victims in 1995, resulting in 8,400 fewer orders than the year before
(Home Office, 1996h).

Perhaps the principal limitation on the use of compensation orders,
however, and the one most difficult to overcome, is the inability of many
defendants to afford what might be thought to be an appropriate amount
in all the circumstances of the case. As with fines, courts are required to
have regard to an offender's means in fixing the level of any compensation order, and it seems that most are anxious to avoid imposing excessive burdens on defendants where it is clear that this will almost inevitably
lead to default and possible imprisonment. In many cases this understandable reserve results in, at best, token orders or no order at all. It can
scarcely be argued, however, that committing people to custody for failing to pay compensation orders serves much useful purpose since the
net result is that the victim receives nothing and the rest of society is left
to pick up the not inconsiderable costs of detaining the defaulter. Courts
do have the power to order the sale of some of the offender's assets to
provide funds for compensation, but, given a natural reluctance to order
the sale of an offender's home (Ashworth, 1995: 259), there is often not
very much of value that can be used for these purposes. The ability to
order payment by instalments mitigates the problem to a certain extent,
but this often only postpones default rather than avoiding it altogether.
Payment by instalments also inevitably means that victims have to wait
lengthy periods before any substantial amount has accrued, engendering
further uncertainty and inconvenience and in many cases prolonging the
impact of the crime.

How could the system for securing compensation for victims be improved without causing any deterioration to the rights of offenders? One
possibility which the last government considered was the establishment
of a sort of 'bridging loan' arrangement under which magistrates' courts
would immediately pay out to victims from public funds the full amount
ordered, then attempt to recoup this expenditure from the offender
through normal enforcement procedures (Home Office, 1988a: para.
3.10). This would not solve the problem of what to do with the

impecunious offender in default, but it would at least pass the risk of loss from the individual victim to the state, a move which would give the clearest possible demonstration of government commitment to enhancing victims' rights. Unfortunately, the previous government considered the likely cost to the Exchequer made such a scheme unrealistic. Given the present government's pledge to stick to their political opponent's spending limits, at least initially, it seems unlikely that this intrinsically fair and sensible proposal will be resurrected in the foreseeable future.

A more radical innovation which, arguably, might eventually save government money, would be to transfer much of the responsibility for securing compensation for victims out of the criminal courts altogether and into a forum where the offender and victim are encouraged to reach a settlement involving some form of reparation including, but not necessarily confined to, financial compensation, and possibly promises as to future behaviour (Bottoms, 1983: 172). Victim–offender mediation schemes, as they are usually called, have been operated successfully in many parts of the world including the United States, Australia and New Zealand. Early experience in this country of using mediation with juvenile offenders to secure reparation in return for diversion from custody or even from prosecution was not particularly encouraging, however, and the government declined to renew the funding it had provided to run several pilot schemes (Marshall and Merry, 1990).

Despite this setback, later examples in Northamptonshire and in Leeds of projects operating successfully with adult offenders, often at the upper end of the offence spectrum, suggest that predictions of the complete demise of this initiative may have been unduly pessimistic. Its proponents argue that, in attempting to remedy emotional and other harms and to restore pre-existing relationships where appropriate, mediation has the potential to secure better and more meaningful forms of reparation for victims beyond the remit of purely financial compensation. Successful mediation and reparation is also said to enhance the prospects of rehabilitating and reintegrating offenders into their local communities. And communities themselves are said to be able to benefit from the participation of lay people in the resolution of local conflicts, with the result that local communitarian structures are established or encouraged and social cohesion is strengthened as a bulwark against disorder and crime. As such, the arguments in favour of an expansion of reparation and mediation schemes resonate very well with the wider contemporary movement towards greater levels of communitarianism (Etzioni, 1995) and towards the model of restorative or relational justice (Braithwaite, 1989; Burnside and Baker, 1994) discussed in Chapter 2, above.

None of these innovative concepts is without its critics, of course. In relation specifically to victim–offender mediation, one could argue that since mediation involves *ex hypothesi* some form of compromise, it contains within it the potential for blaming the victim to a degree that many would find objectionable. There are certainly great difficulties in reconciling restorative and deserts-based principles of sentencing, particularly in relation to more serious crimes of personal violence where renewed contact between a victim and his or her assailant may, in any event, be thought undesirable (Zedner, 1994). Therefore, given the continued pre-eminence of just deserts with its twin emphasis on blaming and punishing, the avenues for any expansion of mediation/reparation schemes are probably quite restricted at present.

Having said that, the new government has already signalled its intention to give effect to its pre-election proposal for a wider form of reparation order under which young offenders could be sentenced to undertake activities which would provide direct reparation for their victims or for their local communities. The precise details of the scheme have yet to be announced, but the move is clearly designed to shift the focus of court-ordered restoration away from purely financial compensation with all the inherent limitations discussed above. Depending upon the extent to which partnership working with the non-statutory sector is to be encouraged under the new order, this may well provide an opportunity for those already engaged in mediation and reparation work to demonstrate its value and relevance to a wider audience.

Forfeiture and other orders affecting property

In addition to the provisions already discussed, the courts have a wide range of powers to deal with property belonging to or in the possession of those who are convicted of criminal offences. In cases of theft, for instance, courts can order anyone having possession of or control of stolen goods to return them to their rightful owner under section 28 of the Theft Act 1968. Courts can also order anyone who is convicted of an offence punishable by imprisonment for two years or more to hand over to the police any property used in or intended to be used in the commission of any crime (Powers of Criminal Courts Act 1973, section 43). Recently, too, there has been a considerable extension of the powers to confiscate the assets of those who are convicted of drug trafficking offences and a range of other crimes (Drug Trafficking Offences Act 1986; Drug Trafficking Act 1994; Proceeds of Crime Act 1995).

While these powers may be, and sometimes are, combined with non-custodial penalties, they are not of themselves community punishments and it is not proposed to discuss their operation in any detail. It is worth alerting the reader to their existence, however, because the extension of such powers provides further evidence of the increasingly punitive tone of criminal justice policy in recent years. Further, the possibility of 'loading' non-custodial sentences by the addition of confiscation and forfeiture orders can add to the punitive 'bite' of community-based penalties, and is thus very much in accord with current official thinking on these matters. In attaching such orders to community sentences, however, courts ought to keep sight of the total effect of the sentence they award, lest the addition of punitive confiscation orders makes the total sentence disproportionate and therefore excessive.

Discharges and other nominal penalties

As briefly mentioned at the head of this chapter, the bottom tier of the sentencing hierarchy is composed of a range of 'nominal' penalties – discharges and binding over – which are used to deal with offences of minimal gravity. In general, such disposals have little rehabilitative effect, being imposed in the main in lieu of punishment. They demand little of offenders other than that they stay out of trouble for the foreseeable future and one – the absolute discharge – does not even require that. For most purposes they do not even count as a conviction at all (see section 13 of the Powers of Criminal Courts Act 1973), although a later court when deciding on the seriousness of any subsequent offence can take into account the fact that an offender has previously been discharged. This last proviso is relatively new, having been inserted into the 1991 Act by the (largely punitive) Criminal Justice and Public Order Act 1994. It could be argued that as a result discharges now have more of a 'net-widening, mesh-thinning' potential than once they had, but the difference must be marginal. Discharges can be combined with restitution and compensation orders (and with a driving disqualification in a Road Traffic case) and some such combination is a useful option when the principal objectives of sentencing are denunciation and reparation.

Discharges may be imposed by virtue of section 1A of the Powers of Criminal Courts Act 1973 (as amended by the 1991 Act) following conviction in cases where it seems 'inexpedient' to the court to inflict any punishment, having regard to the nature of the offence and the character of the offender. They may be granted either absolutely or subject to the condition that the offender should commit no further offence during a period of up to three years. If a discharge is conditional, an offender who is convicted of a subsequent offence committed during the relevant period may be sentenced for the original as well as the later offence. Conditional discharges, therefore, may be thought of as having some deterrent effect and courts make not infrequent use of them, particularly in cases involving theft of small amounts where the offender has little previous criminal history (Moxon, 1988). In 1995 conditional discharges comprised more than 7 per cent of all sentences and orders in criminal cases. There has been a steady increase in their use over the previous decade and much of this has been associated with a decline in the use of the fine caused by rising levels of unemployment among offenders (Ashworth, 1995: 256).

Absolute discharges are less commonly used since they are tantamount to saying that the case should never really have reached court at all if those responsible for the prosecution process had been carrying out their gate-keeping functions properly. In the event less than 1.5 per cent of those sentenced in 1995 were dealt with by way of an absolute discharge, although they were more frequently used in the magistrates' courts than the Crown Court.

Criminal courts also have wide-ranging common-law and statutory powers to 'bind over' anyone who appears before them, whether defendant, complainant or even witness, to keep the peace or to be of good behaviour for such period as the court decides. The penalty for failing to observe the conditions of a bind-over is the forfeiture of a sum of money specifed by the court at the time of binding over. Those being bound over may have the right to make representations to the court, but the Divisional Court have recently made it clear that the operation of the power is not dependent upon the consent of those against whom it is exercised (*R.* v. *Lincoln Crown Court, Ex parte Jude,* [1997] *The Times,* 17 April).

Although a bind-over may be issued as a sentence of the court, this is not its predominant use, and the option of being bound over is not infrequently taken by defendants as part of pre-trial discussions which result in the prosecution being dropped. As may be detected, this ancient and discretionary power is extremely versatile and capable of fulfilling a wide range of functions. For this reason it is very much an adjunct to what is sometimes called in prosecutor's slang 'The Ways and Means Act' through which deals can be done and potential blockages in the system 'smoothed' out. Whether such flexibility is really in the interests of substantive justice may be doubted, and the Law Commission has recently recommended the abolition of the power. Judges, magistrates and prosecutors, on the other hand, all seem to like the flexibility that the bind-over brings them to regulate their caseloads and discipline the otherwise unruly, and it is unlikely that they will readily give it up.

Summary and future reforms

This chapter has reviewed the range of financial and nominal orders which are available to courts to punish offences not thought serious enough to warrant a community penalty or custodial sentence. The main focus has been on the fine, which continues to be the most commonly imposed sentence in England and Wales. Fines are a relatively cost-effective disposal, are not associated with excessive rates of recidivism and have few immediate negative effects on the personal liberty of the majority of those who are sentenced to them; whatever the validity of the 'dispersal of discipline' thesis, it is hard to see that the imposition of a fine contributes much to it. The fine is the quintessential retributive punishment, 'uncontaminated' by any consequentialist ambitions other, perhaps, than the most diffuse of general deterrent effects.

For reasons to do with the efficient administration of the court business (especially in the magistrates' courts) and in the wider interests of justice it is important that the fine should be available to deal equally with all offenders convicted of appropriate offences, irrespective of their personal circumstances. However, given the realities of the wide and growing income inequality between the majority of the population and those whose incomes place them in the bottom 10 per cent of society, it has to be recognised that there are practical obstacles in the way of this universalist ambition. Not least among these obstacles is the fact that the imposition of a fine (or a compensation order) can have radically different consequences because of the differential impact of enforcement practices on the affluent and the impoverished. Until very recently the practice of imprisoning those who were in default of payment was adding substantial numbers of the very poorest and most vulnerable people in society to an already overburdened custodial regime in defiance of the principles of just deserts which were supposed to underpin the whole sentencing framework. Although greatly ameliorated of late, this problem continues to trouble both penal administrators and those concerned with wider considerations of social justice.

At this moment, when a change in the sentencing climate seems at least possible, if not exactly inevitable (see Chapter 8 for a further discussion of likely developments), some minimum changes to sentencing practice may be suggested in an endeavour to secure the greatest degree of fairness possible in the use and administration of financial penalties. First, there must be a genuine acknowledgement at the heart of government that economic factors including, but not confined to, unemployment and income inequality *are* linked to criminal behaviour, even if the precise causal relationships are more complex and non-reductivist than conflict theorists sometimes allege (Tarling, 1982; Coleman and Moynihan, 1996).

Accepting this premise (for which ample evidence now exists: see e.g. Farrington *et al.*, 1986; Field, 1990; Wells, 1995) would exclude any future policy developments likely merely to exacerbate the cycle of poverty, fine default and further exclusion and provide, instead, a motor to drive the search for genuine, workable alternatives. Nothing short of a wide-scale expansion of employment opportunities or (even more utopian) the resolution of the paradoxes of income distribution within capitalist economies will really serve to make the problems of fines and their enforcement less intractable.

In the meantime, however, courts must be encouraged to be even more realistic in their assessments of what offenders can be expected to pay in fines and instalments and in recognising when even small sums have become unpayable through deteriorating circumstances. The conclusion that some form of unit fines system should be restored seems inescapable, particularly if one is serious about implementing the statutory requirement to secure equality of impact of fines.

As far as enforcement practice is concerned, while it may not be feasible even in the medium term to abolish imprisonment for default entirely, legislation could further restrict its use to the clearest cases of wilful refusal to pay, excluding the possibility which exists at present of commitment for 'culpable neglect' (Penal Affairs Consortium, 1995). Restricting the most punitive sanction to those whose default represents a deliberate defiance of the court is in keeping with the generally 'subjective' approach of modern criminal law, and such a move should also reduce the influence of class-based views about the culpability or otherwise of the sorts of coping strategies which people at the economic margins are often forced to adopt in order to survive.

There are clearly limits to the extent that 'defiance' *per se* can be taken into account within a just desert rationale (Wasik and von Hirsch, 1994: 414), but a logical distinction can be drawn between punishing someone for wilfully refusing to pay a fine or compensation order (which is a distinct *actus reus*) and punishing them more severely simply because they *persistently* default. To facilitate this restriction on the use of custody, the extension of non-custodial alternatives contained in the Crime (Sentences) Act 1997 should be implemented and used sensibly by the courts.

Adequate legal representation for those appearing in default courts also seems to be a minimum requirement of justice, even if its cost may not appeal to the Treasury (Young and Wall, 1996). Speed and efficiency in enforcement practice are important too, to prevent the accumulation of debt through repeated appearances which is such a significant factor in eventual default. Alongside these measures, there is an urgent need for systematic counselling and advice to be offered to those who are clearly failing to manage their finances. The recent expansion in the use of the MPSO is a welcome development here, although the suggestion from the Lord Chancellor's Department that this should be achieved through formal agreements with local voluntary groups like the Citizens' Advice Bureau rather than though an expansion of the role of the probation service may prove to be short-sighted. While the voluntary option is undoubtedly cheaper, a case can certainly be made that something more directive like a specifically targeted probation order might actually have more impact on what are characteristically disorganised lifestyles, and that this would be preferable, provided adequate safeguards against possible 'up-tariffing' effects were built in (Allen, 1989: 83). Such an approach would coincidentally assist in challenging the current emphasis on the probation order being essentially a high-tariff 'punishment' rather than a welfare-oriented intervention, but that need not be the prime motivation for such an innovation.

In a penal climate dominated by the 'blame more, understand less' philosophy of recent years such initiatives would seem contradictory, but a new government which is seriously committed to being 'tough on the causes of crime' must endeavour to find novel ways to break the cycle of fine, default and exclusion which patently fails to achieve few of its own objectives in so many individual cases while perpetuating much injustice. Some of these new ways may be quite radical, like decriminalising the problem of the television licence fee by moving instead to a pay-as-you-view system as digital technology develops (Walker and Wall, 1997: 184) or transforming the non-payment of local government taxes into a purely civil debt matter (Penal Affairs Consortium, 1995). Others may be more pragmatic, like abandoning ideological oppositions to electronic monitoring in order to allow the use of curfews to replace custody as the ultimate sanction for default. For innovations like this to happen, however, a new, less punitive climate must prevail, and it is by the extent to which it can deliver such a change that the Labour government elected as this book was being written will be judged by many of its supporters in the criminal justice system and elsewhere.

Chapter 7

Evaluating Community Punishments: Do they Work and are they Fair?

Why evaluate?

At first sight the answer to the question, 'Why evaluate community punishments' may seem so glaringly obvious as to render the question itself quite vacuous. After all, anyone who buys a car or a CD player or whatever wants to know fairly quickly whether the product is up to the job for which it was purchased or if it will have to be modified or even returned. So, a new car is soon driven, reversed, emergency stopped and so on while the CD player is quickly exposed to all its owner's range of musical tastes *pianissimo* to *fortissimo* and back again in order to identify any potential failings or causes for complaint. It hardly seems surprising, therefore, if those who ultimately have to pay for the provision of community-based sanctions want to engage in similar sorts of exercises to make sure that what they have commissioned or sanctioned (or are about to) works in the way that is intended and represents good value for money. Often (as with cars, CD players and community penalties) it is a matter of choosing from among several possibilities the particular option best suited for the immediate task in hand, and so penal policy makers (like motorists and music lovers) look for reliable empirically-based information about how various sentences perform in a variety of practical environments, in order to guide their choices. Expressed in this way, the rationale behind the evaluation of non-custodial penalties seems to be to produce something like a *Which Punishment?* guide to sentencing which will enable the courts to select the most effective sentences from a range of 'off-the-peg' models. Indeed, something very close to this ideal (if that is what it is) appeared in the form of the Home Office publication *The Sentence of the Court*, which through its various editions used the product of empirical research studies to suggest to sentencers the potential benefits and principal limitations of the various disposals available to them (see e.g. Home Office, 1964, 1978).

Having constructed this beguilingly simple analogy between consumer goods and community punishments, I shall use the first part of this chapter to demolish it. Penal policy makers do sometimes use evaluation studies in something like the manner suggested above, but the decision whether to persist with or expand the use of particular sentencing options is rarely entirely research-driven. As we have seen at various points in this book, other considerations, to do with changing financial priorities, a change of personnel in key decision-making positions, or just crude swings in political ideology are usually much more influential in determining the long-term future of sentencing initiatives. The rise and fall of the unit fines system discussed in Chapter 6 above provides one very clear example of the triumph of political expediency over evaluation, but there are others (see e.g. Brownlee, 1995: 603).

Moving closer to the 'front-line', as it were, one finds that the decisions of sentencers as to choice of sentence in particular cases are influenced by so many different considerations as to be best described as 'eclectic' (Walker and Padfield, 1996: 109). 'Reflective' eclecticism might try to take on board some evidence (usually from a pre-sentence report) about whether a particular disposal is likely to achieve the preferred aim at sentencing, but all too often intuitive or emotional responses to the facts of the case outweigh more 'scientific' considerations. The current dominance of just deserts as the first and principal objective for sentencing makes it all the more likely that in the general run of cases judges and magistrates will choose punish-ments on the basis of their retributivist value rather than any future effect they are likely to have. Despite improvements brought about through the activities of the Judicial Studies Board and various more local initiatives (Home Office, 1996d), researchers and academics more generally still lament the lack of awareness among many sentencers about the latest (or even comparatively recent) research into the effectiveness of criminal sanctions and other aspects of the criminal justice process (Ashworth, 1997: 533).

The limitations of evaluation

So, the first point to make about evaluation studies is that they often appear to have depressingly little sustainable impact on the real world of sentencing policy and sentencing practice. One reason for this is the fact (as we shortly see) that the more reflective and sophisticated an evaluation study is, the less likely it is to produce an unequivocal or unqualified conclusion, at least not of the sort that tends to make news headlines or satisfy the politician's yen for a cheap and dramatic 'quick fix'. Because social science research usually has to be undertaken in circumstances as given rather than as created for the purposes of an experiment, researchers face real difficulties in isolating the factors whose impact is to be tested and then controlling for the possible influence of other operative factors. Anyone wanting to do a reputable evaluation study (as opposed to a publicity shot) of a new non-custodial initiative therefore has to try to control for a whole range of human characteristics and tendencies (both at an individual and societal level) some of which may not even be identifiable from the best available data.

Nor is the precise relationship of cause and effect (the 'causal order') likely to be self-evident in any study of the social world (Ryan, 1970: 122). Human beings operate in a universe of *meanings* constructed by the subjects themselves in interaction with each other and, thus, constantly susceptible to change. Observing those interactions and then attributing an 'objective' meaning to them in terms of 'cause' and 'effect' is, in essence, an interpretative activity which brings in a whole range of epistemological and hermeneutic difficulties not generally taken to trouble observers of the natural world (at least in conventional theories of the natural sciences). For this reason the caveat that in social research even high levels of correlation between different variables cannot be taken to demonstrate a causal relationship of any kind has, of necessity, been so often repeated as to be something of an old chestnut by now.

Small wonder then that so much research on sentencing seems to come to the conclusion that no significant difference can be measured between groups which have been subject to this 'treatment' or that, when compared with a control group who have not. Lumping such inconclusive studies together has led some to suggest that 'nothing works' when what is really meant is that, on aggregate, we cannot find any single approach which will work every time with every target group of individuals. Given all of this, the apparently simple question with which we began this chapter seems to have resolved (or dissolved?) itself into the altogether less self-evident query, 'Why evaluate at all?'

The benefits of evaluation

Fortunately, a reasonably robust answer can be given, which should serve to halt this depressing slide into nihilism. Evaluation *does* matter because while it may be acceptable in the short term to be seen to be doing 'something' about, for instance, 'law and order' or the 'prison crisis', initiatives which consistently make the situation worse rather than better cannot be 'talked up' for ever. The legacy of modernity also leads popular opinion to expect that successful innovation will follow rather than precede empirical investigation, in true inductive fashion. Thus, there is a definite pressure on politicians and policy makers to be seen to be trying to find out what the 'right' thing is. This pressure is all the more compelling in a political and economic climate which extols the virtue, indeed the absolute necessity, of 'economy, efficiency and effectiveness' in public spending, a doctrine which is predicated upon the possibility of measurement and evaluation. In this sort of 'market' the appeal of intermediate sanctions between custody and 'straight' probation is strong because they offer politicians and those who run the penal 'industry' the potential to respond to the public call for serious sanctions without breaking the public bank (Clear and Byrne, 1992).

As the tide turned against the 'nothing works' ideology, a gradual reinterpretation of the negative conclusions from the earlier overviews of research on rehabilitative sentencing (see again the discussion in Chapter 2) rekindled an interest in evaluation. The more limited but undoubtedly more realistic conviction that rehabilitative intervention could work under certain closely defined circumstances if accurately targeted and correctly implemented reinvigorated the need for detailed evaluation studies designed to identify and inform 'good practice' and demonstrate 'what works', with whom and under what conditions. Therefore, while the dead hand of the 'nothing works' view of sentencing may have dampened enthusiasm for the product of evaluation studies for a while, the demand for accurate information about the effectiveness of various sentencing options has reasserted itself since at least the beginning of the 1990s.

Methodological advances have improved the reliability of the better studies, and a wider understanding generally of the problems associated with collecting and analysing social data has increased the extent to which what is available can be used sensibly and constructively in policy making and sentencing practice. Effectiveness research is also being used in a reflexive way by probation practitioners in the construction and maintenance of their own programmes, encouraging the emergence of what Raynor (1996b) has called a 'culture of curiosity' among probation workers and managers in which practice is increasingly being informed and modified by a process of integral and ongoing evaluation and feedback. So, while it may still be true that politicians and practitioners do not always receive research findings as gratefully nor apply them as objectively as researchers would like, recognition of the role and importance of evaluative research on sentencing is presently greater than it has been at any time since the early 1970s.

In the remainder of the chapter we shall examine in greater detail some of the major methodological issues which shape and, to a certain degree, limit research into the effectiveness of punishments. Having set those theoretical parameters, we can then take a more informed view of what the existing research literature tells us about the effectiveness of the community-based sentences discussed in Chapter 5. Finally, we can focus on that part of the research which provides information about the extent to which the way in which community sentences are used is influenced by factors of age, gender, class and race.

Methodological problems: identifying what we don't know, and why

What does 'work' mean, exactly?

If, as we have just suggested, the principal purpose of evaluative research into penal sanctions is to identify what is effective, then it is of crucial importance that any research proceeds upon a clear understanding of what will constitute effectiveness and success in the particular case under investigation. Unfortunately, there is no *a priori* definition of success which can be applied universally, and one of the difficulties in comparing results across different studies is that they may very well have been testing for completely different outcomes. It is therefore necessary to recognise the essentially relativistic meaning of 'success' and 'failure' in this context, and to accept that each sentence must be evaluated in terms of the objective or objectives which the person who imposed it sought to achieve.

At first sight that proposition might seem so self-evident as to hardly bear repeating. But it contains within it a range of complications that add to the difficulty of evaluating effectiveness in sentencing. We have already commented on the 'eclectic' nature of many sentencing decisions. The fact is that the sentence which is chosen with one single, clear and carefully articulated objective in mind is a rarity. More often sentences are passed with a range of objectives in mind (some of which may be incompatible with the others), and yet one sentence is supposed to achieve all of them. Even where it is clear that the principal aim of a sentence is to prevent or reduce reoffending by the individual involved, it may be by no means obvious whether this is intended to be achieved through deterrence, rehabilitation or incapacitation.

It is also the case that the majority of evaluation research has tended to focus on the issue of preventing individual recidivism and to ignore or, at least, not attempted to measure other equally valid objectives such as denunciation, reparation and general deterrence. Such an exclusive focus may in the past have led, or contributed, to an element of 'measurement failure' by omitting to look for more generalised outcomes (some of which may have been positive) of sentences which apparently failed to prevent reoffending by the individual who was sentenced. To really succeed, evaluation needs high levels of clarity in its design and implementation strategies, and the fact that the objectives of sentencing are often shrouded with uncertainty can frustrate these needs.

More perniciously, perhaps, while an ability to think beyond the narrow confines of individual recidivism is a necessary adjunct to meaningful evaluation, methodological relativism permits of a certain political legerdemain whereby a measure which is clearly seen to be failing on existing evaluative criteria (like custody, on its patent inability to reduce recidivism) may be redefined as successful when the criterion is changed to emphasise something else (in this example, incapacitation). A more widespread example of this kind of goal substitution took place at the end of the 1970s when the rash of 'nothing works' research overviews encouraged penal policy makers to reject reconviction as the principal criterion for success for non-custodial sentences, and to focus instead on the supposed cost advantages and greater levels of humanity associated with community-based punishments (Brody, 1976: 38). For a time initiatives were evaluated primarily in terms of their ability to divert offenders from custody rather than for their rehabilitative effects, and criteria other than reconviction, such as 'social stability' and 'change in attitude', were emphasised. Increasingly, too, the growing influence of 'managerialism' in criminal justice encouraged a focus on cost and internally validated measures of efficiency rather than on wider social goals.

This flexibility was convenient and probably advantageous from a range of viewpoints since one alternative would presumably have been to have abandoned many non-custodial programmes altogether. However, the ease with which sentencing objectives can be redefined in this way should put us on guard when politicians talk about the future direction of penal policy, what it can and should aim to achieve, and how successful their own preferred sentencing option has been in contributing to that development. Finally, we should also beware a modern tendency towards 'short-termism' in both criminal justice funding and research which arises from the linking of future funding to the 'successful' evaluation of the early stages of many initiatives and which puts pressure on researchers to come up with 'relevant' data after unrealistically short periods of study (Brownlee and Walker, 1997).

The limitations of reconviction as a measure of success

In some ways the focus on individual recidivism and its prevention (which has been and is increasingly again being seen as an essential measure of effectiveness in sentencing) presents fewer methodological problems than researching the success of other aims might. At least in studies of individual recidivism one usually has an identifiable range of subjects about whom reasonable amounts of data can be collected and analysed under some conditions of control. Contrast that with the evaluation of general deterrent effects, for instance, where the task facing researchers is to demonstrate that a particular measure or even a particular individual sentence has so influenced the behaviour of sufficient numbers of otherwise unidentified people as to make a difference – a negative impact – on what, *in the absence of that measure or that sentence alone*, would have been the future levels of offending. Although there have been some attempts at empirical studies of general deterrence (Walker, 1985; and see e.g. Harding and Koffman, 1988: 361–71 for some interesting extracts), it is easy to understand why there are so few and why those that do exist tend to be inconclusive and extremely guarded in their conclusions.

Having said that, even the testing of sentences against their apparent ability to influence individual reoffending is not without its theoretical and methodological difficulties. At a theoretical level, there is some dispute as to whether each and every subsequent offence should constitute 'failure' even if it is a very minor infraction of a technical nature. To put this another way, should all reoffending be attributed the same value in assessing the effectiveness of a sentence? Does the subsequent commission of a shoplifting offence by someone whose stock in trade used to be armed robbery 'invalidate' a probation order (or whatever) to the same degree as an armed robbery committed by an erstwhile habitual shop-lifter? Is it of any value to note that the shoplifter now offends less often than before, even though the behaviour persists to some degree? What counts as success and failure, as far as recidivism goes?

Even where some sort of *de facto* agreement can be reached on these sorts of philosophical issues important methodological limitations on the use of reconviction data remain. One problem that has long been recog-nised (e.g. Hood and Sparks, 1970) is the lack of objectivity in official records of reconvictions. Ever since the reception of social interactionism into criminology in the 1960s it has been acknowledged that between the commission of a criminal offence and its inclusion in the statistics of conviction there are a number of stages of varying predictability. First, the offence must be reported and recorded as such, and then someone (pre-ferably the culprit) must be apprehended for it, charged and convicted.

At each of these stages there is a level of 'wastage' which means, basi-cally, that for various reasons fewer crimes are reported than are com-mitted, fewer are recorded than reported, fewer cleared up than are recorded and so on (Home Office, 1995d: 25). Each of these stages in-volves decision-making by various individuals and agencies and hence there is considerable room for differential enforcement practices pro-ducing distortions in the final figures. In relation to sentences involving probation officers, for instance, research has demonstrated that breach proceedings and the prosecution of reoffending do not follow failure to comply with requirements as rigidly as envisaged in either the law or the National Standards. Vass (1996: 164) sums up this example of the social construction of reconviction as follows:

> [S]upervising officers are capable of determining 'outcomes' by either shielding offenders from further penal sanctions (thus increasing the arithmetical outcomes of 'success') or uncovering and reporting infractions (thus increasing the arithmetical outcomes of 'failure'). Success or failure (apparent recidivism) can be controlled by officials.

Probation officers, it must be emphasised, are not the only officials mak-ing these sorts of potentially distorting decisions, but in the context of community sentencing their influence is of particular importance.

As a result of these processes of attrition it is estimated that for every 100 offences committed only two result in a criminal conviction (Lloyd *et al.*, 1994: 5). It is clear, therefore, that reconviction is not at all the same thing as reoffending and that the use of reconviction rates as a proxy for the extent of reoffending means that underestimation is always present to a greater or lesser (but unknowable) degree. The problem is further compounded by the fact, as the British Crime Survey confirms, that the size of the gap between commission and conviction differs greatly for different types of offences. This means that some forms of reoffending are much less likely to be uncovered than others, making comparisons between different offenders all the more dubious.

Some improvement can be made in smaller studies by the use of self-reported information about reoffending but this is also subject to methodological limitations to do with the increased cost of obtaining such information and the truthfulness or otherwise of respondents. Most evaluation studies therefore make do with officially recorded reconvictions as a measure of recidivism and, although the accuracy and inclusiveness of databases such as that held at the National Identification Bureau in London are constantly improving, the distinction between reoffending and reconviction is unlikely ever to vanish, given the influence of human beings on the construction of both.

When does the counting start and what does it include?

This is not the only problem with the use of reconviction data in evaluation studies. Researchers must also decide the length of time after the 'target' sentence they are going to investigate an individual's offending behaviour and when precisely such a follow-up period should start. Too short a follow-up and significant new offending may not be noticed, particularly as there is inevitably a time lag between apprehension and eventual disposal in court. Too long a period and the impact of the measure that is being evaluated or (probably more importantly) the political enthusiasm for it may have vanished before the results of the evaluation are known. And if reconvictions are to be counted from the day the sentence is passed does this not put community-based disposals at an unfair disadvantage since those punished in the community are at greater liberty to reoffend during the course of their sentence than those who are in custody? Conversely, what is the logical basis for discounting offending during the currency of a probation order if the order itself is supposed to be part of the 'treatment' that is supposed to influence future behaviour? Can its effect be said to have begun only at its termination? These are not trivial questions, and although there is no universally agreed answer to either, it is conventional to use a two-year period follow-up which commences at the date of sentence with a community-based disposal and at the date of release in the case of custody. Neither convention is incontrovertible, however, and care must be taken when comparing different studies to note any divergence in approach on these matters.

Linked with the question of when to start the follow-up is the issue of so-called 'pseudo-reconvictions' (Lloyd et al., 1994: 7). These are reconvictions which occur during the currency of the target sentence but which actually relate to offences committed before the current sentence began. Clearly, since even the most effective 'treatment' cannot be expected to have retrospective effect, the inclusion of these pseudo-convictions seriously distorts the measurement of the sentence under evaluation. This is particularly relevant when comparing community sentences with custody because of the tendency mentioned above of starting to monitor reconvictions in the case of a custodial sentence only after the offender has been released from detention. As a result it is less likely that someone who has completed a custodial sentence will be convicted of an offence pre-dating their sentence than those starting probation or community service simply because the time lapse will be greater. Offences will come to light while they are in custody, or else the CPS will decide that it is not worth proceeding with other offences against someone who is already 'inside' (Lloyd *et al.*, 1994: 7). The fact that those who are eventually imprisoned are less likely to be granted bail pending trial also means that they have less opportunity to commit offences which would count as pseudo-reconvictions than those who are given community sentences and who are more often released on bail in the interim.

Comparing reconviction rates across different sentences

All of these problems which apply to studies that attempt to validate indi-vidual types of sentences are compounded when, as is more usually the case, the purpose of the study is to evaluate how well one sentence works when compared to others of a different kind. The compounding factor has to do with the fact that courts quite patently do not allocate sen-tences at random, nor would most people expect them to. This means that in comparing the subsequent behaviour of offenders who have received, say, a sentence of imprisonment and a probation order it is hard to ensure that we are comparing two like samples of people.

The more rigorous the study, the more effort the researchers will put into trying to 'match' the members of each sample in terms of character-istics thought to influence the chance of reconviction so as to even out background differences between the control and the research group. This is never easy, however, and cannot be guaranteed to be complete. Whereas certain factors such as age, gender, current offence, number of previous convictions and number of previous custodial sentences which have been shown to be associated with reconviction (Copas, 1995) are usually obtain-able from official records, other more socially oriented factors which may also have an influence are routinely absent. Therefore, although approx-imations thought sufficiently robust for most experimental purposes can be made, especially in smaller-scale studies, it is virtually impossible to be certain that the process of matching individuals in the 'treatment' and control groups has compensated for all factors related to reoffending in individual cases.

One way around the 'matching' problem would be to arrange for tot-ally random allocation to sentencing options, but this raises such enorm-ous ethical and practical problems as to be scarcely feasible, especially in a climate dominated by concerns for public protection and giving crim-inals their just deserts. Another more practical approach is to compare samples on the basis of the predicted and actual reconviction rates of the individuals within each sample (Hood and Sparks, 1970). This is a labori-ous process, but it can be done and it then provides a basis on which to compare actually observed outcomes. For example, when all the recorded details of a sample of offenders sentenced to a certain measure were factored in it might be predicted (using information from earlier studies of people possessing that range of characteristics) that 60 per cent of the present sample would be reconvicted within two years. If, in the event, a smaller percentage were actually reconvicted, this would provide some grounds for believing that particular measure had had a beneficial effect on their reoffending. If the same exercise is then carried out for other kinds of sentence it is possible to say which of them performs better against *its own* predicted success rate and thus to make some suggestion as to the superiority of one over the other.

This approach, which has been used in evaluations of the effectiveness of sentences for nearly fifty years now, is thought to be more robust than other forms of comparative method because it does not depend to the same extent on the difficult task of finding matched pairs of individuals in different sentencing groups. There are still problems with it, however, because it obviously hinges on the correct and comprehensive identification of factors associated with reconviction. The state of knowledge here is better than it was, at least on an aggregate or actuarial basis, but, as yet, the partial contribution of social variables such as employment history, marital stability, accommodation and drug or alcohol abuse to the prediction of reconviction is relatively unexplored (McIvor, 1992; Lloyd *et al.*, 1994) and data on these characteristics are routinely absent from the sorts of records used in large-scale studies. It is also impossible to exclude the possibility that it may have been one or more of these unrecorded factors which most influenced the sentencing court in their choice of disposal, and where this has happened offenders who have been dealt with in different ways will not really be comparable even though their offending histories are broadly similar and their reconviction scores the same.

A final possible limitation that must be borne in mind when interpreting studies which purport to compare the 'success' or, rather, the 'failure' rates of different sentences – reconviction, after all, suggests that the preceding sentence failed to impact on the subject's recidivism – is the likelihood that reconviction prediction scores calculated on the basis of aggregate data mask the differential impact that the same measure can have on different individuals at different times of their life (Walker, 1985: 92–3), making generalised conclusions about success or failure misleading. This is linked to the tendency of studies (particularly large-scale, statistically-based studies) to proceed as if sentence types were homogeneous and undifferentiated and as if variations in the specific content and implementation of actual sentences made no difference to their success rates (Bottomley and Pease, 1986: 164). Recently, this tendency has begun to be reversed with greater attention being paid in the design of evaluation studies to the need to specify more clearly the aims of the programme to which the offender has been sentenced and the range of social work inputs involved (Raynor, 1996b). Not only does this bring a greater specificity to the evaluation findings, but it allows evaluation studies to identify and disseminate 'best practice' elements in the approaches that are being employed.

So why evaluate at all?

Faced with this lengthy litany of caveats and cautions, the sceptical reader might conclude that evaluations of the effectiveness of sentences are an expensive luxury yielding heat (at least from the backs of computers) but not much light. This was certainly not the author's objective, however, because recognising the limitations of statistical information is not the same thing as rendering it useless. What is needed is a *critical* appreciation of what evaluation studies can tell us and what, because of the sorts of technical and theoretical limitations summarised above, they cannot. Taking it all together, the critical literature reviewed here does not destroy the case for careful, systematic and rigorous studies of various sentencing options, nor does it suggest that sentencing decisions which take into account the information produced by such studies are in any way invalidated thereby. Far from it, since the alternative basis for choice is dangerously close to personal prejudice and caprice. However, what the evaluation of evaluations does show is that the sort of information which tumbles out of the research machine is a sight more provisional and a good deal less 'scientific' (if that term is taken to mean 'value-neutral' and 'objectively true') than the appearance of all those statistical tables and log linear regressions would suggest. Viewed in this way, research into the effectiveness of punishments provides a great deal of useful information, but it is information that can rarely, if ever, be taken at face value.

How effective are community punishments?

With all of these reservations firmly in mind, it is now time to consider what the existing research evidence tells us about the effectiveness of community sentences. Most of the discussion which follows focuses on the issue of recidivism, taking that as an indication of success and failure. The reader will by now appreciate that recidivism is but one of the possible criteria by which effectiveness might be judged and that it is pre-eminent in the literature primarily because it reflects the value judgement of policy makers that punishments, if they are working, *should* reduce reoffending. Much of the research which is discussed uses reconvictions as a proxy for reoffending and I shall not trouble the reader with the caveats about that approach, each time it is encountered. It bears repeating, however, that any attempt to compare the effectiveness of sentences through the simple comparison of reconviction rates is likely to produce misleading results (Lloyd *et al.*, 1994: 43). The review presented here cannot hope to be comprehensive. It reports on probation and youth supervision, community service, combination orders and curfews, but not on attendance centre or financial penalties for which little by way of consolidated data is available. Readers who want a more detailed account of the issues involved are referred to the suggestions for further reading at the end of the book

The use and effectiveness of probation orders

Despite the intentional escalation in the seriousness of offenders with whom probation officers now deal, nearly three-quarters of all probation orders run their full course without breach for reoffending (Home Office, 1996g). If this genuinely represents two or even three crime-free years in the lives of a group of people who have quite often been regularly in trouble with the law, then it is no mean achievement of itself. This conclusion is by no means certain, however, since, as we have seen in Chapter 5, courts do have the discretion when dealing with subsequent offences to allow an existing probation order to continue. Statistics for 1994, for example, record that 46 per cent of those whose probation orders were completed in that year had been reconvicted before termination (Home Office, 1996g: para. 46).

Attempting to measure what may be called the suppression of offending or 'holding' effect of probation orders in this way from aggregated statistical data is fraught with methodological difficulties, not the least of which is the problem of filtering out those 'pseudo-reconvictions' which actually relate to offences committed before the commencement of the community order. Nonetheless, if it can be done properly, calculating the 'holding' or incapacitation effect of a probation order is one way of measuring the order's effectiveness, and there is room for believing that, in general, probation orders perform reasonably well on this criteria, although, obviously, they cannot hope to obtain the same incapacitation effects as custody.

Reports in the press in the middle of 1997 highlighted Home Office research which suggested that one in ten of all murders committed in England and Wales in a year were carried out by someone under probation supervision either as a community sentence or after release from prison (*The Times*, 2 July 1997). The ideological impact of the stories and their timing has been discussed, above, in Chapter 5 but for present purposes it is important to set this bald statistic in context. The study on which the news stories were based related to 204 serious incident reports received in the 13 months to December 1996. While one should not attempt to trivialise the impact on their victims of offences as serious as murder or attempted murder (101 incidents), rape (36) or indecent assault (10), it has to be remembered that there are about 200,000 people under probation supervision at any one time. Two hundred and four serious offenders represents about 0.1 per cent of that total. Set against this light, the statistics in that particular study clearly give rise to some proper concern but do not invalidate the general proposition that while it continues probation supervision can offer reasonable protection against renewed offending.

Turning to information about offending *after* the completion of a probation order, the empirical evidence shows mixed results. The recent large-scale Home Office study of reconvictions already referred to in the section on methodology suggested that whereas a probation order without additional conditions fared better than prison in terms of reconviction after two years by about 11 per cent, 'strengthened' probation orders fared less well by about 9 per cent (Lloyd *et al.*, 1994: 41). In a similar vein, the latest available official figures on reconviction following probation (Home Office, 1997c) show that 60 per cent of those starting probation in 1993 had been reconvicted for a notifiable offence (i.e. one serious enough to warrant inclusion in the annual criminal statistics) within two years of commencement of the order. 'Strengthened' probation orders fared even less well on this measure. Where the original order had included a 'specified activities' requirement the reconviction rate was 61 per cent, while 74 per cent of those required to attend a probation centre as a condition of their order were reconvicted within two years.

Devotees of the 'prison works' faith seized upon these figures and compared them unfavourably with similar information about the reconviction of those released from prison in 1993 which pointed to a reconviction rate for adult ex-prisoners of 53 per cent after two years (Home Office, 1997b). Such a simple comparison does not really hold up to any more detailed scrutiny, however, as the Home Office's own researchers have been at pains to point out. Once necessary adjustments are made to equalise personal characteristics known to be linked to reconviction (such as age, sex and past criminal history), and once those 'pseudo-reconvictions' which actually related to offences committed *before* the commencement of the sentence are removed, the difference in the latest study between the overall reconviction rates for immediate custody and all community penalties was reduced to one percentage point after rounding.

Indeed, adult probation orders may actually do better than this if reconviction is measured from the date of termination rather than commencement of the order (and, after all, custody reconviction rates are calculated from the *end* not the *beginning* of the sentence). Such an adjustment tends to reduce overall reconviction rates for probation by between 10 and 12 percentage points to levels below those of custodial sentences (ACOP, 1996: 4; Home Office, 1996g: Table 4.3). Therefore, the Home Office research itself concludes that there is currently no significant difference between reconviction rates for custody and all community penalties including probation, a statement that was strikingly at odds with claims by the Conservative government during the 1997 election campaign (Conservative Party, 1997: 36).

Further, other more localised studies have produced evidence suggesting that probation, whether strengthened or not, performs at least as well as prison on this measure and usually a good deal better, particularly if reoffending is tracked over five years rather than two (Brownlee, 1995; ACOP, 1996; Oldfield, 1996). Indeed, some probation programmes which incorporate variants of the 'cognitive behavioural' approach (see Chapter 4 again) claim to have produced significantly greater reductions in recidivism over a number of years than immediate imprisonment. Internal evaluations of the STOP ('straight thinking on probation') programme run by Mid Glamorgan Probation Service, for instance, suggest that whereas those offenders who are released from custody have actual reconviction rates some 6 per cent higher than would be forecast on standard predictive scales, those who complete a STOP programme are reconvicted 7 per cent *less often* than predicted, and for less serious offences (Raynor and Vanstone, 1994).

Sweeping generalisations from localised studies like these would be unwise, at least until a great many more replication studies have been completed and the evaluations themselves have been subjected to more rigorous external scrutiny. One must also remember the potential that supervising officers more generally have for distorting the figures when they do not enforce requirements in some cases as rigorously as the National Standards require because of humane considerations like empathy with, or sympathy for, those they continue to see as 'clients'. As a result, offenders on probation may appear to be doing better in terms of reconviction rates than offenders given custody, not because probationers commit fewer new offences after conviction but because they receive preferential treatment (although this advantage must logically disappear when supervision has ended and any reconvictions involve offences detected by persons other than probation officers). Nonetheless, the evidence that is currently available supports the proposition that in aggregate probation orders compare favourably with custodial sentencing when their effectiveness is tested in terms of recidivism, and that in some more specific instances they outperform custody by some margin. Given this, and given that custodial sentencing is significantly more expensive and certainly more personally damaging to many of those who undergo it, the case for favouring community-based penalties, including probation, remains persuasive on a number of grounds.

Moreover, noting that probation orders with special conditions have a higher 'failure' rate than other forms of supervision or custody does not necessarily mean that 'straight' probation is more effective in reducing recidivism than 'strengthened' probation. Once the offending history of those assigned to each disposal is examined it becomes clear that offenders with very different characteristics (and therefore different risks

of reconviction) are being sentenced to these different disposals (Lloyd
et al., 1994: 51). As probation is required by government policy to move
higher up the tariff and to work with ever more serious offenders, it would
be naïve to expect reconviction rates that were markedly better than other
disposals dealing with similarly recidivist offenders (Mair and Nee, 1992:
338). Criticisms of probation's apparently high rate of 'failure' have often
been based on the premise that since those put on probation are generally less 'criminal' than those given custody, they are less likely to be
reconvicted in any event and, therefore, there should always be a significant gap between the reconviction rates of the two sentences (Hood and
Sparks, 1970: 181).

This premise is extremely dubious in the current sentencing climate
for the reasons just explained, and because it appears to confuse seriousness of offence at conviction with a demonstrable commitment to offending. A seriously recidivist shoplifter is more likely to be sentenced to
probation than someone who inflicts grievous bodily harm in an uncharacteristic but nonetheless intentional assault, yet it is the violent offender
who represents the 'better bet' in terms of reconviction (Lloyd *et al.*, 1994:
35). In the circumstances in which it now works, a generally low reconviction rate for probation would be more likely to imply recruitment of
low-tariff offenders than to indicate that the probation service had dis-
covered a miracle cure for crime (Raynor, 1988: 30; Morris and Tonry,
1990: 240). On the one hand this could raise the question of whether
the probation service has been *too* successful in diverting from custody
offenders with a high rate of reconviction, thereby condemning probation, especially intensive probation programmes, to high rates of failure
when measured on reconviction rates. On another view, however, that
sort of dilemma merely illustrates the futility of relying solely on reconviction rates to measure success or failure of a community sentence and
the difficulties that arise when there is insufficient clarity about what a
particular sentence is supposed to achieve.

Supervision orders

About three-quarters of the orders terminated in 1994 had run their full
course, while termination for failure to comply with requirements or
because of conviction for another offence occurred in only 14 per cent
of cases (Home Office, 1996g). Given that a good many of those on supervision will have been within the peak age range for offending, this completion rate represents a solid achievement, although, as has been pointed
out above, it does not guarantee an absence of reoffending, just an absence
of breach proceedings.

Surprisingly, perhaps, the effectiveness of different kinds of community sentences imposed on young offenders in terms of reoffending is
not measured on a regular basis in many parts of England and Wales
(Audit Commission, 1996: para. 68). It is worth noting, however, that given

the strong positive correlation between youthfulness and reconviction it is unlikely that any particular disposal will influence recidivism to any great extent in this age group. Certainly custodial sentences do not, given that 75 per cent of male young offenders were reconvicted within two years of release (Home Office, 1997b). It is hard to imagine that even on aggregate figures for supervision and other community penalties for young offenders do not compare favourably with such a dismal record.

Community service

Taking the latest available figures (Home Office, 1996g) as indicative of general trends on reoffending, some 70 per cent of community service orders which came to an end in 1994 had run their full course, with the rate of successful completions, unsurprisingly, being higher the fewer hours that had been ordered. It should be noted once again that this does not necessarily mean a complete absence of further offences during the currency of the order because, as with probation orders, courts dealing with new offences have a discretion to allow an existing CSO to continue. Only 6 per cent of orders were terminated in 1994 as a consequence of reconviction, despite the fact that 35 per cent of those whose orders were terminated (whether on completion or otherwise) in that year had collected at least one reconviction by the termination date. In addition, 15 per cent of orders in 1994 were terminated because of a failure to comply with requirements. Few conclusions can be safely drawn from these data on how far CS operates to suppress offending and, therefore, to offer an element of public protection during the currency of an order, although, given the continuance of orders in the great majority of cases, it is likely that most reoffending involved relatively minor offences.

Overall, some 56 per cent of those given community service in England and Wales were reconvicted within two years of commencement on the latest available figures (Home Office, 1996g: Table 4.1(d)). Reconviction rates after community service vary considerably, however, depending on whether the specified number of hours had been completed or not, the sort of offence for which the original order had been made and, most crucially, the number of previous convictions. The simple fact is that whatever type of sentence is being evaluated in this way, reconviction rates rise as the number of recorded previous convictions increase. For community service, reconviction rates measured in 1994 over two years ranged from 31 per cent for those with no previous conviction on commencement to 69 per cent for those with 11 or more previous convictions. Reconviction rates were also significantly higher for those whose original offence had been burglary (a finding that was common across all types of sentences). Males were reconvicted more than females in all age groups and younger males were reconvicted most often of all, in line with expectations.

Given these complexities and variations, it is difficult to draw any general conclusion from these data regarding the efficacy of community service in curbing recidivism. The Home Office study of the reconvictions of those sentenced in 1987 (Lloyd *et al.*, 1994) reported that, once allowance was made for pseudo-reconvictions, CSOs had an overall reconviction rate 3 per cent lower than predicted on the basis of current offence, offending history and other significant variables. Despite all the caution necessarily attached to interpretations of that finding, it represents a mildly encouraging sign that CS may have some positive effect, albeit small, on reoffending. The safest claim that can be made is that community service performs no worse than sentences of immediate custody in this respect (a sentiment which echoes research findings in other jurisdictions: see McDonald, 1986: 166). Indeed, as we have seen above in relation to probation orders, measuring reconviction from the date of termination rather than commencement of an order tends to reduce overall reconviction rates by between 10 and 12 percentage points to levels much below those of custodial sentences (ACOP, 1996: 4; Home Office, 1996g: para. 47). As we noted in Chapter 2, there has always been an ambivalence about the aims which CS should attempt to secure; rehabilitation is not the only objective, nor even the prime one that sentencers may have in mind when imposing a CSO.

Therefore, while it is clearly no panacea for offending behaviour (a claim which few would make, in any event), community service is certainly not ruled out on grounds on public protection, and may be favoured on other grounds such as cost and because the element of reparation associated with it can benefit offenders, victims and the general community (McIvor, 1992, 1993: 400). And, as the National Standards indicate (Home Office *et al.*, 1995: 34), community service labour can even be harnessed to reducing future opportunities for crime, by, for example, fitting home security devices or distributing crime prevention literature. This remains an intriguing and even an ironic possibility, but while there are examples of it working in practice (e.g. Forrester *et al.*, 1990), there are a number of aspects of community service, to do with the limited skills of those on CSOs and the possible risk to the public, which limit its usefulness for crime prevention work (Barker *et al.*, 1992: 28).

Combined orders

Given its relative novelty, information on the reconvictions of those who have been sentenced to a combination order is somewhat limited. Details from a special sampling exercise of 1,262 offenders who commenced combination orders in the last quarter of 1992 show that 63 per cent had been reconvicted within two years (Home Office, 1996g: Table 4.9). While this finding was based on relatively small numbers, it was very close to the 61 per cent recorded in the larger study comparing the reconvictions of those commencing community penalties in 1993 (Home Office, 1997c). At first sight, this is a disappointingly high figure, but all of the caveats which have been applied above to the measurement of reoffending after probation and community service as separate orders must also be borne in mind here. In addition, it should be noted that in terms of predicted reconvictions, combination orders performed better, on average, than probation orders alone. Nor should one forget that as a supposedly 'high-tariff' disposal the combination order may be used for sentencing some of the more committed recidivist offenders. It is hardly surprising, therefore, that many of those who were routinely committed to law-breaking before such a sentence remain so afterwards. Nonetheless, the combination order comes within the general conclusion of the Home Office studies that on generally accepted measures there is currently no significant difference between the reconviction rates for custody and all community sentences.

Since the intention which lay behind the decision to create this sentence was to provide sentencers with a tough new option for punishing some persistent property offenders – those guilty of burglary, theft, handling and fraud offences – in the community rather than in custody, a more meaningful measure of its effectiveness might be the extent to which it has succeeded in diverting that type of offender from detention. There is no published research which deals specifically with this aspect, but indirect evidence inferred from the latest available Criminal Statistics (Home Office, 1996h) points to a lack of success. Since its introduction in 1992 the combination order has gradually attracted proportionately more of those sentenced for property offences so that 2 per cent of those dealt with for burglary and 3 per cent of those dealt with for theft for handling in 1995, for instance, were given a combination order. However, these small advances have been accompanied by increases at least as big in the proportionate use of immediate custodial sentences in these offence categories.

While one cannot say for certain that the rise in the use of custody would not have been even greater in the absence of the combination order, these figures lead one to suspect that little or no diversion effect is present. This disappointing outcome is undoubtedly one further consequence of the conversion of the last government to the belief that 'prison works' which led to a rise in both the use of community penalties *and* custodial sentencing since 1993. It remains to be seen whether a more rational sentencing climate will prevail with the election of a new government and, if so, whether this will enable the combination order to achieve more by way of what it was intended to do.

Curfew orders

In view of the fact that curfew orders are not, as yet, in normal use as a community sentence, any attempt to say how effective these are in terms of reconvictions would be premature, even if the evidence from the American experience of house arrest sanctions was less equivocal. For the record, however, one can note that the evaluation of the pre-1991 trials in England and Wales reported 18 breaches and 11 further offences in the 50 curfew orders in the sample (Mair and Nee, 1990). The initial evaluation of the second wave of pilots from 1995 onwards suggests that some improvement may have taken place in terms of this measure in the interim. Of 83 curfew orders made in the three pilot areas in the first twelve months, 56 (75 per cent) were completed successfully although seven of this had involved breach action short of termination. Nineteen of the offenders (23 per cent) had their orders revoked and were resentenced (Mair and Mortimer, 1997). The short time-scale involved in this first study did not allow for a follow-up study of reconvictions to be undertaken and we must therefore wait for the fuller picture to emerge.

The case for community sentences

In summary, the evidence reviewed above gives some grounds for believing that in aggregate community-based punishments are at least as effective in tackling recidivism as an institutional sentence. Or, to put it the other way round, the research evidence certainly does not rule out the use of community sentences on the grounds of public protection, especially when what is being looked for is long-term efficacy against recidivism rather than some shorter-term incapacitative effect. It is also clear from what has been said here and in Chapter 4 that by focusing not on the general effect but on specific sentencing 'programmes', one finds firmer grounds for believing that, in relation to community penalties and the prevention of reoffending, some things do work with some people under some conditions. The principal prerequisites of success seem to be that programmes are accurately targeted at those most likely to benefit from them, are delivered in a consistent matter by appropriately trained and committed staff and are subject to monitoring and evaluation to maintain what may be called 'programme integrity' and ensure that intended outcomes are met (Raynor, 1996b: 250).

Of course, generalised statements like these must be treated with great caution for all the reasons rehearsed in the first part of this chapter; and the evidence is nowhere like clear enough to dispel entirely what Bottomley and Pease (1986: 164) have dubbed the 'penal agnosticism' of objective observers. But given what we know (or think we know) about other advantages of punishment in the community, such as its lower unit costs, and its general tendency to be less dehumanising than custody and to drive fewer of those who endure it to self-harm and suicide, the lack of any demonstrable superiority on the part of institutional sentencing in controlling recidivism should mean that it is the use of *custody* not community sentencing that has to be justified and defended, as indeed the schema of the 1991 Act implies.

Community sentences and the 'dispersal of discipline'

Before leaving the subject, however, we must pick up on a promise made at the end of Chapter 1 and discuss in more detail the possibility which has been raised by Scull (1977), Cohen (1979, 1985), Mathiesen (1983) and others that in reality the expansion of community sentencing merely adds to the overall level of state control of deviant populations without reducing the use of imprisonment in any way. Cohen, for instance, has asserted that because community-based sanctions do little, if anything, to challenge the pre-eminence of the prison in penal thinking, the net effect of the expansion of 'punishment in the community' has been that the apparatus of social control now 'penetrates' more deeply and widely across and through society, having moved out beyond the confines of the prison to extend the potential for 'discipline' into society's informal networks. In Cohen's view these new forms of discipline supplement the existing prison system, they do not replace it. Because of the growth of community-based sanctions, more and more people who would not previously have been incarcerated are brought within the ambit of social control ('the net is widened'). The 'strengthening' of community sanctions means that these new recruits are subjected to levels of control that would not have accompanied older penalties, like the fine ('the mesh is thinned'). Finally, Cohen argues that, because of the expansion of control beyond the confines of the institution (prison, reformatory or asylum) and because many of the new community programmes are justified on welfarist principles, the distinction between punishment and treatment is 'blurred' to a point where it will eventually be impossible to determine who exactly is enmeshed in the social control system and who is not.

For a time in the 1980s Cohen's 'dispersal of discipline' thesis represented something of an orthodoxy among radical criminologists and it received support from a number of other scholars (e.g. Hylton, 1981). On one level it is hard to dispute the evidence from a wide range of different countries that the range and take-up of community-based sanctions *can* expand alongside a rising prison population. This is very much what has happened in England and Wales between 1993 and 1996, for instance. Even Bottoms, who, as we saw in Chapter 6, is generally critical of the dispersal of discipline thesis, is pessimistic about the capacity of community penalties, 'in a gradual way, [to] erode the central importance of the prison in modern penality' (1987: 177). But does it necessarily follow that there is an inevitable link between the expansion of community penalties and a rising prison population, and that punishment in the community is really a 'Trojan horse' ushering in an intensification of social control? The claim that it does has been hotly contested on both theoretical and empirical grounds (e.g. Bottoms, 1983; McMahon,

1990, 1992; Matthews, 1987; Vass, 1990, and see Chapter 5 again, where some of the empirical evidence is reviewed).

To some extent the protagonists in this debate are arguing past each other. Critics of community penalties, being the inheritors, indeed in some cases the originators, of the radical non-interventionist, anti-correctionalist tradition in sociology, generally take the view that, far from being humane replacements for an inhumane custodial regime, community punishments are actually disguised forms of coercion, rendering those sentenced to them liable to a whole swathe of largely untrammelled discretionary powers in the hands of 'experts' to intervene in and control their lives.

Needless to say, this nightmarish and totally negative picture is rejected by those who continue to advocate the use and, indeed, the expansion of community-based sentences under conditions of critical scrutiny. Peter Raynor, for instance, has recently argued (1996b: 250) that the emerging focus on cognitive behavioural techniques in probation programmes is about *increasing* the ability of erstwhile offenders to take greater responsibility for their own lives and choices, rather than a search for more effective forms of social control. Clearly, such opposing views cannot both be correct, and given that they are predicated on such widely divergent sets of values, there seems little possibility of reconciling them, other than on the purely pragmatic (and not entirely convincing) ground that, for the present, the gradualist approach seems the only feasible way to make any progress towards the wider goals of the abolitionist project.

Comprehensive and readable summaries of the main contributions to this debate are available elsewhere (see e.g. Vass, 1996: 166–73; Cavadino and Dignan, 1997: 231–42) and it is not proposed to go over the same ground here. However, two general conclusions will be suggested. First, although there has tended to be a defensive reaction among practitioners to the criticisms levelled at community punishments, there is little doubt that the critique has been effective in illustrating discrepancies between objectives and actual outcomes which, in turn, has highlighted the need for improved working practices. So, while convincing evidence can be produced of non-custodial initiatives which do appear to have had some success in keeping out of custody those who would otherwise have been sent there (e.g. McDonald, 1986; Raynor, 1988; Mair *et al.*, 1994), no one can now ignore the *potential* for 'alternatives' to draw into intensive forms of intervention those whose offending behaviour does not really justify such a response. Therefore, more attention is being given to 'gate-keeping' procedures to ensure, as far as is possible, that 'up-tariff' initiatives are targeted only at those genuinely at risk of custody (McRoberts, 1989; Brownlee, 1990).

Secondly, while the implicit thesis that there is a necessary association between an expanding system of community punishments and a rising prison population has not been universally accepted, the contrary and rather naïve belief that extending the range of non-custodial sentences will inevitably lead to a reduction in the use of custody has also been dispelled. Therefore, rather more sophisticated explanations of the complex relationship between the level of recorded crime, the range of available sentences and the size of the prison population have had to be explored. This has led to the recognition that factors such as changes in the age and ethnic composition of the offending population, a toughening of policing policies (like the adoption of the so-called 'zero tolerance' approach) and a hardening of rhetoric among policy makers and in the media all function to distort this complex relationship.

As a result, the resolution of the several crises in criminal justice that come to a head in the crisis of prison overcrowding is seen to require action at a variety of levels and at a multiplicity of sites, rather than merely a return to the 'beauty contest' approach to sentencing options described in Chapter 1. In particular, the activities and policies of the government of the day as the apex of a highly complex matrix of social, political and judicial processes are seen to be crucial in creating the sort of penal climate which determines the precise relationship between custodial and non-custodial sentences and the proportion of offenders assigned to each (Vass, 1996).

But are community punishments implemented fairly?

We shall return to the tricky issue of government policy and its impact on the penal climate in Chapter 8, but one further important issue is still left hanging over from the end of the first chapter. This concerns the assertion, by Vass (1990), Hudson (1989, 1993) and others, that disparities in the use of community punishments along the lines of class, age, gender and ethnic origin are reproducing and accentuating social inequalities and injustice within the penal system. The general argument is that decisions on suitability for non-custodial options are being unduly influenced by consideration of personal characteristics in a discriminatory fashion, and that this bias helps to account for the unrepresentative nature of the 'remnant' prison population who are thought unsuitable for punishment in the community.

Class

Neither the *Criminal Statistics* nor the *Prison Statistics* series routinely present information on the social class of defendants within the criminal process. However, other sources of information like the National Prison Survey (Walmsley *et al.*, 1992) and smaller studies of specific sentencing programmes provide ample evidence on which to assert that the overwhelming majority of those caught up in the penal system are working class, unskilled and unemployed and that this part of the general population is particularly over-represented in custodial institutions (Cavadino and Dignan, 1997: 270). The influence of age is more difficult to demonstrate because of a lack of detailed research on the point, but we did note in Chapter 5 that the age profile of those receiving community penalties is shifting slowly upward to reflect the diversion from formal criminal proceedings of younger offenders as well as the demographic shift to an older population. In 1985 half of all community service orders, for instance, went to under-21s; by 1994 this proportion had fallen to a quarter (Home Office, 1996g: 7).

Gender

Statistical evidence on the issue of gender is more complete and this suggests that women are indeed sentenced in different ways than men. Taking the figures for 1992 as indicative, 38 per cent of women convicted of indictable offences were given absolute or conditional discharges compared with 19 per cent of men, and 17 per cent were given a probation or supervision order compared with 10 per cent of men. Only 5 per cent of female offenders were given a sentence of immediate custody, 5 per cent were given a CSO and 26 per cent were fined, compared with 16, 10 and 35 per cent of men respectively (Hedderman, 1995: 152). In the same year 61 per cent of all female offenders proceeded against were cautioned: for men the equivalent figure was 36 per cent (Hedderman and Hough, 1994).

It would seem, therefore that women are being diverted away both from prosecution and from custody in different proportions than men and that the use of community service and probation also shows gendered differences. The raw figures are silent, of course, as to the explanation for these observed disparities and can offer no evidence to resolve the controversy over whether *different* treatment amounts to *more severe* or *more lenient* treatment (cf. Allen, 1989; Bottomley and Pease, 1986; Carlen, 1983; Hedderman and Hough, 1994; Walker and Wall, 1997). The wider point, however, is that a system which promotes justice and fairness should not tolerate differences in treatment, whether for chivalrous or vindictive motives, which cannot be justified on strictly legal grounds.

Race

As regards race, information on the prison population in England and Wales in 1995 indicates that (excluding foreign nationals) 13 per cent of male prisoners and 14 per cent of female prisoners were from non-white ethnic groups compared with a 5 per cent representation in both the male and female general populations (Home Office, 1996j). These statistics point immediately to a gross over-representation of people from settled ethnic minorities at the 'deep-end' of the penal system, and although the explanation for this empirical observation is highly contentious, the possibility that the disproportionate exclusion of non-whites from consideration for non-custodial sentences is a contributory factor cannot simply be excluded.

An influential research study by Hood (1992) on the impact of race on sentencing in five Crown Court centres in the West Midlands reported that there were significant racial disparities in the distribution of sentences along the scale of punishments from long sentences of imprisonment at the one end through suspended sentences, CSOs, probation and fines, to discharges at the other. After taking account of legally relevant factors influencing the severity of the sentence, such as current offence and previous record, Hood found that black (but not Asian) adults were given sentences higher up the 'tariff' than whites and were, therefore, put at more risk of getting a prison sentence should they reappear on fresh charges. Black offenders were more likely than whites to receive a suspended sentence and less likely to have been placed on probation or given a CSO.

Similar conclusions arose from a smaller study by Kirk of the sentencing of juveniles in Wolverhampton. This also found that Afro-Caribbean defendants received significantly more 'high-tariff' non-custodial sentences (particularly supervision orders with requirements and community service orders) than white or Asian defendants. Once again, this distinction could not be explained by differences in the seriousness of offences, and it occurred even though Afro-Caribbean defendants had on average committed fewer current offences and had shorter previous criminal records (Penal Affairs Consortium, 1997b).

Subsequent Home Office figures (Home Office, 1996e) reveal that the percentage of commencements for probation, CS and combination orders among the ethnic minorities increased between 1993 and 1994/95, but as the data are not related to the *predictive* imposition of those orders it is impossible to say whether this represents an improvement on the situation reported by Hood. Racial disparities in the allocation of sentences are important not only because some sentences intrude more into the sentenced person's daily life than others but also because, as has been noted, the type of sentence passed may have a strong impact on the likelihood of a person receiving a custodial sentence if he or she should reoffend.

As we saw in Chapter 5, the origins, extent and impact of discrimination on racial and other grounds is an enormously contentious subject (Reiner, 1989; Hood, 1992; Smith, 1994) and it would be impossible to deal adequately with this controversy within the confines of the present chapter. Readers are, therefore, directed, once again, to the references given and to the suggestions for further reading at the end of the book. But even if the channels through which discrimination operates and the degree to which it affects eventual outcomes remain opaque and indeterminate, the empirical evidence referred to above demonstrates that we cannot simply dismiss as ungrounded the assertion that there are disparities in the way that offenders are allocated to community and other non-custodial sentences (Fitzgerald, 1993) and that these reflect and tend to reinforce existing differences of advantage and disadvantage in society.

The role of the probation service

Given its responsibility for preparing pre-sentence reports for courts, the probation service is in a position to play a key role in this battle against discrimination in the allocation of community sentences, and its potential for perpetuating or reducing present disparities should not be underestimated. Recently the service, in common with other parts of the criminal justice system, has been making determined efforts to monitor and improve its race relation and anti-discrimination practices, and to recruit and promote larger numbers of officers from ethnic minorities. There is, however, some evidence that probation officers perceive black offenders in a manner reflecting overt and covert racism; and that even where these attitudes do not come through into the working practices of individual officers, institutional structures and conventions and the need to construct reality in report writing through the official discourse of personal responsibility and blame mean that not enough is done to exclude potentially discriminatory material from PSRs for black defendants (Denney, 1992; 1996; Penal Affairs Consortium, 1997b, citing Kirk's Wolverhampton Study). Therefore, the current emphasis in the service on anti-discriminatory monitoring and training is both timely and necessary. It should be persisted with, despite the 'hit-and-run' criticisms of the populist (and not so populist) press, and the resistance of individual officers, who sometimes see it only in terms of another management form to complete.

Much has been done to begin to combat the influence of discrimination, on grounds of race and sex, particularly since the implementation of section 95 of the Criminal Justice Act 1991 made monitoring and publication of information on these issues compulsory (see Penal Affairs Consortium, 1997b for a summary of current policy and practice against unjustifiable discrimination). However, much work still remains, and in face of continuing disparities in the sentencing figures and in other statistical pictures of the criminal justice system, only a supreme optimist or a fool would suppose that the problem has been eradicated. While it persists, the possibility (putting it no higher than that) that people are being treated less favourably in their access to non-custodial sentences on grounds of their class, race or gender (or the interrelation of all three) challenges the legitimacy claims of the criminal justice system. For if, as Duff (1996: 23) argues, formal equality is not enough and,

> [w]e cannot simply say that a penal system is just so long as it inflicts proportionate punishments on all those who are actually, and correctly, convicted: justice is not done if, for example, those who are prosecuted and convicted form only a small proportion, selected by unjustly discriminatory methods of those who are actually guilty,

then any system which perpetuates those same methods into the allocation of punishment itself surely loses all claim to be 'just'.

Chapter 8

Concluding Remarks: Some Pointers for a Journey of Hope?

In this book I have attempted to provided an overview of the range of non-custodial penalties available to sentencers in England and Wales, together with an indication of how they have evolved, the philosophical and ideological beliefs which sustain them, and the practical difficulties associated with their implementation. It is not my intention to summarise again what has already been summarised at the end of each chapter. Rather, I shall try to draw out in this final chapter some of the themes which have run through the analysis in the book and to point to some of the lessons that can be learnt from the experience so far of punishment in the community. I was tempted to call the chapter 'back to the future', because it seems to me that community-based punishments will only flourish as viable sentencing options in a climate similar to that which prevailed in the period shortly before and after the passing of the 1991 Act. Although there was a good deal of punitive rhetoric flying around (in the tradition of a 'twin-track' or 'bifurcated' penal policy), there was also the beginnings of an articulation of the distinction between the *purposes* of custody and the *purposes* of the various non-custodial sentences. In the pre-legislative period from 1987 onwards there was, in addition, an unmistakable bias *against* the use of imprisonment except for a minority of the most serious offenders. 'For most offenders', the 1990 White Paper declared (Home Office, 1990a: para. 2.7, emphasis supplied), 'imprisonment has to be justified in terms of public protection, denunciation and retribution. Otherwise it can be an *expensive way of making bad people worse.*' If the momentum of that period is to be recaptured and decarceration is to become a serious prospect again, then something of that ideological climate must be restored and, indeed, redoubled, and the legacy of 'prison works' will have to be dissolved, once and for all.

It would be a misreading of history to present that period unequivocally as a high-water mark for tolerance and compassion towards transgressors. Clearly, there was a strong punitive message in the way in which the reforms were justified (Windlesham, 1993: 226–9) which Vass, in a telling and prophetic commentary (1990: 169–70), attacked even then as paradoxical and ultimately self-defeating. Yet, with hindsight, one can see that for a brief period a combination of relatively liberal sentiments among politicians and their advisers and civil servants and a pragmatic recognition of the unacceptable burden of continuing with a pro-custody policy *had* produced a moment at which it might have been possible not only to reduce the number of people in custody but, more importantly, to reduce the ideological commitment to custody as the only 'real' punishment (Windlesham, 1993: 221–4; Downes, 1997: 8). Moreover, there was at that moment in history the political will to drive this policy through, once it had been determined upon, and a more or less bipartisan atmosphere that made the attempt seem less of a political risk than it might otherwise have been. The sentencing framework which emerged from the convergence of all these factors in the shape of the 1991 Act was not perfect, as the discussions above have shown. Some further development of the basic structure was needed, for instance, to disentangle the various types of community penalty, in terms of the aims that they might serve and the types of offences for which they might be appropriate. However, had the climate of reform endured, the necessary jurisprudence could have been developed, with the occasional 'touch' on the policy tiller from government to keep the boat moving in the right direction.

Populist punitiveness and the 'failure' of alternatives to custody

As a result of the steady development of penal policy over the last thirty years and especially over the last fifteen, courts in England and Wales now have more community-based sentencing options than almost any other jurisdiction. Yet the stark fact remains that, despite an overall increase in the use of non-custodial sentences since 1991, the prison population has risen by 50 per cent in the past five years and now stands at over 62,000 persons, with little realistic prospect of any substantial reduction in the foreseeable future. Does this inability to stem the rising torrent of incarceration demonstrate that non-custodial penalties are, at best, peripheral to penality in this country, at worst merely an adjunct to an increasingly punitive system centred now, as always, on the supremacy of the custodial sentence?

As with most of the questions about the penal system, this is not an easy one to answer. There is no simple mathematical relationship between custody and alternatives to it (nor between the crime rate and the numbers in prison for that matter), and the reasons for the failure of community-based penalties to make greater inroads into the use of custodial sentences are complex and difficult to delineate precisely. But as the discussion above has demonstrated at various points, the kind of political climate which surrounds the activities of the sentencers is of particular importance. The increasingly populist approach to setting sentencing policy since at least 1993 has contributed to the establishment of a particularly punitive climate in which even community-based sentences are expected to fulfil essentially retributivist functions. The Lord Chief Justice, Lord Bingham, speaking extra-judicially, has recently expressed this relationship most clearly in a speech to the Police Foundation:

> Given the temper of our society in the last five years, I do not find it surprising that the prison population should have increased by 50%, reflecting the more ready resort to custody by sentencers and an increase in the length of sentences imposed. The tenor of political rhetoric has strongly favoured the imposition of severe sentences; this rhetoric has been faithfully reflected in certain elements of the media; and judges accused of passing lenient sentences have found themselves routinely castigated in some newspapers . . . The increase in the prison population is not explained by any recent increase in sentencing powers, and I have no doubt that it is related to the pressure of public opinion.
>
> (Bingham, 1997)

The discovery of a relationship between the populist punitiveness of politicians and the failure of non-custodial penalties to impact upon the prison population is not, of course, particularly novel (Pitts, 1988; Vass, 1990: 169–70). It seems clear that no matter how cost effectively they are delivered, the mere existence of even a wide range of community-based penalties will do nothing to secure a reduction in the prison population if the overriding objective of the criminal justice system is punishment-based. Under such conditions, community penalties can too easily become mere adjuncts, add-ons to the penal regime which, by facilitating the (semi-) incapacitation of a greater number of offenders, help to sustain the ideology that an exclusively punitive response to the problems of crime and criminal victimisation is a viable policy, despite abundant evidence to the contrary. The concomitant focus on individual pathology or maladjustment, and the taken-for-granted moral superiority of correctionalism over respect and understanding excludes a great deal that is meaningful and constructive in the interaction between those who are punished in the community and those who supervise them. Reform becomes devalued in comparison with the promotion of control, and it becomes too easy to lose sight of the basic humanity of those on whom the penalties have been imposed. In such a climate, too, where the essential role of community penalties is expressed in the language of punishment, the stigmatising potential of having been on what is perceived as a 'heavy-end' or 'up-tariff' sentence is magnified, increasing, in turn, the risk of being treated more severely on subsequent court appearances. Although it is hard to substantiate empirically, it may well be in this way that the greatest amount of 'net-widening' occurs.

Most informed observers would agree, perhaps sadly, that politicians of left and right (and now the 'radical centre') in Britain and in many other countries have recently been scrambling to outdo each other in emphasising the need for tougher rather than more humane patterns of sentencing. One result of this in England and Wales, as Chapter 1 outlined, has been that, while an espousal of non-custodial sentences in proper cases has endured as part of the legacy of the Criminal Justice Act 1991, the language used in the official discourse around community-based punishments has tended to supplant the more familiar reformative or rehabilitative purposes of, say, a probation or a community service order, with a direct appeal to, and endorsement of, the punitive potentialities of those sentences.

More generally, rather than confront traditional understandings of the meaning of 'punishment', many governments have chosen to present non-custodial penalties in ways which make them appear punitive in a *traditionalist* sense (Carlen, 1989: 20; Brownlee and Joanes, 1993: 217). For some involved in the provision of community-based sanctions, this change in emphasis has been acceptable, if only on the pragmatic ground that it might encourage traditionally-minded sentencers to make more use of non-custodial options. For others, however, this whole discourse amounts to a redefinition of non-custodial sanctions and an undermining of the philosophy that sustains them which some, at least, have resisted. The result has been a lack of consensus on the nature and purpose of community punishments among those most directly involved in their provision, and a concomitant confusion over how they might best be integrated into an anti-custodial strategy.

New Labour, new penology?

For some of the 'refuseniks' and for a large number of other people with an interest in the promotion of a more humane approach to crime and crime control, the immanence of a change of party in government seemed for a time to offer the possibility of some change in this climate. So far as it is possible to discern at this point, however, the commitment to the punitive discourse has survived the dramatic demise of the Conservative Party in the 1997 election. The new Labour administration does have innovative proposals to put to parliament which, if implemented, will result, for example, in greater use of reparation as a punishment for young offenders and an enhanced role for local authority youth justice teams in dealing with youth crime. However, the presentation of these and other potentially welcome measures continues to reflect the perceived need to 'talk tough on crime'. So, for instance, plans to increase the use of community sentences by the extension of electronic monitoring were trailered in the populist press by 'a senior government source' as 'the tough option' under a headline which proclaimed that 'Straw extends tagging in big blitz on soft sentences' (*Daily Mail,* 28 July 1997). The same report also announced that the new training regime for probation officers would 'ensure they spend less time on social work theory and instead learn more about making community service "punishment-orientated" ', a sentiment with which the new Home Secretary apparently associated himself a couple of days later (*The Guardian*, 30 July 1967).

On the day that he announced his plans for youth justice and for tagging to parliament the Home Secretary could be heard on the radio defending his strategy in language that would not have much alarmed his predecessor (Straw, 1997b). Prisons, he confided, were 'essentially a demand-led service' (a feature that apparently distinguishes them from the health and education services), and his priority was not to reduce the prison population but 'to secure the safety of the public', as if to imply that the former objective was invariably opposed to the latter. Conceding that the prison population would probably rise 'in the short term', Mr Straw then went on to 'talk down' the significance of that statement by suggesting that *by comparison with the United States* Britain did not really imprison very many of its population. Perhaps the dazzling effrontery of the remark stunned the interviewer, but he declined to reply that comparison with a country in which on any given day there are *1.1 million* in state or federal prisons and where, on reliable estimates, one in three black men aged 20–29 are 'under the control' of the criminal justice system (Currie, 1996: 6) hardly resounds to our credit.

Nor did the new government lose much time in announcing its intention to implement most of the mandatory sentence provisions in the Crime (Sentences) Act 1997 against violent and sexual offenders and drug traffickers, in the face of continuing opposition both from senior members of the judiciary and penal reform groups. Given the decision not (yet) to complete the hat-trick by bringing in the minimum sentence arrangements for repeat burglars (by far the most numerous of the categories of offenders affected by the 1997 provisions), the proposals will perhaps not necessarily add greatly to the prison population (Home Affairs Committee, 1997: xvi), but the announcement is of great symbolic value. Michael Howard announced his 'three strikes and you're out' intentions as part of a 27-point plan to 'toughen up' the criminal justice system at the Conservative Party conference in October 1993 in a speech in which he relaunched the 'prison works' credo. Most commentators view that speech as marking, if not the beginning, certainly the maturing of the counter-reforms that unravelled the liberal aspects of the 1991 sentencing framework. Labour in their later stages in opposition were, at best, lukewarm in their attempts to undo what a broad consensus of opinion regarded as a very illiberal, unjustifiably punitive policy. Labour in government have signalled their intention to embrace it as their own.

None of this is entirely unpredictable. In the lead up to and during the 1997 election campaign the Labour Party talked a great deal about the failure of the Conservatives to control crime and disorder in language which could not but increase general fear of crime among many of those at whom it was targeted. Having wrested the baton of the party of law and order from their political opponents, and having carried it so prominently as they marched to their historic victory, 'new' Labour could not really be seen to be casting it aside so soon. The party which claims to be 'tough on crime, tough on the causes of crime' knows that reducing the criminogenic influences of a society composed more than ever of 'winners and losers' is not something that can be easily accomplished in the short run; and in the meantime it obviously intends to deliver on the first part of its promise. Nor could this be said to be inherently objectionable. Crime *does* diminish the quality of life of those who are its victims and it is almost trite now to remark that its impact falls heaviest on those who are already disadvantaged in other ways: the poor, the inhabitants of inner-city areas and members of ethnic minorities. Therefore, it is indeed the duty of government to secure the safety of its citizens, and to take all reasonable and effective steps towards that end.

The problem with opting for tougher sentencing policies, even ostensibly in the short term, is that it is not necessarily the same thing as taking reasonable and effective steps against crime. It is certainly a high-cost and ultimately high-risk strategy for restoring public confidence in the law because, once embarked upon, the political costs of withdrawing from tough policies are so high that no politician is going to want to pay them (Hough, 1996: 209). Moreover, the evidence from this country and elsewhere suggests strongly that the public will never be satisfied with tougher new regimes unless widespread misperceptions about leniency in sentencing are challenged and changed. By persisting with the punitive language and retributivist justifications of their predecessors, rather than attempting to change public attitudes to crime and sentencing through information and education (Fattah, 1980) Labour risk creating for themselves the sort of 'punishment deficit' which comes from a mismatch between the supply and demand of forms of punishment that will make society safer (Leadbeater, 1996).

Promises which imply that the only feasible approach is to deal with crime aggressively and assertively stimulate a (perhaps pre-existing) 'taste' in the public for punishment which, once excited, can become almost insatiable, as appears to have happened in the United States (Tonry, 1994b; Currie, 1996). And meeting the expectations that more and more criminals will be severely punished seems almost inevitably to undercut the viability of any measure other than custody, as well as putting at risk other forms of social spending of a kind more likely to be associated with the social causes of crime. In the United States between 1980 and 1993, for instance, total federal spending on employment and training programmes was cut nearly in half while spending on correctional facilities increased by 521 per cent (Currie, 1996: 7).

Of course, this may be an unduly pessimistic premonition about the future in Britain. The new government, after all, is committed to spending more, not less, of GDP on education and training over the full period of its first term. And it is clear that Jack Straw's purpose in 'talking up' the 'toughness' of community penalties is to encourage sentencers to make greater use of them, thus reducing the proportionate use of custody. As we have seen in Chapter 1, an almost identical policy pursued by an earlier administration did have the desired effect, at least for a short time between 1992 and 1993. As the switches in sentencing practice (in both directions) between 1992 and 1995 have shown, judicial thinking of the magnitude required to effect an appreciable change in sentencing patterns can be achieved. Reductions in the use of custody can be encouraged, for instance, by meaningful communication between those who sentence and those who provide disposals outside the custodial regime (Brownlee and Joanes, 1993: 219; Brownlee, 1994a: 91; Home Office, 1996d).

The aim of this communication is not to persuade sentencers away from the view that offences against the person or of house burglary deserve more severe sentences than, say, offences of minor damage. Rather, the ambition, from a reductionist's point of view, is to persuade those with the discretionary power to choose between possible sentences that this or that particular form of non-custodial disposal is commensurate with serious offending. Such discussions about the proper range and form of punishment do now take place more regularly in a more structured way through the auspices of the Criminal Justice Consultative Council, local Area Criminal Justice Committees and, in certain areas, local steering groups on community sentences (Ashworth, 1995: 48–9; Home Office, 1996d: para. 3 and for an example of even fuller discussions see Christie, 1993: 40–3).

Realistically, however, the extent to which the general tenor of sentencing policy can be influenced by even high-powered dialogue between practitioners is always going to be subject to constraints imposed by the legislative framework set by the government of the day (Vass, 1996: 177–8). And it is here that the seeds of destruction of the new initiative on non-custodial sentencing lie, for the government seems unwilling or unable to surrender any of the ideological ground recaptured from those who, from 1993 onward, set about dispersing the climate of restraint which had taken six years to establish and which, alone, made progress in reducing custody a possibility. Therefore, the Home Secretary's policy, which seems to be one of 'tough and tougher' and which aims to rebuild the liberal balance implicit in the bifurcatory 1991 arrangements upon the punitive rhetoric of the 1993 counter-reforms, appears self-contradictory and may, therefore, prove self-defeating in the longer run.

Turning the journey around: the first steps

If we are to have a sensible system of graduated punishments in the community which reduces the reliance on the use of custody, then it is surely time to abandon the pretence that 'prison works'. Imprisonment does not work: it is not ordinarily a therapeutic experience; it can have a devastating effect on individuals and their families; it can and with depressing regularity does, lead to suicide; it confronts the offender with great difficulty in obtaining a job and re-establishing his life on release. Not my words, but those of the present Lord Chief Justice of England (Bingham, 1997: 11). In the present state of society we may have to persist with the institution of imprisonment, but we should not glory in that failing; and in recognizing that for the state to deprive a citizen of his or her liberty is a gross invasion of their ordinary rights as human beings, we should restrict the use of custody to those whose crimes are either so heinous or so threatening to the public that no other course of action seems justifiable. The limits of proportionality which mark this minority out from the great majority of those sentenced by the courts must be drawn with even greater clarity and restraint (Ashworth and von Hirsch, 1997).

Outside of those strict boundaries, we need a graduated system of realistic, demanding and constructive community punishments. These will have to be differentiated from each other with considerable clarity, since they will not all impose the same demands on those sentenced to them, nor target the same offender populations. It may be that in fine-tuning that targeting, the differences between individuals and the specificity of each case mean that the search for 'uniform sentencing outcomes' is an 'inappropriate aim' (Matthews, 1989: 141). In other words, in what is essentially a realm of ethical choice, sentencers may actually achieve a greater level of substantive justice by pursuing some sort of hybrid objective rather than a strict desert model, subject always to the outer constraints of *dis*proportionality. The ultimate aim must be to fashion a comprehensive system of punishments in which a range of non-custodial penalties provide the successive steps for a ladder of scaled punishments outside prison, to replace the present 'binary' system in which imprisonment is seen as punishment and everything else is seen as an alternative, a letting off (Morris and Tonry, 1990: 224).

Managing public opinion

Of course, such a scaled system would not necessarily lead to a reduction in the overall severity of sentencing, while a climate of populist punitiveness prevailed. As Vass's critique of the 1991 system (Chapter 5, above) reminds us, there is an essential contradiction in intending to keep people out of prisons and at the same time promising to exercise punitive and inflexible power over them. Yet, while there is an appetite among the public for punitiveness amounting at times to vindictiveness towards the 'other' of crime, the sort of non-custodial regimes that politicians will feel safe in offering are likely to be characterised by structure, rigidity and quick, tough responses to breach of requirements (Vass, 1990: 169–70). Public tolerance places limits on the possibility of developing effective decarceration policies and, therefore, it is essential for any radical reform strategy to engage directly with misconceptions among the public about the supposed leniency of existing practices (Matthews, 1989: 146). Rather than trying to dress non-custodial sentences up to appear indistinguishable from the 'real thing' – custody – the government should be attempting to tackle the belief, deeply rooted in the public and the penal culture (Windlesham, 1993: 208), that imprisonment is the proper penalty for all save the most minor or out-of-character offences. The effects of not doing so were spelled out recently by the Lord Chief Justice in the speech referred to above:

> In the public mind, I think that custody is generally seen as the only true retributive or punitive sentence. Anyone who commits a crime of any seriousness and is not sentenced to custody is generally perceived to have got away with it. This is very unfortunate, because of the inherent drawbacks of imprisonment . . . because the efficacy of imprisonment is in many cases open to question; because the cost of imprisoning offenders is very high, and inevitably absorbs resources which would otherwise be available for schools, hospitals and other facilities of more obvious benefit to the public than prisons; and because the prison system is already bursting at the seams.
>
> (Bingham, 1997: 11)

Realists on the left now tend to take everything seriously, including public opinion (Matthews, 1989: 145), but taking public opinion seriously is not the same as taking it 'as read'. The small but consistent body of research on public attitudes to punishment which was reviewed in Chapter 2 demonstrates that there is a clear lack of understanding of probation and rehabilitative sentences but that, given appropriate information, the general public will accept levels of sentencing they previously condemned as far too soft. No one would imagine that effecting so widespread a change in attitude could be achieved without some considerable effort, nor that all of the media would be willing allies in such an endeavour. One has only to see how the speech of the Lord Chief Justice quoted above was reported in certain newspapers (e.g. the *Daily Mail* for 11 July 1997, which ran the story on its front page in rather incredulous terms under the banner headline 'Keep the Criminals Out of Prison') to appreciate the level of resistance displayed by the populist press to progressive ideas. But the importance of engendering public tolerance of non-custodial penal policies cannot be doubted (Fatah, 1980; Matthews, 1989; Christie, 1993) and, as the example of the death penalty in Great Britain reveals, even if a government does not succeed in carrying the whole population with it on a liberal initiative, with the necessary political will it can still take steps to manage rather than to surrender to the resultant hostile opinion (Hough, 1996: 191).

What kind of community punishments? The quality issue

Of course, the general public cannot, nor should they, be asked to endorse non-custodial sentences unless they reflect genuine public interests by providing adequate retribution for offending behaviour together with reasonable levels of protection from further offending at a cost which is not out of proportion to that spent on other social programmes. To borrow a consumerist phrase, there is a 'quality of service' issue here, and the public can only be expected to 'buy into' community-based punishments which are demonstrably well run, as effective as possible in achieving the purposes held out for them, and not obviously contributing any appreciable amount to existing fears and insecurities (a condition which will be more readily met when politicians have less to gain from 'talking up' the level of crime).

These requirements establish the case for the continuous, rigorous monitoring of programmes in ways which make their strengths and weaknesses transparent to those who are running them, and which make individual programmes accountable to the wider public. Part of that monitoring must involve a self-critical approach to 'client' selection, for if non-custodial sanctions, particularly 'heavy-end' orders, are to avoid the problems of 'net-widening' they must be targeted accurately on those whose offending behaviour is such as to justify the added interference with liberty which is represented by many of the measures now being associated with probation and community service in the interests of public safety.

Careful targeting and programme integrity also seems to be a necessary adjunct to such rehabilitative effect as may be obtained, at least if the evidence from the cognitive-behavioural approach is to be relied upon, although targeting in this sense may have the different meaning of selecting those with the most chance of 'succeeding' on the programme. This confusion of terms raises new problems and calls for the construction of strict guidelines to determine whether the demands of rehabilitation or proportionality are to be paramount in 'gate-keeping' decisions. Choosing between them is, once more, essentially an ethical issue, but a choice must inevitably be made because a position of deliberate 'obfuscation' which tries to combine the two objectives by some kind of 'sleight of hand' (Harris, 1992: 160) carries with it unacceptably high risks of 'net-widening' and the 'blurring' of boundaries between care and control.

As far as the future of the probation service is concerned, it is unlikely that it will be able to maintain a distinct role purely as an 'social work' agency for offenders, even in a climate of opinion a good deal less punitive than at present. Systemic pressures and financial considerations as well as changing public expectations probably mean that the service will have to function more and more as a multi-agency partner in an integrated criminal justice system, delivering and managing the sorts of non-custodial sentences that form part of the structured and differentiated system of punishments sketched out above. If so, this will continue to have profound implications for the knowledge and skills base of the service and for the basic motivations of its members (Clear and Byrne, 1992: 323–6). It also raises the intriguing prospect of a split between the traditional 'care' and 'control' functions, with the probation service fulfilling only the latter and someone else (latter-day, more pluralist court missionaries?) taking up the rest (Harris, 1992: 173).

Such a development is not inevitable, however, and given the necessary political will to work towards a less punitive climate more generally, there will almost certainly be a place within the criminal justice system for an organisation that continues to be motivated by humanitarian and anti-custodial values. The probation service will better equip itself to fulfil this role if it continues to work towards an ethic which embraces the interests of victims as well as offenders, perhaps through an extension of its work in mediation and reparation schemes (Cavadino and Dignan, 1997: 307). But it cannot produce its own resources; and if the government is seriously commited to finding credible and workable community punishments it must be prepared to acknowledge that the probation service and other organisations working with it in fostering restorative, reparative approaches to justice are essentially demand-led, too. The recent trend of cutting costs in this area must be reversed, if realistic alternatives to imprisonment are to stand a chance of demonstrating their value (Downes, 1997: 9).

Looking further ahead: solving the crisis of crime and punishment

In the longer term, even more radical changes will be needed if we are not simply to repeat the cyclical crises of rises in crime, declines in tolerance, and consequential 'hikes' in sentencing severity. The time has surely come, if not to remove the determination of sentencing policy from the political arena altogether (which may be impossible in a parliamentary democracy), at least to find better ways of insulating it from the immediate influences of political fortune hunting that have led in the past to ambivalence, inconsistency and injustice. One possible way to do this is to legislate for the establishment of the sort of Sentencing Council advocated by Andrew Ashworth as an appropriate vehicle for setting sentencing levels and declaring sentencing principles (Ashworth, 1995: ch. 13). Such a body could have an important influence on sentencing policy by setting the sort of 'cardinal' anchoring points for the range of sentences (Chapter 2) that ensured restraint in punishment in a way which, as I have sought to demonstrate, deserts theory on its own cannot do. The Council could also take the lead in disseminating more accurate information about sentencing practice in an effort to educate and influence public opinion (Ashworth and Hough, 1996: 786).

Attractive as this proposal might sound, the Labour government appear to have allowed their earlier enthusiasm for a Sentencing Council to shrink to a pledge to request the Court of Appeal to introduce sentencing guidelines for all main criminal offences. For reasons that were explored in

Chapter 1, this policy is unlikely to secure either the consistency looked for by the Home Secretary or the reduction in overall severity advocated by proponents of parsimony: even the Lord Chief Justice takes the view that in most of the leading cases in which guidance on levels of sentencing has been given, the effect has been to increase the level of sentencing (Bingham, 1997: 11).

Ultimately, there is no penal answer to the problem of crime. For this reason, the government must begin without delay to deliver on the second half of its famous commitment and attack the social conditions in which crime becomes, if not a pre-determined response, at least an understandable option for so many, especially those at the economic margins. If it merely hides behind the rhetoric of blame and continues, as its precedessor did, to heap *all* the blame for social ills at the feet of maladjusted individuals, the new government will find that it merely preserves the conditions under which a growing number of people turn to crime and, as a result, *managing* rather than reducing the offender population will remain its priority. Under such conditions it would continue to face serious problems of legitimacy (Garland, 1996), and, having promised to do *something* about the high levels of crime bequeathed to it by eighteen years of 'market solutions', might well find itself under irresistible pressures to go once more for an authoritarian response.

Therefore, there are sound political as well as moral reasons for setting out now on a journey that would bring hope and optimism to those in the bottom third of British society who have suffered most of all in the past two decades (Downes, 1997). Lessening the impoverishment of a whole section of the population through positive action on employment, housing, education and inequality should be an end in itself, not simply a means to reducing the criminogenic influences of a society based overwhelmingly at present on a culture of winners and losers and an ethic of greed.

The fact that such affirmative action also offers the only hope of a long-term solution to the problems of crime and the fear and insecurity that afflicts even the so-called 'contented' classes of post-modern society, merely provides one further, instrumentalist incentive to act. Punishments in the community based on some principle of reintegration and reprieve will seem more attractive when there is felt to be less need for punishments at all, and less fear of the consequences of not reacting in an aggressive and punitive way to each and every breach of the law. Such a time seems distant from us now, but to set out to reach it is to embark on a journey of hope, and there are already some signs of the way that we should go.

Suggestions for Further Reading

Readers will already have noted that each of the chapters is copiously supplied with references to other sources. Without wishing to diminish the importance of each of those individual references, I set out below under individual chapter headings some suggestions as to further reading which might be of particular interest and assistance.

Chapter 1: Evolving punishment in the community

Bottoms, A. E. (1987) Limiting Prison Use: The Experience of England and Wales, *Howard Journal*, 26, 2, 177–202.

Bottoms, A. E. (1995) The Philosophy and Politics of Sentencing, in Clarkson, C. M. V. and Morgan, R. (eds) (1995) *The Politics of Sentencing Reform*, Oxford: Clarendon Press.

Downes, D. and Morgan, R. (1994) 'Dumping the Hostages to Fortune'? The Politics of Law and Order in Post-War Britain, in Maguire, M., Morgan, R. and Reiner, R. (eds) (1997) (2nd edn) *The Oxford Handbook of Criminology*, Oxford: Clarendon Press.

Garland, D. (1996) The Limits of the Sovereign State: Strategies of Crime Control in Contemporary Society, *British Journal of Criminology*, 36, 4, 445–71.

Sparks, R. (1996) Prisons, Punishment and Penality, in McLaughlin, E. and Muncie, J. (eds) (1996) *Controlling Crime*, London: Sage.

Windlesham, Lord (1993) *Responses to Crime. Vol. 2: Penal Policy in the Making*, Oxford: Clarendon Press, ch. 5.

Chapter 2: Justifying community punishments

Duff, R. A. (1996) Penal Communications: Recent Work in the Philosophy of Punishment, *Crime and Justice: An Annual Review*, Vol. 20, Chicago: University of Chicago Press.

Duff, R. A. and Garland, D. (1994) *A Reader on Punishment*, Oxford: Oxford University Press, Introduction.

von Hirsch, A. (1993) *Censure and Sanctions*, Oxford: Clarendon Press.

Walker, N. (1991) *Why Punish?* Oxford: Oxford University Press.

Wasik, M. and von Hirsch, A. (1988) Non-Custodial Penalties and the Principle of Desert, *Criminal Law Review*, 555.

Chapter 3: The changing role of the probation service (1): missionaries in the age of welfare

Bochel, D. (1977) *Probation and After-Care: Its Development in England and Wales*, Edinburgh: Scottish Academic Press.

Harris, R. (1995) Probation Around the World: Origins and Development, in Hamai, K., Villé, R., Harris, R., Hough, M. and Zvekic, U. (eds) (1995) *Probation Around the World: A Comparative Study*, London: Routledge.

McWilliams, W. (1983) The Mission to the English Police Courts 1876–1936, *Howard Journal*, XII, 129–47.

McWilliams, W. (1985) The Mission Transformed: Professionalisation of Probation Between the Wars, *Howard Journal*, 24, 4, 257–74.

McWilliams, W. (1986) The English Probation System and the Diagnostic Ideal, *Howard Journal*, 25, 4, 241–60.

Chapter 4: The changing role of the probation service (2): probation in the age of the actuary

Feeley, M. and Simon, J. (1992) The New Penology: Notes on the Emerging Strategy of Corrections and its Implications, *Criminology*, 30, 4, 449–74.

Feeley, M. and Simon, J. (1994) Actuarial Justice: The Emerging New Criminal Law, in Nelken, D. (ed.) (1994) *The Futures of Criminology*, London: Sage.

May, T. (1991) Under Siege: Probation in a Changing Environment, in Reiner, R. and Cross, M. (1991) (eds) *Beyond Law and Order: Criminal Justice Policy and Politics into the 1990s*, Basingstoke: Macmillan.

May, T. (1994) Probation and Community Sanctions, in Maguire, M., Morgan, R. and Reiner, R. (eds) (1994) *The Oxford Handbook of Criminology*, Oxford: Clarendon Press.

Nellis, M. (1995) Probation Values for the 1990s, *Howard Journal*, 34, 1, 19–41.

Peters, A. (1986) Main Currents in Criminal Law Theory, in Van Dijk, J., Haffman, C., Rutter, F. and Schutte, J. (eds) (1986) *Criminal Law in Action*, Arnhem: Gouda Quint.

Rhodes, R. (1996) Governing without Government, *Political Studies* (1996), XLIV, 652–67.

Chapter 5: Community penalties

Ashworth, A. J. (1992) Non-Custodial Sentences, *Criminal Law Review*, 242–51.

Ashworth, A. J. (1995) (2nd edn) *Sentencing and Criminal Justice*, London: Butterworths, ch. 10.

Ellis, T., Hedderman, C. and Mortimer, E. (1996) *Enforcing Community Sentences: Supervisors' Perspectives on Ensuring Compliance and Dealing with Breach*, Home Office Research Study No. 158, London: Home Office.

Wasik, M. and Taylor, R. (1994) (2nd edn) *Guide to the Criminal Justice Act 1991*, London: Blackstone Press, ch. 2.

Chapter 6: Financial and nominal penalties

Bottoms, A. E. (1983) Neglected Features of Contemporary Penal Systems, in Garland, D. and Young, P. (eds) (1983) *The Power to Punish: Contemporary Penality and Social Analysis*, London: Heinemann.

Penal Affairs Consortium (1995) *The Imprisonment of Fine Defaulters*, London: The Penal Affairs Consortium.

Shaw, S. (1989) Monetary Penalties and Imprisonment: The Realistic Alternatives, in Carlen, P. and Cook, D. (eds) (1989) *Paying for Crime*, Milton Keynes: Open University Press.

Young, P. (1989) Punishment, Money and a Sense of Justice, in Carlen, P. and Cook, D. (eds) (1989) *Paying for Crime*, Milton Keynes: Open University Press.

Chapter 7: Evaluating community punishments: do they work and are they fair?

Bottomley, A. K. and Pease, K. (1986) *Crime and Punishment: Interpreting the Data*, Buckingham: Open University Press, ch. 4.

Copas, J. (1995) On Using Crime Statistics for Prediction, in Walker, M. A. (ed.) (1995) *Interpreting Crime Statistics*, Oxford: Clarendon Press.

Lloyd, C., Mair, G. and Hough, M. (1994) *Explaining Reconviction Rates: A Critical Analysis*, Home Office Research Study No. 136, London: HMSO.

Penal Affairs Consortium (1997) *Race and Criminal Justice*, London: The Penal Affairs Consortium.

Vass, A. A. (1996) Community Penalties: The Politics of Punishment, in May, T. and Vass, A. A. (eds) (1996) *Working with Offenders: Issues, Contexts and Outcomes*, London: Sage.

Chapter 8: Concluding remarks: some pointers for a journey of hope

Christie, N. (1993) (2nd edn) *Crime Control as Industry: Towards Gulags, Western Style*, London: Routledge.

Currie, E. (1996) *Is America Really Winning the War against Crime and Should Britain Follow its Example?* NACRO 30th Anniversary Lecture, London: National Association for the Care and Resettlement of Offenders.

Downes, D. (1997) What the Next Government should do about Crime, *Howard Journal*, 36, 1, 1–13.

Hough, M. (1996) People Talking about Punishment, *Howard Journal*, 35, 3, 191–214.

Bibliography

Abel, R. L. (ed.) (1982) *The Politics of Informal Justice, Vols. 1 and 2*, New York: Academic Press.

ACOP (1988) *More Demanding than Prison*, Wakefield: Association of Chief Officers of Probation.

ACOP (1996) *Probation Works Better than Prison: A Briefing Paper*, London: Association of Chief Officers of Probation.

Advisory Council on the Penal System (1970) *Non-Custodial and Semi-Custodial Penalties*, London: HMSO.

Allen, F. A. (1964) *The Borderland of Criminal Justice*, Chicago: University of Chicago Press.

Allen, H. (1989) Fines for Women: Paradoxes and Paradigms, in Carlen and Cook (eds) (1989).

Allen, R. (1991) Out of Jail: The Reduction of the Use of Penal Custody for Male Juveniles 1981–88, *Howard Journal*, 30, 1, 30–52.

Ashworth, A. J. (1986) Punishment, and Compensation: Offender, Victim and the State, *Oxford Journal of Legal Studies*, 6, 86–122.

Ashworth, A. J. (1992) Non-Custodial Sentences, *Criminal Law Review*, 242–51.

Ashworth, A. J. (1993) Victim Impact Statements and Sentencing, *Criminal Law Review*, 498–509.

Ashworth, A. J. (1994) Justifying the Grounds of Mitigation, *Criminal Justice Ethics*, Winter/Spring, 5–10.

Ashworth, A. J. (1995) (2nd edn) *Sentencing and Criminal Justice*, London: Butterworths.

Ashworth, A. J. (1996) Editorial in the June edition of *Criminal Law Review*, 365–9.

Ashworth, A. J. (1997) Editorial in the August edition of *Criminal Law Review*, 533–4.

Ashworth, A. J. and Gibson, B. (1994) The Criminal Justice Act 1993: Altering the Sentencing Framework, *Criminal Law Review*, 101–9.

Ashworth, A. J. and Hough, M. (1996) Sentencing and the Climate of Opinion, *Criminal Law Review*, 776–87.

Ashworth, A. J. and von Hirsch, A. (1997) Recognising Elephants: The Problem of the Custody Threshold, *Criminal Law Review*, 187–200.

Ashworth, A. J., von Hirsch, A., Bottoms, A. E. and Wasik, M. (1995) Bespoke Tailoring Won't Suit Community Sentences, *New Law Journal*, 30 June, 970–2.

Audit Commission for Local Authorities in England and Wales (1989) *The Probation Service: Promoting Value for Money*, London: HMSO.

Audit Commission for Local Authorities in England and Wales (1996) *Misspent Youth: Young People and Crime*, London: HMSO.

Bailey, R. and Brake, M. (eds) (1975) *Radical Social Work*, London: Edward Arnold.

Ball, R., Huff, C. and Lilly, R. (1988) *House Arrest and Correctional Policy: Doing Time at Home*, Newbury Park, Calif: Sage.

Barker, M., Pease, K. and Webb, B. (1992) *Community Service and Crime Prevention: The Cheadle Heath Project*, Crime Prevention Unit Paper 39, London: Home Office Crime Prevention Unit.

Barnes, W. (ed.) (1995) *Taking Responsibility: Citizen Involvement in the Criminal Justice System*, Toronto: Centre of Criminology.

Baumer, T. and Mendelsohn, R. (1992) Electronically Monitored Home Confinement: Does It Work?, in Byrne *et al.* (eds) (1992).

Bingham, Lord Bingham of Cornhill (1997) *The Sentence of the Court: Police Foundation Lecture 1997*, London: The Police Foundation.

Blair, T. (1997) Statement by Rt Hon. Tony Blair, MP, Leader of the Labour Party, at a Press Conference, 25 April 1997, London: Labour Party Press Office.

Blomberg, T. and Lucken, K. (1994) Stacking the Deck by Piling Up Sanctions: Is Intermediate Punishment Destined to Fail?, *Howard Journal*, 33, 1, 62–80.

Bochel, D. (1976) *Probation and After-Care: Its Development in England and Wales*, Edinburgh: Scottish Academic Press.

Bottomley, A. K. and Pease, K. (1986) *Crime and Punishment: Interpreting the Data*, Buckingham: Open University Press.

Bottoms, A. E. (1973) The Efficacy of the Fine: A Case for Scepticism, *Criminal Law Review*, 543–81.

Bottoms, A. E. (1977) Reflections on the Renaissance of Dangerousness, *Howard Journal*, XVI, 2, 70–96.

Bottoms, A. E. (1980) An Introduction to 'The Coming Crisis', in Bottoms and Preston (eds) (1980).

Bottoms, A. E. (1983) Neglected Features of Contemporary Penal Systems, in Garland and Young (eds) (1983).

Bottoms, A. E. (1987) Limiting Prison Use: The Experience of England and Wales, *Howard Journal*, 26, 2, 177–202.

Bottoms, A. E. (1995a) The Philosophy and Politics of Sentencing, in Clarkson and Morgan (eds) (1995).

Bottoms, A. E. (1995b) *Intensive Community Supervision for Young Offenders: Outcomes, Process and Cost*, Cambridge: Institute of Criminology.

Bottoms, A. E. and McWilliams, W. (1979) A Non-Treatment Paradigm for Probation Practice, *British Journal of Social Work*, 9, 2, 159–202.

Bottoms, A. E. and Preston, R. H. (eds) (1980) *The Coming Penal Crisis: A Criminological and Theological Exploration*, Edinburgh: Scottish Academic Press.

Bottoms, A. E. and Stevenson, S. (1992) What Went Wrong? Criminal Justice Policy in England and Wales, 1945–70, in Downes, D. (ed.) (1992).

Box, S. (1987) *Recession, Crime and Punishment*, Basingstoke: Macmillan.

Box, S., Hale, C. and Andrews, G. (1988) Explaining Fear of Crime, *British Journal of Criminology*, 28, 340–56.

Braithwaite, J. (1989) *Crime, Shame and Reintegration*, Cambridge: Cambridge University Press.

Braithwaite, J. and Mugford, S. (1994) Conditions of Successful Reintegration Ceremonies, *British Journal of Criminology*, 34, 2, 139–71.

Braithwaite, J. and Pettit, P. (1990) *Not Just Deserts: A Republican Theory of Justice*, Oxford: Oxford University Press.

Brake, M. and Hale, C. (1992) *Public Order and Private Lives: The Politics of Law and Order*, London: Routledge.

Broad, B. (1996) New Partnerships in Work with Offenders and Crime Partnership Work, in May and Vass (eds) (1996).

Brody, S. (1976) *The Effectiveness of Sentencing*, Home Office Research Study No. 35, London: HMSO.

Brownlee, I. D. (1990) Targeting the Young Adult Offender, *Criminal Law Review*, 852–8.

Brownlee, I. D. (1994a) Hanging Judges and Wayward Mechanics: A Reply to Michael Tonry, in Duff *et al.* (eds) (1994).

Brownlee, I. D. (1994b) Taking the Strait-Jacket Off: Persistence and the Distribution of Punishment in England and Wales, *Legal Studies*, 14, 3, 295–312.

Brownlee, I. D. (1995) Intensive Probation with Young Adult Offenders: A Short Reconviction Study, *British Journal of Criminology*, 35, 4, 599–612.

Brownlee, I. D. and Joanes, D. (1993) Intensive Probation for Young Adult Offenders, *British Journal of Criminology*, 33, 2, 216–30.

Brownlee, I. D. and Walker, C. P. (1997) The Urban Crime Fund and Total Geographic Initiatives in West Yorkshire, *Policing and Society* (forthcoming).

Burnside, J. and Baker, N. (1994) *Relational Justice: Repairing the Breach*, Winchester: Waterside.

Byrne, J. M. and Pattavina, A. (1992) The Effectiveness Issue: Assessing What Works in the Adult Community Corrections System, in Byrne *et al.* (eds) (1992).

Byrne, J. M., Lurigio, A. J. and Petersilia, J. (eds) (1992) *Smart Sentencing: The Emergence of Intermediate Sanctions*, Newbury Park, Calif.: Sage.

Carlen, P. (1983) *Women's Imprisonment: A Study in Social Control*, London: Routledge Kegan Paul.

Carlen, P. (1989) Crime, Inequality and Sentencing, in Carlen and Cook (eds) (1990).

Carlen, P. (1990) *Alternatives to Women's Imprisonment*, Milton Keynes: Open University Press.

Carlen, P. and Cook, D. (eds) (1989) *Paying for Crime*, Milton Keynes: Open University Press.

Carr, Lord Carr of Hadley (1996) Speech in the House of Lords, House of Lords Debates, 5th Series, Vol. 572, col. 1051, 23 May 1996.

Carter, P., Jeffs, T. and Smith, M. (1992) (eds) *Changing Social Work and Welfare*, Milton Keynes: Open University Press.

Cavadino, M. and Dignan, J. (1997) (2nd edn) The Penal System: An Introduction, London: Sage.

Cavadino, P. (1994) The Opening Door: Reflections on the Criminal Justice Act, *Criminal Justice Matters*, No. 9, Autumn, London: Institute for the Study and Treatment of Delinquency.

Charman, E., Gibson, B., Honess, T. and Morgan, R. (1996) *Fine Imposition and Enforcement Following the Criminal Justice Act 1993*, Research Findings No. 36, London: Home Office Research and Statistics Directorate.

Christie, N. (1977) Conflicts as Property, *British Journal of Criminology*, 17, 1–15.

Christie, N. (1993) (2nd edn) *Crime Control as Industry: Towards Gulags, Western Style*, London: Routledge.

Christie, N. (1995) Against Just Deserts, in Barnes (ed.) (1995).

Clarkson, C. M. V. and Morgan, R. (eds) (1995) *The Politics of Sentencing Reform*, Oxford: Clarendon Press.

Clear, T. and Byrne, J. (1992) The Future of Intermediate Sanctions: Questions to Consider, in Byrne *et al.* (eds) (1992).

Cohen, S. (1975) It's Alright for You to Talk: Political and Sociological Manifestos for Social Work Action, in Bailey and Brake (eds) (1975).

Cohen, S. (1979) The Punitive City: Notes on the Dispersal of Social Control, *Contemporary Crises*, 3, 339–63.

Cohen, S. (1985) *Visions of Social Control: Crime Punishment and Classification*, Cambridge: Polity Press.

Coleman, C. and Moynihan, J. (1996) *Understanding Crime Data: Haunted by the Dark Figure*, Buckingham: Open University Press.

Conservative Party, The (1997) *You Can Only be Sure with the Conservatives: The Conservative Manifesto 1997*, London: Conservative Central Office.

Cook, T., Cooper, H., Cordray, D., Hartmann, L., Light, R., Louis, T. and Mosteller, F. (eds) (1992) *Meta-Analysis for Explanation: A Casebook*, New York: Russell Sage Foundation.

Copas, J. (1995) On Using Crime Statistics for Prediction, in Walker, M. A. (ed.) (1995).

Cottingham, J. (1979) Varieties of Retribution, *Philosophical Quarterly*, 29, 238–46.

Crawford, A. (1994a) The Partnership Approach to Community Crime Prevention: Corporatism at the Local Level?, *Social and Legal Studies*, 3, 497–519.

Crawford, A. (1994b) Social Values and Managerial Goals: Police and Probation Officers' Experiences and Views of Interagency Co-operation, *Policing and Society*, 323–39.

Crawford, A. (1997) *The Local Governance of Crime: Appeals to Community and Partnerships*, Oxford: Clarendon Press.

Croft, J. (1978) *Research in Criminal Justice*, Home Office Research Study No. 44, London: HMSO.

Cross, R. (1975) *The English Sentencing System*, London: Butterworths.

Crow, I. and Simon, F. (1987) *Unemployment and Magistrates' Courts*, London: National Association for the Care and Resettlement of Offenders.

Crow, I., Richardson, P., Riddington, C. and Simon, F. (1989) *Unemployment, Crime and Offenders*, London: Routledge.

Crow, I., Johnson, V., Dignan, J., Cavadino, M. and Walker, M. (1994) Magistrates' Views of the Criminal Justice Act 1991, *Justice of the Peace*, 158, 37–40.

Cullen, F. and Gilbert, K. (1982) *Reaffirming Rehabilitation*, Cincinatti: Anderson.

Currie, E. (1996) *Is America Really Winning the War against Crime and Should Britain Follow its Example?* NACRO 30th Anniversary Lecture, London: National Association for the Care and Resettlement of Offenders.

de Haan, W. (1990) *The Politics of Redress: Crime Punishment and Penal Abolition*, London: Unwin Hyman.

de Haan, W. (1991) Abolitionism and Crime Control: A Contradiction in Terms, in Stenson and Cowell (eds) (1991).

Denney, D. (1992) *Racism and Anti-Racism in the Probation Service*, London: Routledge.

Denney, D. (1996) Discrimination and Anti-Discrimination in Probation, in May and Vass (eds) (1996).

Dignan, J., Sorsby, A. and Hibbert, J. (1997) *Neighbour Disputes: Comparing the Cost Effectiveness of Mediation and Conventional Approaches*, Sheffield: Centre for Criminological and Legal Research.

Downes, D. (1988) *Contrasts in Tolerance*, Oxford: Oxford University Press.

Downes, D. (1992) *Unravelling Criminal Justice*, Basingstoke: Macmillan.

Downes, D. (1997) What the Next Government should do about Crime, *Howard Journal*, 36, 1, 1–13.

Downes, D. and Morgan, R. (1994) 'Hostages to Fortune'? The Politics of Law and Order in Post-War Britain, in Maguire *et al.* (eds) (1994).

Downes, D. and Rock, P. (1995) *Understanding Deviance* (rev. 2nd edn), Oxford: Clarendon Press.

Drakeford, M. and Vanstone, M. (eds) (1996a) *Beyond Offending Behaviour*, Aldershot: Arena.

Drakeford, M. and Vanstone, M. (1996b) Rescuing the Social, *Probation Journal*, April, 16–19.

Dressler, D. (1959) *Practice and Theory of Probation and Parole*, New York: Columbia University Press.

Duff, R. A. (1986) *Trials and Punishments*, Cambridge: Cambridge University Press.

Duff, R. A. (1996) Penal Communications: Recent Work in the Philosophy of Punishment, *Crime and Justice: An Annual Review*, Vol. 20, Chicago: University of Chicago Press.

Duff, R. A. and Garland, D. (1994) *A Reader on Punishment*, Oxford: Oxford University Press.

Duff, R. A., Marshall, S., Dobash, R. E. and Dobash, R. P. (eds) (1994) *Penal Theory and Practice: Tradition and Innovation in Criminal Justice*, Manchester: Manchester University Press.

Ellis, T., Hedderman, C. and Mortimer, E. (1996) *Enforcing Community Sentences: Supervisors' Perspectives on Ensuring Compliance and Dealing with Breach*, Home Office Research Study No. 158, London: Home Office.

English, J. (1997) *The Rise and Fall of Unit Fines*, Unpublished Ph.D. Thesis, University of Leeds.

Etizioni, A. (1995) *The Spirit of Community: Rights, Responsibilities and the Communitarian Agenda,* London: Fontana Press.

Farrington, D., Gallagher, B., Morley L., St Leger, R. and West, D. (1986) Unemployment, School Leaving and Crime, *British Journal of Criminology,* 26, 4, 335–56.

Fattah, E. (1980) Towards a Better Penal System, *Howard Journal,* 19, 27–39.

Faulkner, D. (1989) The Future of the Probation Service: A View from Government, in Shaw and Haines (eds) (1989).

Faulkner, D. (1993) All Flaws and Disorder, *The Guardian,* 11 November.

Feeley, M. and Simon, J. (1992) The New Penology: Notes on the Emerging Strategy of Corrections and its Implications, *Criminology,* 30, 4, 449–74.

Feeley, M. and Simon, J. (1994) Actuarial Justice: The Emerging New Criminal Law, in Nelken (ed.) (1994).

Feest, J. (1988) *Reducing the Prison Population: The West German Experience,* London: National Association For the Care and Resettlement of Offenders.

Field, S. (1990) *Trends in Crime and Their Interpretation: A Study of Recorded Crime in Post War England and Wales,* Home Office Research Study No. 119, London: HMSO.

Finkelstein, E. (1996) Values in Context: Quality Assurance, Autonomy and Accountability, in May and Vass (eds) (1996).

Fitzgerald, M. (1993) *Ethnic Minorities and the Criminal Justice System,* The Royal Commission on Criminal Justice, Research Study 20, London: HMSO.

Fitzgerald, M. and Sim, J. (1992) (2nd edn) *British Prisons,* Oxford: Blackwell.

Fitzpatrick, P. (1992) The Impossibility of Popular Justice, *Social and Legal Studies,* 1, 2, 199–215.

Folkard, M., Smith, D. E. and Smith D. D. (1976) *Impact: Intensive Matched Probation and After Care Treatment. Vol. 2: The Results of the Experiment,* Home Office Research Study No. 36, London: HMSO.

Forrester, D., Frenz, S., O'Connell, M. and Pease, K. (1990) *The Kirkholt Burglary Prevention Project: Phase II,* London: Home Office Crime Prevention Unit.

Foucault, M. (1977) *Discipline and Punish: The Birth of the Prison,* London: Allen Lane.

Frankel, M. E. (1972) *Criminal Sentences: Law Without Order,* New York: Hill & Wang.

Frost, M. L. (ed.) (1992) *Sentencing Reform: Experiments in Reducing Disparity,* Beverly Hills: Sage.

Frost, S. and Stephenson, G. (1989) A Simulation Study of Electronic Tagging as a Sentencing Option, *Howard Journal,* 28, 2, 91–104.

Galbraith, J. (1992) *The Culture of Contentment,* Harmondsworth: Penguin.

Garland, D. (1985) *Punishment and Welfare: A History of Penal Strategies,* Aldershot: Gower.

Garland, D. (1990) *Punishment and Modern Society: A Study in Social Theory,* Oxford: Clarendon Press.

Garland, D. (1996) The Limits of the Sovereign State: Strategies of Crime Control in Contemporary Society, *British Journal of Criminology,* 36, 4, 445–71.

Garland, D. and Young, P. (eds) (1983) *The Power to Punish: Contemporary Penality and Social Analysis,* London: Heinemann.

Gendreau, P. and Ross, R. (1987) Revivification of Rehabilitation: Evidence from the 1980s, *Justice Quarterly*, 349–407.

Gibson, B. (1990) *Unit Fines*, Winchester: Waterside Press.

Gibson, B. (ed.) (1995) *The Sentence of the Court: A Handbook for Magistrates*, Winchester: Waterside Press.

Gibson, B. and Levy, G. (1993) A Method of Achieving Fair Unit Fines, *Justice of the Peace*, 157, 147.

Gibson, B., Cavadino, P., Rutherford, A., Ashworth, A. and Harding, J. (1994) *Criminal Justice in Transition*, Winchester: Waterside Press.

Gilling, D. (1996) Crime Prevention, in May and Vass (eds) (1996).

Habermas, J. (1976) *Legitimation Crisis*, London: Heinemann.

Hall, S. (1980) *Drifting into a Law and Order Society*, London: Cobden Trust.

Hall, S., Critcher, C., Jefferson, T., Clarke, J. and Roberts, B. (1978) *Policing the Crisis*, London: Macmillan.

Hamai, K., Villé, R., Harris, R., Hough, M. and Zvekic, U. (eds) (1995) *Probation Around the World: A Comparative Study*, London: Routledge.

Harding, C. and Koffman, L. (1988) (1st edn) *Sentencing and the Penal System: Test and Materials*, London: Sweet and Maxwell.

Harding, C. and Koffman, L. (1995) (2nd edn) *Sentencing and the Penal System: Test and Materials*, London: Sweet and Maxwell.

Harris, R. (1992) *Crime, Criminal Justice and the Probation Service*, London: Tavistock/Routledge.

Harris, R. (1994) Continuity and Change: Probation and Politics in Contemporary Britain, *International Journal of Offenders Therapy and Comparative Criminology*, 31, 1, 33–45.

Harris, R. (1996) Probation Around the World: Origins and Development, in Hamai *et al.* (eds) (1995).

Hart, H. L. A. (1968) *Punishment and Responsibility*, Oxford: Oxford University Press.

Haxby, D. (1978) *Probation: A Changing Service*, London: Constable.

Hedderman, C. (1995) Gender, Crime and the Criminal Justice System, in Walker, M. A. (ed.) (1995).

Hedderman, C. and Hough, M. (1994) *Does the Criminal Justice System Treat Men and Women Differently?* Research Findings No. 10, London: Home Office Research and Statistical Directorate.

Heidensohn, F. (1994) Gender and Crime, in Maguire *et al.* (eds) (1994).

Home Affairs Committee (1997) *Second Report: The Management of the Prison Service (Public and Private)*, House of Commons Papers, Vol. 57, session 1996–97.

Home Office (1910) *Report of the Departmental Committee on the Probation of Offenders Act 1907 Cmd 5001*, London: HMSO.

Home Office (1927) *Report of the Departmental Committee on the Treatment of Young Offenders*, Cmd 2831, London: HMSO.

Home Office (1936) *Report of the Departmental Committee on the Social Services in Courts of Summary Jurisdiction*, Cmd 5122, London: HMSO.

Home Office (1961) *Report of the Interdepartmental Committee on the Business of the Criminal Courts* (the Streatfield Report), Cmnd 1289, London: HMSO.

Home Office (1962) *Report of the Departmental Committee on Probation* (The Morison Report), Cmnd 1650, London: HMSO.

Home Office (1963) *The Organisation of After-Care* (The Wooton Report), London: Home Office.

Home Office (1964) *The Sentence of the Court: A Handbook for Courts on the Treatment of Offenders* (1st edn), London: HMSO.

Home Office (1965) *The Child, the Family and the Young Offender*, Cmnd. 2742, London: HMSO.

Home Office (1970) *Report of the Advisory Council on the Penal System: Non-Custodial and Semi-Custodial Penalties*, London: Home Office.

Home Office (1974) *Report of the Advisory Council on the Penal System: Young Adult Offenders*, London: HMSO.

Home Office (1978) *The Sentence of the Court: A Handbook for Courts on the Treatment of Offenders* (3rd edn), London: HMSO.

Home Office (1985) *The Cautioning of Offenders, Home Office Circular* 14/1985, London: Home Office.

Home Office (1986) *Criminal Justice: A Working Paper* (rev. edn), London: HMSO.

Home Office (1988a) *Punishment, Custody and the Community*, Cm 424, London: HMSO.

Home Office (1988b) *Tackling Offending: An Action Plan*, London: Home Office.

Home Office (1989) National Standards for Community Service Orders Circular 18/1989.

Home Office (1990a) *Crime, Justice and Protecting the Public*, Cm 965, London: HMSO.

Home Office (1990b) *Supervision and Punishment in the Community: A Framework for Action*, Cm 966, London: HMSO.

Home Office (1991a) *A General Guide to the Criminal Justice Act 1991*, London: Home Office.

Home Office (1991b) *Criminal Justice Act 1991: Custodial Sentences and the Sentencing Framework*, London: Home Office.

Home Office (1991c) *Criminal Justice Act 1991: Fines and Other Financial Penalties*, London: Home Office.

Home Office (1992) *Effect of Reclassification of Offences in the 1988 Criminal Justice Act*, Home Office Statistical Bulletin 18/92, London: Home Office.

Home Office (1993) *Monitoring of the Criminal Justice Act 1991: Data from a Special Data Collection Exercise*, Home Office Statistical Bulletin 25/93, London: Home Office.

Home Office (1994a) *Monitoring of the Criminal Justice Acts 1991 and 1993: Results from a Special Data Collection Exercise*, Home Office Statistical Bulletin 20/94, London: Home Office.

Home Office (1994b) *Home Office Review of Recruitment and Qualifying Training of Probation Officers*, Probation Circular 31/94.

Home Office (1994c) *Introducing Competences: Building on Strengths: A Guide for the Probation Service*, London: Home Office Probation Training Unit.

Home Office (1995a) *Strengthening Punishment in the Community*, London: HMSO.

Home Office (1995b) *Review of Probation Officers Recruitment and Qualifying Training: Discussion Paper by the Home Office*, London: Home Office.

Home Office (1995c) *Measuring the Satisfaction of Courts with the Probation Service,* Home Office Research Study No. 144, London: HMSO.

Home Office (1995d) *Digest 3: Information on the Criminal Justice System in England and Wales,* Home Office: Research and Statistics Department.

Home Office (1996a) *Protecting the Public: The Government's Strategy on Crime in England and Wales,* Cm 3190, London: HMSO.

Home Office (1996b) *Annual Report for the Home Office and the Charity Commissioners,* Cm 3208, London: Home Office.

Home Office (1996c) *Projections in the Long Term Trends in the Prison Population to 2004,* Home Office Statistical Bulletin 4/96.

Home Office (1996d) *Community Sentence Demonstration Projects.* Probation Circular No. 50/1996, London: Home Office.

Home Office (1996e) *Summary Probation Statistics: England and Wales 1995,* Home Office Statistical Bulletin 10/96.

Home Office (1996f) *Cautions, Court Proceedings and Sentencing: England and Wales 1995,* Home Office Statistical Bulletin 16/96.

Home Office (1996g) *Probation Statistics for England and Wales 1994,* London: Home Office.

Home Office (1996h) *Criminal Statistics for England and Wales 1995,* Cm 3421, London: HMSO.

Home Office (1996i) *Prison Statistics for England and Wales 1995,* Cm 3355, London: HMSO.

Home Office (1996j) *The Prison Population in 1995,* Home Office Statistical Bulletin 14/96.

Home Office (1997a) *Sentencing without a Pre-Sentence Report,* Research Findings No. 47, London: Home Office Research and Statistics Directorate.

Home Office (1997b) *Reconvictions of Prisoners Discharged from Prison in 1993, England and Wales,* Home Office Statistical Bulletin 5/97.

Home Office (1997c) *Reconvictions of those Commencing Community Penalties in 1993, England and Wales,* Home Office Statistical Bulletin 6/97.

Home Office (1997d) *Magistrates' Views of the Probation Service,* Research Findings No. 48, London: Home Office Research and Statistics Directorate.

Home Office (1997e) *The Prison Statistics for England and Wales 1996,* Cm 3732, London: HMSO.

Home Office (1997f) *Notifiable Offences: England and Wales 1996,* Home Office Statistical Bulletin 3/97.

Home Office, Department of Health and the Welsh Office (1995) *National Standards for the Supervision of Offenders in the Community,* London: Home Office.

Honderich, T. (1984) *Punishment: The Supposed Justifications* (rev. edn), Harmondsworth: Penguin.

Hood, C. (1991) A Public Management for All Seasons? *Public Administration,* 69, 3–19.

Hood, R. (ed.) (1974) *Crime, Criminology and Public Policy,* London: Heinemann.

Hood, R. (1992) *Race and Sentencing: A Study in the Crown Court,* Oxford: Clarendon Press.

Hood, R. and Shute, S. (1996) Protecting the Public: Automatic Life Sentences, Parole and High Risk Offenders, *Criminal Law Review,* 788–800.

Hood, R. and Sparks, R. (1970) *Key Issues in Criminology*, London: Weidenfeld and Nicolson.

Hough, M. (1996) People Talking about Punishment, *Howard Journal*, 35, 3, 191–214.

Hough, M. (1997) High Cost of Keeping Peace, *The Guardian*, 23 April 1997.

Hough, M. and Moxon, D. (1985) Dealing with Offenders: Popular Opinion and the Views of Victims, *Howard Journal*, 24, 3, 160.

Howard, M. (1995) Speech by Rt Hon. Michael Howard QC, MP, to the National Probation Conference, reported in *The Guardian*, 17 March 1995.

–Hudson, B. A. (1987) *Justice Through Punishment*, Basingstoke: Macmillan.

⋗ Hudson, B. A. (1989) Discrimination and Disparity: The Influence of Race on Sentencing, *New Community*, 16, 1, 23–34.

· Hudson, B. A. (1993) *Penal Policy and Social Justice*, Basingstoke: Macmillan.

Humphrey, C. (1991) Calling in the Experts: The Financial Management Initiative, Private Sector Management Consultants and the Probation Service, *Howard Journal*, 30, 1, 1–18.

Humphrey, C. and Pease, K. (1992) Effectiveness Measurement in Probation: A View from the Troops, *Howard Journal*, 31, 1, 31–52.

Hylton, J. (1981) The Growth of Punishment: Imprisonment and Community Corrections in Canada, *Crime and Social Justice*, Summer, 18–28.

Issit, M. and Woodward, M. (1992) Competence and Contradiction, in Carter, Jeffs and Smith (eds) (1992).

ISTD (Institute for the Study and Treatment of Delinquency) (1997) *The ISTD Handbook of Community Programmes for Young and Juvenile Offenders*, Winchester: Waterside Press.

James, A. (1995) Probation Values for the 1990s – and Beyond? *Howard Journal*, 34, 4, 326–43.

James, A. and Bottomley, A. K. (1994) Probation Partnerships Revisited, *Howard Journal*, 33, 2, 158–68.

Jones, P. R. (1990) Expanding the Use of Non-Custodial Sentencing Options: An Evaluation of the Kansas Community Corrections Act, *Howard Journal*, 29, 114–29.

Kemsley, J. (1992) Are We All Accountants Now?, *Probation Journal*.

Knott, C. (1995) The STOP Programme: Reasoning and Rehabilitation in a British Setting, in McGuire (ed.) (1995).

Labour Party, The (1996) *Tackling Youth Crime: Reforming Youth Justice*, London: The Labour Party.

Labour Party, The (1997a) *Time to Act: Labour's Proposals for Tackling Crime and Disorder*, London: The Labour Party.

Labour Party, The (1997b) *New Labour: Because Britain Deserves Better: The 1997 Manifesto*, London: Labour Party.

Lacey, N. (1988) *State Punishment: Political Principles and Community Values*, London: Routledge.

Lacey, N. and Zedner, L. (1995) Discourses of Community in Criminal Justice, *Journal of Law and Society*, 23, 3, 301–25.

Lawson, C. (1978) *The Probation Officer as Prosecutor: A Study of Proceedings for Breach of Requirements in Probation*, Cambridge: Institute of Criminology.

Le Mesurier, L. (1935) *A Handbook of Probation and Social Work of the Courts*, London: NAPO.

Leadbeater, C. (1996) *The Self-Policing Society*, London: Demos Publications.

Lipsey, M. (1992) Juvenile Delinquency Treatment: A Meta-Analytical Inquiry into the Variability of Results, in Cook *et al.* (eds) (1992).

Lipton, D., Martinson, R. and Wilks, J. (1975) *Effectiveness of Treatment Evaluation Studies*, New York: Praeger.

Lloyd, C., Mair, G. and Hough, M. (1994) *Explaining Reconviction Rates: A Critical Analysis*, Home Office Research Study No. 136, London: HMSO.

Lloyd, J. (1997) The Blair Story, *New Statesman*, May 1997 Special Edition, London: New Statesman Ltd.

Lowman, J., Menzies, R. J. and Palys, T. S. (eds) (1987) *Transcarceration: Essays in the Sociology of Social Control*, Aldershot: Gower.

Lurigio, A. J. and Petersilia, J. (1992) The Emergence of Intensive Probation Supervision Programs in the United States, in Byrne *et al.* (eds) (1992).

McDonald, D. (1986) *Punishment Without Walls: Community Service Sentences in New York City*, New Brunswick: Rutgers University Press.

McGuire, J. (ed.) (1995) *What Works: Reducing Reoffending: Guidelines from Research and Practice*, Chichester: John Wiley.

McGuire, J. (1996) *Cognitive Behavioural Approaches: An Introductory Course on Theory and Research*, Liverpool: University of Liverpool Department of Clinical Psychology.

McGuire, J. and Priestley, P. (1995) Reviewing What Works: Past, Present and Future, in McGuire (ed.) (1995).

McIvor, G. (1992) *Sentenced to Serve: The Operation and Impact of Community Service by Offenders*, Aldershot: Avebury.

McIvor, G. (1993) Community Service by Offenders: How Much Does the Community Benefit? *Social Work Practice*, 3, 385–403.

McLaughlin, E. and Muncie, J. (eds) (1996) *Controlling Crime*, London: Sage.

McMahon, M. (1990) 'Net-Widening': Vagaries in the Use of a Concept, *British Journal of Criminology*, 30, 121–49.

McMahon, M. (1992) *The Persistent Prison? Rethinking Decarceration and Penal Reform*, Toronto: University of Toronto Press.

McRoberts, C. (1989) *Hereford and Worcester Young Offender Project: First Evaluation Report*, University of Oxford: Department of Social and Administrative Studies.

McWilliams, W. (1983) The Mission to the English Police Courts 1876–1936, *Howard Journal*, 12, 129–47.

McWilliams, W. (1985) The Mission Transformed: Professionalisation of Probation Between the Wars, *Howard Journal*, 24, 4, 257–74.

McWilliams, W. (1986) The English Probation System and the Diagnostic Ideal, *Howard Journal*, 25, 4, 241–60.

McWilliams, W. (1987) Probation, Pragmatism and Policy, *Howard Journal*, 26, 2, 97–121.

Maguire, M. (1992) Parole, in Stockdale and Casale (eds) (1992).

Maguire, M., Morgan, R. and Reiner, R. (eds) (1994) *The Oxford Handbook of Criminology*, Oxford: Clarendon Press.

Mair, G. and Mortimer, E. (1997) *Curfew Orders with Electronic Monitoring: An Evaluation of the First Twelve Months of the Trials in Greater Manchester, Norfolk and Berkshire, 1995–1996*, Home Office Research Study No. 163, London: HMSO.

Mair, G. and Nee, C. (1990) *Electronic Monitoring: The Trials and their Results*, Home Office Research Study No. 120, London: HMSO.

Mair, G. and Nee, C. (1992) Day Centre Reconviction Rates, *British Journal of Criminology*, 32, 2, 329–39.

Mair, G., Lloyd, C. and Nee, C. (1994) *Intensive Probation in England and Wales: An Evaluation*, Home Office Research Study No. 133, London: HMSO.

Major, J. (1993) Interview by Rt Hon. John Major MP in the *Mail on Sunday*, 21 February 1993, cited in Cavadino and Dignan (1997).

Marshall, T. F. and Merry, S. (1990) *Crime and Accountability: Victim/Offender Mediation in Practice*, London: HMSO.

Martinson, R. (1974) What Works? *The Public Interest*, March, 22–54.

Martinson, R. (1979) New Findings, New Views: A Note of Caution regarding Sentencing Reform, *Hofstra Law Review*, 7, 243–58.

Mathiesen, T. (1983) The Future of Control Systems: The Case of Norway, in Garland and Young (eds) (1983).

Mathieson, D. (1992) The Probation Service, in Stockdale and Casale (eds) (1992).

Matthews, R. (1987) Decarceration and Social Control: Fantasies and Realities, *International Journal of the Sociology of Law*, 15, 39–60.

Matthews. R. (1989) Alternatives to and in Prison: A Realist Approach, in Carlen and Cook (eds) (1989).

Maxwell, G. and Morris, A. (1993) *Family, Victims and Culture: Youth Justice in New Zealand*, Wellington: Social Policy Agency and Institute of Criminology.

May, T. (1991a) *Probation: Politics, Policy and Practice*, Milton Keynes: Open University Press.

May, T. (1991b) Under Siege: Probation in a Changing Environment, in Reiner and Cross (eds) (1991).

May, T. (1994) Probation and Community Sanctions, in Maguire *et al.* (eds) (1994).

May, T. and Vass, A. A. (eds) (1996) *Working with Offenders: Issues, Contexts and Outcomes*, London: Sage.

Mayhew, P. (1994) *Findings from the International Crime Survey*, Home Office Reseach Finding 8, London: Home Office.

Moore, M. (1987) The Moral Worth of Retribution, in Schoeman (ed.) (1987).

Morris, A. and Gelsthorpe, L. (1990) Not Paying for Crime: Issues in Fine Enforcement, *Criminal Law Review*, 839.

Morris, N. (1974) *The Future of Imprisonment*, Chicago: University of Chicago Press.

Morris, N. and Tonry, M. (1990) *Between Prison and Probation: Intermediate Punishments in a Rational Sentencing System*, New York: Oxford University Press.

Moss, N. (1989) *Tackling Fine Default*, London: Prison Reform Trust.

Moxon, D. (1983) *Fine Default, Unemployment and the Use of Imprisonment*, Home Office Research Bulletin 16, London: Home Office.

Moxon, D. (1988) *Sentencing Practice in the Crown Court*, Home Office Research Study No. 103, London: HMSO.

Moxon, D. and Whittaker, C. (1996) *Imprisonment for Fine Default*, Home Office Research Findings No. 36, London: Home Office.

Moxon, D., Corkery, J. and Hedderman, C. (1992) *Developments in the Use of Compensation Orders in the Magistrates' Courts since October 1988*, Home Office Research Study No. 126, London: HMSO.

Moxon, D., Sutton, M. and Hedderman, C. (1990) *Unit Fines: Experiments in Four Courts*, Home Office Research and Planning Unit Paper 59, London: Home Office.

Murray, C. (1990) *The Emerging British Underclass*, London: Institute of Economic Affairs.

NACRO (1987) *Diverting Juveniles from Custody: Findings from the Fourth Census of Projects Funded under the DHSS Intermediate Treatment Initiative*, London: National Association for the Care and Resettlement of Offenders, Youth Section.

NACRO (1989) *The Electronic Monitoring of Offenders*, Briefing Paper, London: National Association for the Care and Resettlement of Offenders.

NACRO (1997) *Criminal Justice Digest No. 91*, London: National Association for the Care and Resettlement of Offenders.

Narayan, U. (1993) Appropriate Responses and Preventive Benefits: Justifying Censure and Hard Treatment in Legal Punishment, *Oxford Journal of Legal Studies*, 13, 2, 166–82.

Nelken, D. (ed.) (1994) *The Futures of Criminology*, London: Sage.

Nellis, M. (1991) The Electronic Monitoring of Offenders in England and Wales, *British Journal of Criminology*, 31, 165–81.

Nellis, M. (1995a) Probation Values for the 1990s, *Howard Journal*, 34, 1, 19–41.

Nellis, M. (1995b) The 'Third Way' for Probation: A Reply to Spencer and James, *Howard Journal*, 34, 4, 350–3.

Nellis, M. (1996) Probation Training: The Links with Social Work, in May and Vass (eds) (1996).

Newburn, T. (1995) *Crime and Criminal Justice Policy*, London: Longman.

Nuttall, C. and Pease, K. (1994) Changes in the Use of Imprisonment in England and Wales 1950–1991, *Criminal Law Review*, 316–23.

Oatham, E. and Simon, F. (1972) Are Suspended Sentences Working? *New Society*, 3 August, 233–5.

Oldfield, M. (1994) Talking Quality, Meaning Control: McDonalds, the Market and the Probation Service, *Probation Journal*, 186–92.

Oldfield, M. (1996) *The Kent Reconviction Study*, Maidstone: Kent Probation Service.

Osborne, D. and Gaebler, T. (1992) *Reinventing Government: How the Entrepreneurial Spirit is Transforming the Public Sector*, Reading, Mass.: Addison-Wesley.

Pease, K., Billingham, S. and Earnshaw, I. (1977) *Community Service Assessed in 1976*, Home Office Research Study No. 39, London: HMSO.

Penal Affairs Consortium (1995) *The Imprisonment of Fine Defaulters*, London: The Penal Affairs Consortium.

Penal Affairs Consortium (1997a) *Reducing Offending*, London: The Penal Affairs Consortium.

Penal Affairs Consortium (1997b) *Race and Criminal Justice*, London: The Penal Affairs Consortium.

Peters, A. (1986) Main Currents in Criminal Law Theory, in Van Dijk *et al.* (1986).

Phillpotts, G. and Lancucki, L. (1979) *Previous Convictions, Sentence and Reconvictions: A Statistical Survey of a Sample of 5,000 Offenders Convicted in 1971*, Home Office Research Study No. 53, London: HMSO.

Pitts, J. (1988) *The Politics of Juvenile Justice*, London: Sage.

Pitts, J. (1992) The End of an Era, *Howard Journal*, 31, 133–48.

Pointing, J. (ed.) (1986) *Alternatives to Custody*, Oxford: Blackwell.

Pratt, J. (1989) Corporatism: The Third Model of Juvenile Justice, *British Journal of Criminology*, 29, 236–54.

Raine, J. W. and Willson, M. J. (1993) *Managing Criminal Justice*, Hemel Hempstead: Harvester Wheatsheaf.

Raynor, P. (1988) *Probation as an Alternative to Custody*, Aldershot: Avebury.

Raynor, P. (1996a) The Criminal Justice System, in Drakeford and Vanstone (eds) (1996a).

Raynor, P. (1996b) Evaluating Probation: The Rehabilitation of Effectiveness, in May and Vass (eds) (1996).

Raynor, P. and Vanstone, M. (1994) *'Straight Thinking on Probation': 3rd Interim Evaluation Report*, Mid Glamorgan Probation Service.

Raynor, P., Smith, D. and Vanstone, M. (1994) *Effective Probation Practice*, Basingstoke: Macmillan.

Reiner, R. (1989) Race and Criminal Justice, *New Community*, 16, 1, 5–21.

Reiner, R. and Cross, M. (1991) (eds) *Beyond Law and Order: Criminal Justice Policy and Politics into the 1990s*, Basingstoke: Macmillan.

Renzema, M. (1992) Home Confinement Programmes: Development, Implementation and Impact, in Byrne *et al.* (eds) (1992).

Rhodes, R. (1994) The Hollowing Out of the State: The Changing Role of the Public Service in Britain, *The Political Quarterly*, 138–51.

Rhodes, R. (1996) Governing without Government, *Political Studies*, XLIV, 652–67.

Robinson, P. (1987) Hybrid Principles for the Distribution of Criminal Sanctions, *Northwestern University Law Review*, 82, 19–42.

Robinson, P. (1994) Desert, Crime Control, Disparity, and Units of Punishment, in Duff *et al.* (eds) (1994).

Ross, R., Fabiano, E. and Ewles, C. (1988) Reasoning and Rehabilitation, *International Journal of Offender Therapy and Comparative Criminology*, 32, 29–35.

Rotman, E. (1990) *Beyond Punishment: A New View of the Rehabilitation of Offenders*, Westport, Conn.: Greenwood Press.

Rumgay, J. (1989) Talking Tough: Empty Threats in Probation Practice, *Howard Journal*, 28, 3, 177–86.

Rutherford, A. (1993) *Criminal Justice and the Pursuit of Decency*, Oxford: Oxford University Press.

Ryan, A. (1970) *The Philosophy of the Social Sciences*, London: Macmillan.

Schlesinger, P. and Tumber, H. (1994) *Reporting Crime: The Media and the Politics of Criminal Justice*, Oxford: Clarendon Press.

Schoeman, F. (ed.) (1987) *Responsibility, Character, and the Emotions: New Essays in Moral Psychology*, Cambridge: Cambridge University Press.

Scull, A. (1977) *Decarceration: Community Treatment and the Deviant: A Radical View*, Cambridge: Polity Press.

Shaw, R. and Haines, K. (eds) (1989) *The Criminal Justice System: A Central Role for the Probation Service*, Cambridge: University of Cambridge Institute of Criminology.

Shaw, S. (1989) Monetary Penalties and Imprisonment: The Realistic Alternatives, in Carlen and Cook (eds) (1989).

Smith, D. J. (1994) Race, Crime and Criminal Justice, in Maguire *et al.* (eds) (1994).

Smith, D. J. (1996) Pre-Sentence Reports, in May and Vass (eds) (1996).

Sparks, R. (1996) Prisons, Punishment and Penality, in McLaughlin and Muncie (eds) (1996).

Spencer, J. (1995) A Response to Mike Nellis: Probation Values for the 1990s, *Howard Journal*, 34, 4, 344–9.

Stenson, K. and Cowell, D. (eds) (1991) *The Politics of Crime Control*, London: Sage.

Stockdale, E. and Casale, S. (eds) (1992) *Criminal Justice Under Stress*, London: Blackstones.

Straw, J. (1997a) Interview with the Home Secretary, Rt Hon. Jack Straw, MP on BBC Radio's *The World at One*, 16 May 1997.

Straw, J. (1997b) Interview with the Home Secretary, Rt Hon. Jack Straw, MP on BBC Radio's *Today*, 30 July 1997.

Tarling, R. (1982) *Crime and Unemployment*, Home Office Research Bulletin 12, London: Home Office Research and Planning Unit.

Taylor, I., Walton, P. and Young, J. (1973) *The New Criminology: For A Social Theory of Deviance*, London: Routledge Kegan Paul.

Lord Taylor of Gosforth, Lord Chief Justice (1993) Speech to the Law Society of Scotland, *Journal of the Law Society of Scotland*, April, 129–31.

Thomas, D. A. (1992) Criminal Justice Act 1991: Custodial Sentences, *Criminal Law Review*, 232–41.

Thomas, D. A. (1993) Commentary on *R.* v. *Cox*, *Criminal Law Review*, 152–3.

Thorpe, D., Smith, D., Green, C. and Paley, J. (1980) *Out of Care: The Community Support of Juvenile Offenders*, London: Allen and Unwin.

Tonry, M. (1994a) Proportionality, Parsimony, and Interchangeability of Punishments, in Duff *et al.* (eds) (1994).

Tonry, M. (1994b) *Malign Neglect: Race, Crime and Punishment in America*, New York: Oxford University Press.

Travis, A. (1997) Tougher Times Ahead, *Society, The Guardian*, 23 July 1997.

Unger, R. (1976) *Law in Modern Society*, New York: Free Press.

Utting, D. (1996) *Reducing Criminality among Young People: A Sample of Relevant Programmes in the United Kingdom*, Home Office Research Study No. 161, London: Home Office.

Van Dijk, J., Haffman, C., Rutter, F. and Schutte, J. (eds) (1986) *Criminal Law in Action*, Arnhem: Gouda Quint.

Vass, A. A. (1990) *Alternatives to Prison: Punishment, Custody and the Community*, London: Sage.

Vass, A. A. (1996) Community Penalties: The Politics of Punishment, in May and Vass (eds) (1996).

von Hirsch, A. (1976) *Doing Justice: The Choice of Punishment*, New York: Hill and Wang.

von Hirsch, A. (1981) Desert and Previous Convictions in Sentencing, *Minnesota Law Review*, 65, 591–634.

von Hirsch, A. (1986) *Past or Future Crimes*, Manchester: Manchester University Press.

von Hirsch, A. (1990a) Proportionality in the Philosophy of Punishment: From 'Why Punish?' to 'How Much?', *Criminal Law Forum*, 1, 2, 259–90.

von Hirsch, A. (1990b) The Ethics of Community-Based Sanctions, *Crime and Delinquency*, 36, 1, 162–73.

von Hirsch, A. (1991) Criminal Record Rides Again, *Criminal Justice Ethics*, 10, 2, 54–7.

von Hirsch, A. (1992) Scaling Intermediate Punishments: A Comparison of Two Models, in Byrne *et al.* (eds) (1992).

von Hirsch, A. (1993) *Censure and Sanctions*, Oxford: Clarendon Press.

von Hirsch, A. and Ashworth, A. J. (eds) (1992a) *Principled Sentencing*, Boston: Northeastern University Press.

von Hirsch, A. and Ashworth, A. (1992b) Not Not Just Deserts: A Response to Braithwaite and Pettit, *Oxford Journal of Legal Studies*, 12, 83–98.

von Hirsch, A. and Jareborg, N. (1991) Gauging Criminal Harm: a Living Standard Analysis 11 *Oxford Journal of Legal Studies*, 1.

von Hirsch, A., Wasik, M. and Greene, J. (1989) Punishments in the Community and the Principles of Desert, *Rutgers Law Journal*, 20, 595–618.

Walker, C. and Wall, D. (1997) Imprisoning the Poor: Television Licence Evaders and the Criminal Justice System, *Criminal Law Review*, 173–86.

Walker, M. A. (1978) Measuring the Seriousness of Crime, *British Journal of Criminology*, 18, 4, 348.

Walker, M. A. (ed.) (1995) *Interpreting Crime Statistics*, Oxford: Clarendon Press.

Walker, N. (1980) *Punishment, Danger and Stigma*, Oxford: Blackwell.

Walker, N. (1985) (1st edn) *Sentencing: Law, Theory and Practice*, London: Butterworths.

Walker, N. (1991) *Why Punish?* Oxford: Oxford University Press.

Walker, N. (1992) Legislating the Transcendental: von Hirsch's Proportionality, *Cambridge Law Journal*, 51, 3, 530–7.

Walker, N. and Hough, M. (1988) *Public Attitudes to Sentencing: Surveys from Five Countries*, Aldershot: Gower.

Walker, N. and Marsh, C. (1984) Do Sentences Affect Public Disapproval? *British Journal of Criminology*, 24, 1, 27–48.

Walker, N. and Padfield, N. (1996) (2nd edn) *Sentencing: Law and Practice, Theory*, London: Butterworths.

Wall, D. and Bradshaw, J. (1994) The Message of the Medium: The Social Impact of the TV Licensing System, *New Law Journal*, 144, 1198.

Walmsley, R., Howard, L. and White, S. (1992) *The National Prison Survey 1991: Main Findings*, Home Office Research Study No. 128, London: HMSO.

Wasik, M. (1992a) Sentencing: A Fresh Look at Aims and Objectives, in Stockdale and Casale (eds) (1992).

Wasik. M. (1992b) Arrangements for Early Release, *Criminal Law Review*, 252–61.

Wasik, M. (1993) (2nd edn) *Emmins on Sentencing*, London: Blackstone Press.

Wasik, M. and Taylor, R. (1994) (2nd edn) *Guide to the Criminal Justice Act 1991*, London: Blackstone Press.

Wasik, M. and Taylor, R. (1995) *Guide to the Criminal Justice and Public Order Act 1994*, London: Blackstone Press.

Wasik, M. and von Hirsch, A. (1988) Non-Custodial Penalties and the Principles of Desert, *Criminal Law Review*, 555.

Wasik, M. and von Hirsch, A. (1994) Section 29 Revised: Previous Convictions in Sentencing, *Criminal Law Review*, 409–18.

Wells, J. (1995) *Crime and Unemployment*, Economic Report Vol. 9. London: Employment Policy Institute.

Whitehead, P. (1990) *Community Supervision for Offenders*, Aldershot: Avebury.

Whittaker, C. and Mackie A. (1997) *Enforcing Financial Penalties*, Home Office Research Study No. 165, London: Home Office.

Williams, B. (1996) The Probation Service and Victims of Crime: Paradigm Shift or Cop Out?, *Journal of Social Welfare and Family Law*, 18, 4, 461–74.

Williams, Lord Williams of Mostyn (1996) Speech in the House of Lords, House of Lords Debates, 5th Series, Vol. 572, cols 1025–76, 23 May 1996.

Willis, A. (1977) Community Service as an Alternative to Imprisonment, *Probation Journal*, 24, 120–2.

Willis, A. (1981) *Social Welfare and Social Control: A Survey of Young Men on Probation*, Research and Planning Unit Bulletin 8, London: Home Office.

Willis, A. (1986) Alternatives to Imprisonment, in Pointing (ed.) (1986).

Wilson, J. Q. (1975) *Thinking About Crime*, New York: Basic Books.

Windlesham, Lord (1993) *Responses to Crime. Vol. 2: Penal Policy in the Making*, Oxford: Clarendon Press.

Young, P. (1989) Punishment, Money and a Sense of Justice, in Carlen and Cook (eds) (1989).

Young, R. and Wall, D. (1996) Criminal Justice, Legal Aid and the Defence of Liberty, in Young, R. and Wall, D. (eds) (1996) *Access to Criminal Justice*, London: Blackstone Press.

Young, W. (1979) *Community Service Orders: The Development and Use of a New Penal Measure*, London: Heinemann.

Zedner, L. (1994) Reparation and Retribution: Are They Reconcilable? *Modern Law Review*, 57, 2, 228–52.

Index